GLORIOUS GENTLEMEN

Also available by Bruce Sandison

ANGLING LINES
RIVERS & LOCHS OF SCOTLAND
LIES, DAMNED LIES AND ANGLERS
SANDISON'S SCOTLAND

Bruce Sandison

GLORIOUS GENTLEMEN

Tales from Scotland's Stalkers, Keepers and Gillies

BLACK & WHITE PUBLISHING

First published 2012
by Black & White Publishing Ltd
29 Ocean Drive, Edinburgh EH6 6JL

1 3 5 7 9 10 8 6 4 2   12 13 14 15

ISBN: 978 1 84502 460 4

A CIP catalogue record for this book is available from the British Library.

Typeset by Ellipsis Digital Ltd, Glasgow
Printed and bound by ScandBook AB, Sweden

For Ann

For there is good news yet to hear and fine things to be seen,
Before we go to paradise by way of Kensal Green.

Contents

Foreword
by Geoffrey Palmer

I started fishing in what can only charitably be called 'my later middle' years. I have few regrets, but one is that during the previous fifty years, when all I seemed to do was grow older trying to earn a crust, get married and have a family, was, of course, that I could also have been fishing.

Like most converts to a new cause, I have become an enthusiastic angler and in recent years have enjoyed some lovely fishing on the English chalk streams and a bit in New Zealand and Montana. But now much of my fishing is done in Scotland, where I spend most of my days chasing salmon.

My introduction to salmon fishing was at Tillmouth, on the Lower Tweed under the expert guidance of the then head gillie, Michael Chapman. For a novice coming face to face for the first time with Michael and his team who looked like a bunch of out-of-work pirates, it was just a touch intimidating. But Michael was wonderful, the most skilled of boatmen, delightful company and a tolerant and gentle advisor.

Since then I have been fortunate enough to fish a number of top Tweed beats – which might explain to the curious why I am still working at my ripe old age – and the prolific Helmsdale River and the Lower Oykel, which is my favourite salmon stream.

One of the delights of this book is meeting again on its pages some of the many gillies and boatmen with whom I have spent so many happy hours in the past. Men in the mould of Michael Chapman, like Billy Jack on Junction Pool and Colin Pringle at Makerstoun, without whose skills and patience my daughter would never have caught that first salmon on Upper Floors, and Steven Mackenzie, and wisest and most glorious gentleman of them all, George Ross on the Oykel.

Bruce Sandison has put together a fascinating mix of history, amusing stories, opinions and memories. But what is most refreshing is that neither he nor his subjects fight shy of speaking their minds. It is interesting to read what some of the men charged with ensuring that we return to the river the salmon that we catch actually think of the catch and release policy.

As an actor, I have always thought that the most diverse group of individuals you could ever come across were stage door keepers, but later experience has introduced me to an even more diverse, though thankfully less weird group, our gillies – the long-suffering men who, on a Monday morning after weeks of low water conditions and east winds, will still greet us with a smile and at least an outward show of optimism. These are the men who spend a lot of their days thinking, as they watch us cast, "My God, is that the best he can do?"

According to Atty MacDonald, a renowned Lower Oykel gillie, a gillie's most important attribute is the ability to 'be able to yawn with his mouth shut'. This is a warm, humorous, nostalgic and informative book that lets us into the thoughts and lives of those men who guide our fishing and are our daily companions.

Geoffrey Palmer
July 2012

Preface

This book has taken about three years to write. It would have taken a lot longer without the help of Hazel Buckley of Chartered Accountants and James Paterson Reid in Kelso. James Paterson, an expert angler and Sandison family friend for more that twenty-five years, kindly volunteered to provide hard-copy transcripts of my recorded interviews with the stalkers, keepers and gillies, and Hazel Buckley tackled the work on my behalf. This involved Hazel listening in to and deciphering the recordings I had made and then typing out what must have amounted to some 300,000 words. As such, this book is as much Hazel's and James's as it is mine, and I would like to record here my heartfelt thanks to them both for such unprecedented support.

I published a similar work in the 1980s, *The Sporting Gentleman's Gentlemen*, and I wanted to see what, if anything, had changed during the intervening years. In the course of doing so I soon found that, although most of the men that I had spoken to in the 1980s had gone off to stalk, fish and shoot in another place, they are still fondly remembered by their successors, the men I spoke to on my recent travels round Scotland. Many started their working careers under the guidance and tutelage of my departed friends – wonderful characters like Frank Binnie at Tweedmill and Jimmy Wallace across the river at Tillmouth; Willie Drysdale at Hopetoun and Colin Leslie on the Tay; David MacDonald and Tom MacPhearson at Invercauld on Deeside; and Walter Maxwell and Andrew Hunter at Thornhill.

I think the greatest difference I noticed was that those who hold these positions today are in some ways more professional in their approach than their predecessors were, in as much as they will not tolerate some of the abuses and antics that the men I spoke to in the 1980s had to put up with. Essentially, however, they are just as committed to the rivers, moors and lochs in their care as the previous generations of the stalkers, keepers and gillies were in times past. But the nature of our sport and those who enjoy it has changed, and mightily. I don't think that it would be entirely unfair to suggest that in the past stalking, shooting and fishing on Scottish estates was very much the preserve of the so-called 'upper echelons' of society, whereas today it is universally enjoyed by a much wider range of people; basically, I suppose, if you can pay, then you are welcome.

Thus, the pressure on field sport activities has increased in recent years. This has caused some estates to take a short-term view of management practices for financial reasons, rather than pursuing longer-term objectives of sustainability to preserve the wildlife on their lands. As that great Scottish poet Norman MacCaig once put it in 'A Man in Assynt', "Who owns this landscape? The millionaire who bought it, or the poacher staggering downhill in the early morning with a deer on his back?" And certainly, it is true to say that more and more of Scotland's landscape is being taken into the hands of millionaires, many of whom hail from overseas. I don't have a problem with this; after all, they can't pack it up and take it away with them, can they? And, at least as far as I am concerned, regardless of who 'owns' it, the land remains the common heritage of the Scottish people.

I found that this view was generally shared by those I spoke to, but many expressed concerns about the damage being caused to salmonid populations by the industrial-scale fish farms and indiscriminating, interceptory netting at sea and in our coastal waters, as well as the alleged over-zealous culling of deer, approved and sanctioned by Scottish Natural Heritage. But one thing hasn't change and I don't think that it ever will change: their knowledge of the lands they manage and their kindness, courtesy and patience with those of us who come to them seeking guidance and assistance, and of course, their wonderful, matchless sense of humour. I would like to thank them all for sharing with me the stories and tales of their lives and times. In doing so they have made this book a celebration of more than one hundred years of stalking, shooting and fishing in the land I love.

Bruce Sandison
Hysbackie, August 2012

1
Colin Pringle
Makerstoun, Tweed

Colin Pringle is head gillie on the Makerstoun Beat of the River Tweed, the 'Queen of Scottish Rivers'. The Tweed at Makerstoun is considered to be one of the loveliest parts of the river, where it forces its flow between red sandstone cliffs that are bordered by mature woodlands, fertile fields and meadows resplendent with wildflowers.

Colin was born in 1963 and lives with his wife, Lesley, a civil servant, twins Ben and Sarah, and a friendly black Labrador named Tweed. Their home is a splendid cottage close to the banks of the river at the end of a long driveway from the main road between Melrose and Kelso.

When I arrived, Colin came out to greet me followed by Tweed, who cold-nosed my hand. We all trooped through to Colin's sitting room and settled comfortably to talk by the spark and scent of a cheerful log fire.

Colin was brought up in the Ettrick and Yarrow Valley where his father, who loved fishing, was a shepherd. Another well-known shepherd who worked there and also loved fishing was the Scottish poet and author, James Hogg, the 'Ettrick Shepherd' (1770–1835). A memorial to Hogg stands at the head of St Mary's Loch; the poet, with his sheepdog by his side, looking out over the loch he so often fished when staying at Tibbie Shiels, an Inn that has been caring for anglers for almost two hundred years.

Colin told me, "We used to fish the burns around St Mary's Loch. If it had been raining all day and the burns were in spate, Father would send me out to dig the worms. We would fish together in the evening and rarely went home empty-handed. That's how I got started. I have fished the Yarrow and Ettrick all my life." The family subsequently moved to the town of Selkirk where Colin went to school. He told me, somewhat ruefully, "I was asked to leave school when I was fifteen, and the feeling was mutual. Exams were coming up and I wasn't really interested. I was the one sitting gazing out the window and was ready for work."

His first job was with Kendal Fish Farm, next to the rugby field in Selkirk near Philiphaugh. Colin got to know the rugby field very well in later life, as he played for Selkirk as a back-row forward for forty years, prior to taking up judo, where he soon gained his black belt. But he soon left the fish farm, and on a self-employed basis, worked for a number of years in forestry – mainly in the Tweed Valley at Walkerburn, Innerleithen and Peebles, but also tree planting on Eskdalemuir. As an angler, he noticed the depth of the ploughing furrows dug to accommodate the trees. "They were seven feet deep," he said, "and there are no peat bogs there now, nothing to hold back the water like a sponge until slowly releasing it into rivers in spring." Colin stopped forestry work when he was thirty-two years of age. "I realised that during the trout-fishing season I had only managed out for a cast once in six months, and that was not the way I wanted to live. At the same time, I saw an advert in the local paper for a second boatman on the Dryburgh beat of the Tweed, so I applied for the job.

"The beat was owned by Ian Gregg, a former chairman of the

Tweed Commissioners and founder of the famous north-east chain of bakery shops, the firm that organised the petition against George Osborne's daft hot pastie tax at the last budget. Ian lived at Dryburgh and he employed a new man every season to train with Stewart McIntyre, his full-time boatman; that was his way of putting something back into fishing, helping someone get a job." But at the end of the season there were no jobs available on the river, so Colin had to go back to forestry. He continued, "Then, much to my surprise, I got a phone call from Ian Gregg one evening to say that there was a job going on the Upper Floors beat at Kelso and that he had spoken to the owner, the Duke of Roxburghe, and I was to contact the Duke's factor to arrange an interview. Ian Gregg was a gentleman, and I am indebted to him for his help."

Colin spent seven years as a gillie at Upper Floors and loved it. "The Duke reserved the beat for himself and his family on bank holidays and Saturdays. He was a keen sportsman, and if there was some special happening on a Saturday afternoon – horse racing, golf, whatever – he would tell us gillies to fish the beat in his absence. I suppose that I must have had about 130 salmon during the seven years I was there. I got on well with the Duke, but you couldn't pull the wool over his eyes.

"I remember one Saturday morning during my first spring there, when nothing much was doing on the river, the Duke told me that he had guests staying and could I catch a few trout for their breakfast the following morning. I thought this must be the best job in the world, to be paid for trout fishing on Upper Floors. I went home, got my trout rod and soon had a couple of decent fish in my bag. Then the rise went quiet. Normally, in these conditions, I would be happy enough to sit on the bank and wait for the trout to start rising again, but I wanted to impress the Duke, so I thought that I had better work a little bit harder at this.

"I mounted a small, wet fly and a few moments later hooked a fish. But it wasn't a trout. It was an 8lb fresh-run salmon and it gave me a merry dance on my trout rod before I managed to land it. That night I went up to the back door of the castle, knocked and left the trout and the salmon on the doorstep. As I was walking back to my car, I heard this shout, 'Where the blazes did you get that from?' There was the Duke standing at the door, looking down at the fish. So I told him that I had caught the trout and the salmon that afternoon on my trout rod using a small, wet fly."

On another occasion when a party of Americans had the beat, a huge spate made the river virtually unfishable. They had their own aeroplane at Edinburgh, so they just went off home early. This did nothing for the number of fish in the game book, so on the Friday, when the flood was subsiding, the Duke asked the gillies to fish the beat themselves. Colin remembered, "I had Dougie Laing with me; he was a retired policeman from Melrose who used to help us out at the back end of the season if were short of a gillie. Dougie and I had ten salmon in the morning and at lunchtime I asked my wife Lesley to leave the children with her mother for the afternoon and join us. She hadn't fished much, but I was sure that if she caught a salmon it would encourage her to fish more.

"We went up to the Slates Pool and I put her in the boat with Dougie and roped the boat down the pool. She had a few casts, and then Dougie took the rod and hooked a really good fish. I pulled the boat into the bank and Dougie gave Lesely the rod and asked her to play it. I told her to give it line, to let it run, because the rod was almost bent double, but she was gritting her teeth and holding on like grim death with this big fish thrashing at her feet. So Dougie winked at me and said to Lesley, 'Well done, hen, give me the rod and I'll get it in.' She handed the rod back to Dougie, who landed the salmon, which we estimated weighed 23lbs. With a smile, I asked her what she thought of fishing now and Lesely replied, 'Not much.' Well, I thought, if that doesn't do it, nothing will!"

Colin had clearly enjoyed the time he spent at Upper Floors, so I asked him why he had decided to leave. The idea was put into his mind one day when he was walking up from Floors and Eoin Fairgrieve, the gillie on the next beat, Makerstoun, was walking down. They stopped to talk and Eoin asked, "Colin, if you weren't at Floors, which other beat would you like to be on?" Junction Pool was the leading beat on the river, but Colin said that he didn't really know. "What about Makerstoun then?" said Eoin.

Colin looked at him had replied, "Eoin, you are much younger than I am and you will be there for a good while yet." But it turned out that because of a back injury, he had to leave. Eoin said that he wanted the person who took his place to be the right man to look after his guests. "It's your own place at Makerstoun. You are your own boss, and it's like running your own business."

Colin told him, "I've never thought about it, but it would all depend upon what Lesley thinks, and the house."

"Bring her up at the weekend," said Eoin.

When Colin told Lesley the news, she seemed to be less than

enthusiastic, but Colin said, "Come on, there's no harm in just having a look. It was a lovely house, as was everything else about the place, and I felt that it was time to move on from Floors, so that's how I ended up getting the job at Makerstoun. This is my eleventh season here. Nobody bothers you and it is not so commercial as Floors.

"When I handed my notice in at Floors, the Duke was in London and he phoned and asked me to think about it carefully and not to do anything until he got back. When I spoke to him on his return, I told the Duke that I had made up my mind and that was it. He reminded me that I wouldn't catch as many fish up there, but I said there was more to life than just the number of fish caught. He said, 'Yes, you're right,' and we left it at that."

Of course, Floors is more productive than Makerstoun, but Makerstoun also has its place in angling legend, thanks to a fish landed by Robert Kerse almost two hundred years ago. The story of the incident was famously recounted shortly after it happened by another great Tweed character, the angling writer William Scrope (1772–1852): "In the year 1815, Robert Kerse hooked a clean salmon of about 40lbs in the Makerstoun water, the largest, he says, he ever encountered: fair work he had with him for some hours; till at last Rob, to use his own expression, was 'clean dune out'. He landed the fish, however, in the end, and laid him out on the channel; astonished, and rejoicing at his prodigious size, he called out to a man on the opposite bank of the river, who had been watching for some time: 'Hey, mon, sic a fish!'

"He then went for a stone to fell him with, but as soon as his back was turned, the fish began to wamble towards the water, and Kerse turned, and jumped upon it; over they both tumbled, and they, line, hook and all, went into the Tweed. The fish was too much for Rob, having broke the line, which got twisted round his leg, and made its escape, to his great disappointment and loss, for at the price clean salmon were then selling, he could have got five pounds for it."

However, my favourite story from these 'airts', and the finest angling put-down that I have ever read, comes from Tibbie Shiels. The Inn was much used by anglers who came to fish St Mary's Loch and famous because of its association with people such as James Hogg, Thomas Tod Stoddart, Sir Walter Scott and his friends, Robert Louis Stevenson, Thomas Carlyle and other literary luminaries. One of Scott's friends was Christopher North, the pen name of John Wilson, lawyer and professor of moral philosophy at Edinburgh University in 1820. He was a well-known sportsman and keen angler and bestowed upon himself such titles as MA, Master of Angling, and FRS, Fisherman Royal of Scotland, but he is most remembered for his columns in *Blackwood's Magazine*. The articles were written under his pen name and described the angling exploits of himself (North) and James Hogg (The Shepherd) and John Gibson Lockhart (Tickler), who married Sophia, Sir Walter Scott's elder daughter.

Someone had been boasting about all the fish they had caught and of their great size, much to the amusement of the Shepherd, who replied, "Poo, that was nae day's fishin' ava, man, in comparison to ane o' mine on St Mary's Loch. To say naething about the countless sma' anes, twa hunder about half a pun', ae hunder about a haill pun', fifty about twa pun', five-and-twenty about fowre pun', and the lave rinnin' frae half a stane up to a stane and a half, except about half a dizzen, aboon a' weicht that put

Geordie Gudefallow and Huntly Gordon to their mettle to carry them pechin to Mount Benger on a haun-barrow."

Another of Hogg's friends and fishing companions was Thomas Tod Stoddart (1810–1880), angler and author of the first book on Scottish fishing, *The Art of Angling as Practised in Scotland*, published in 1835 and later republished as *The Angler's Companion to the Rivers and Lakes of Scotland*; I suppose the precursor of my own book, *The Rivers and Lochs of Scotland*, published in 1997. Stoddart and James Hogg were expert anglers and often fished together on St Mary's. One of their most notable days was 4 May 1833, when they shared a boat and took seventy-nine trout weighing 36lbs. No doubt they celebrated their victory over a dram or two with Tibbie. She was always known as Tibbie, but her real name was Isobel Richardson, and she had been widowed at an early age when she opened the Inn to support herself and her children. It was rumoured that Hogg was fond of her, because in later life she said of him, "Yon Hogg, the Shepherd, ye ken, was an awfu' fine man. He should hae tae'n me, for he cam coortin' for years, but he just gaed away and took another." Tibbie and Hogg's wife nursed him through his last illness; she herself outlived all her illustrious clients and died in July 1878 at the age of ninety-six.

Earlier in our conversation, Colin had mentioned the fish farm on the Ettrick at Philiphaugh where he briefly worked after leaving school, and the impact of forestry on the Eskdalemuir catchment and the rivers it fed. I was very much involved in a controversy over a similar situation further north, the mass-afforestation of the Flow Country of Caithness and East Sutherland, where more than 100,000 acres of virgin peatlands were ploughed and planted with foreign conifers, lodge pole pine and Sitka spruce. The planting had a deplorable effect on the water quality of rivers and lochs, as well as on the flora and fauna of the area. At that time, back in 1988, I remember attending the Game Fair, which was held that year at Floors Castle. Because of heavy rain, it was a sea of mud and I recall seeing the then Scottish Secretary, Malcolm Rifkind, currently MP for Kensington and Chelsea, plodding about the site in Wellingtons.

After much urging and unpleasant publicity, his government eventually closed the tax-loophole that allowed the factory tree planting to flourish, but sadly not soon enough to save much of the Flow Country, where the tax-payer is once again forking out cash to have trees removed and the land reinstated. Another former Scottish Secretary, Michael Forsyth, who has fished with Colin Pringle, played an important part in preventing the reopening and expansion of the smolt-rearing farm at Philiphaugh where Colin had worked. Uproar ensued in 2002 when the proposal was lodged; the Tweed Proprietors and Commissioners were rightly concerned about the impact of escapes from the farm into the Ettrick and thence the Tweed. Michael Forsyth published a hard-hitting letter in *The Scotsman* highlighting these dangers.

During a telephone conversation with Michael Forsyth, I asked him why he was so firmly opposed to a fish farm on the Ettrick, and yet, as Scottish Secretary, had allowed hundreds of primarily foreign-owned fish farms to be established in the West Highlands and Islands – responsible, in my view, for the catastrophic collapse of wild salmonids in these areas. I will never forget his reply. He told me that the responsible minister at the time, Lord Jamie Lindsay, had assured him and his colleagues that salmon farms posed no danger to wild fish and that they had accepted this reassurance. Indeed, Mr Forsyth told me that such was Lord Lindsay's enthusiasm for fish farms that he had acquired the nickname amongst his colleagues of 'Norwegian Jamie'. In due course, when the conservative government lost power, 'Norwegian Jaime' became chairman of Scottish Quality Salmon, the public mouthpiece of the industry.

The end of this story came in June 2008, when the world's largest producer of farm salmon, the Norwegian multi-national company Marine Harvest, who had been forced to abandon their plan on the Ettrick, sold the Philiphaugh site to a local firm of property developers. The Ettrick and the Tweed thus escaped the ungentle administrations of fish farms, but the degradation these farms cause continues unabated in the West Highlands and Islands of Scotland to this day and, indeed, in many other countries around the globe.

Colin's comment, listening to these stories, was precise and well reasoned. "I try not to get involved," he said. "After all, there are people paid a lot more than I am to sort out the politics of angling. I just focus on my job and the river." And at times, Colin told me, he also has to focus on the recovery of luxury motorcars. One morning, an angler had parked his Rolls-Royce at the top of a steep bank above the beat so that his wife could sit in the car and write postcards and at the same time keep an eye on Colin and her husband fishing. Colin said, "We were in the boat and could see her sitting there, scribbling away, when we heard a scream. We looked up and saw the car slide forward, almost in slow motion, and then roll sixty feet down the bank, ending up, on its side, barely two yards from the river.

"She had been getting hot and tried to reach over from the passenger seat to turn the ignition on so that she could lower her window, but couldn't reach it. So she got out, went round the back of the car and opened the driver's door. With one foot in the vehicle and half sitting on the driver's seat, the car suddenly started to roll forward. She jumped out just before the door was crushed by the branch of an oak tree which could have trapped her if she had been inside; the poor woman got a terrible fright.

"But that was not the end of it. My guest told me that he had money in the boot and his wife's jewelry in the glove compartment and would I get it. Well, I had my thigh waders on, with tungsten studs in the soles, and with the car on its side I had to stand on the paintwork to heave the door open and jump in. He was shouting down instructions to me about which lever to pull to open the boot; the cash was under the carpet and I got it and also the jewelry from the glove compartment. But I had a hell of a job to get the door back open so that I could get out. I don't know what it did for the walnut interior or the leather upholstery, but eventually, after a struggle, I managed. All in a day's work, I suppose. The next day they had to bring a crane down to the river to recover the car. They got it back on its wheels and winched it up the slope, where, after lying on its side all night, it started with the first turn of the key."

Apart from the odd Rolls-Royce, Colin once had to recover a guest who had gone astray. Colin's friend and colleague, Eoin Fairgreve, who had persuaded Colin to take over from him as head gillie at Makerstoun, is still involved with the beat through a fishing course held there and run in conjunction with the magazine, *Trout & Salmon*, a magazine that I wrote for over a period of twenty-five years, beginning in 1975 when Jack Thorndike was editor, followed by the late Roy Eaton, and latterly, Sandy Leventon. The casting course is very popular and well organised. Each day the guests have one hour's instruction with Eoin and an hour in the boat with each of the two gillies in attendance. An elderly guest in his eighties and whose first name was Jack was on the course, and everyone kept an eye on him to make sure that he didn't get into difficulties. After Jack's hour with Eoin he was supposed to go up to the top of the beat to join Colin in the boat, a walk of no more than twelve minutes. When he didn't appear at the appointed place at the appointed hour, Colin thought that he might have stopped off for a cast along the way, but phoned Eoin to ask when he had left the bottom fishing hut. The answer was at least half an hour ago. It was a foggy day and Colin was worried that he might have fallen into a ditch or had a heart attack. So everybody had to stop fishing and search parties were arranged to look for him.

Colin eventually met up with Eoin on the hill near Makerstoun House, some distance from the river, where they saw their missing guest standing in the mist, with his balaclava on, waders, big jacket and rod over his shoulder. Colin shouted, "Jack, where have you been!"

Jack replied, "Oh, I must have taken a wrong turn when I was walking up the river." He had gone up the private drive towards the house where he had met the postman and had asked if he could tell him where the river was. The postman had looked askance and replied, "I don't know, but I would have thought from the way you are dressed that you would have more of an idea where the river was than me." You can't see the river from the house and old Jack had been purposefully heading off down the road towards Kelso.

Inevitably, anglers fall in, particularly more elderly piscators. Colin said, "Oh yes, aye, we've had a couple of drookings, but nothing too serious. I did get a fright once when one of my guests, again well into his eighties, slipped and went right under. He dropped his rod and crawled ashore and we later found his rod washed up about eighty yards downstream. He told his wife about the incident and from then on she insisted that he always wore a life jacket. He did as he was told, but used to take it off and hang it from a tree whilst he fished, then put it on again, just in case his wife was waiting for him at the fishing hut when he got back."

Colin also remembered another guest from his days at Upper Floors, a farmer who had come the previous year and returned the next year with a party of friends. By this time he, of course, was the expert and told Colin and Colin Bell, the head gillie at Floors, to look after the other guests, as he could look after himself. Colin told me, "I was passing the fishing hut and stopped to put some more logs on the fire, as we all did, especially in the early months of the season. There he was, in his underpants, with all his clothes draped round the room on the backs of chairs to dry. I asked what had happened and he seemed quite unconcerned and very happy with himself. 'Oh,' he said, 'I've just been speaking to the Duke of Marlborough.' I asked where, because I knew that he wasn't fishing my beat, but down on Lower Floors. 'Well,' the dripping guest replied, 'I was near the end of the beat when I fell into a deep hole and dropped my rod. I swam ashore and ran down the bank into Lower Floors where I saw the boatman Ian

Simm and a guest on the river. I called across and asked them if they would be kind enough to pick up my rod as it came by, and I saw the guest get it. They rowed ashore and we introduced ourselves, which is when I found out that I was speaking to the Duke of Marlborough.' He had damn near drowned himself, was still freezing and near naked, but he was very proud about his encounter with a duke. Oh aye, you get some good laughs."

I asked Colin what he thought of the policy that every fish had to be returned, and like most of the gillies I spoke to throughout Scotland, he had reservations – although, of course, he complies with the rule and ensures that his guests do as well. "I'm not sure that it will make much difference, putting one hundred per cent of the fish back rather than, say, seventy-five to eighty per cent of them. It's very hard on the guests. One who has been putting back all the fish he caught for two or three years now, told me recently that he and his wife were hosting a special dinner party and that he would dearly love to be able to serve salmon. Another, an elderly lady, pointed out to me that in all probability she wouldn't be here in a year or so, dead and gone, never mind being able to keep any of the fish she caught. I think that other gillies probably share my view, particularly since our river is producing so many fish now. Perhaps the rule might be just a bit draconian?"

However, the rule does not apply to sea-trout, and the Tweed can produce excellent sport with these fine fish. The guest, if he wishes, can take one home for the pot. When I was speaking to Colin on the phone recently, he told me that four sea-trout had been caught that day, two at 7lbs and two weighing 8lbs. And that his guests went home happy.

Colin was always keen to get his children, the twins Sarah and

Ben, interested in fishing and shooting, but so far, he has not been entirely successful in doing so. "I think that they probably get bored with me talking about it so much," he said. "One evening, when Ben was about ten years old, I said that I could guarantee him a fish if he came down to the river with me. Reluctantly, he did, and after about fifteen or twenty casts turned to me and said, 'I thought I was guaranteed a fish?' when suddenly he was into one, and because of the strength of the salmon, he had to put his feet on the back of the boat to hold on to the rod. He said that his arms were aching and asked me to take the rod, but I refused, telling him that if I did, then it would be my fish, not his, and that I had to row the boat. Later, at the Game Fair, Sandy Leventon of *Trout & Salmon* asked me if I had any photographs of Ben landing his first salmon, which I had, and it duly appeared in the magazine, much to Ben's delight."

Ben's sister Sarah was the same when it came to fishing. On a day in 2011 when conditions were perfect, Colin tried to persuade Ben to come with him to the river, but to no avail. However, Sarah said she would go. Almost immediately, she missed one, then another, but she hooked the next one and finally landed her first salmon. "I am sure she would go again," said Colin, "but just now she is more interested in her horse. However, she shot her first pigeon last Saturday. Again, I had asked Ben to join me but he said he was busy, and when Sarah heard this she complained that I never asked her. I had given her a clay pigeon shooting lesson for a birthday present and she seemed to enjoy it, so off we went to the wood at about 5am. There were two birds sitting on a branch and I told her to shoot between them, which she did, and both pigeons came down. 'I've got two!' she shouted. 'I've got two. How did I manage that with just one bullet?' She was delighted with herself and we took them home for the larder."

I asked Colin if he was happy with the way he had spent his life to date and would he, if he could, change anything. "No," he said. "I wouldn't change a thing. Now and again I have regrets, particularly on a Saturday afternoon when there is an international rugby match being broadcast on television, Scotland v England, and I am on the river. But apart from that, I am more than content with my lot. No, I wouldn't change a thing."

Night had arrived when I left. Lesley came through to say goodbye and Sarah and Ben were upstairs, busy with homework. Colin, with Tweed tail-wagging at his heels, waved me off. As I drove up the winding road I glanced back at the cottage in the trees, the warm glow from its windows fading into the darkness. But the warm glow from Colin's good company remained with me.

2
Chris McManus, Loch Tay

Chris McManus is unique. He is an experienced angler and stalker with a great knowledge and love of Scotland's precious environment and all that it contains, and yet he has no family history of involvement in the countryside or with field sports. Chris was born in 1950 on the south side of Glasgow, the 'dear green place', and he went to school there. His father had a road haulage business and when Chris left school at the age of fifteen he went to work with his dad. As a young man, he discovered Loch Lomond and used to go there to shoot geese and to canoe. Inevitably, he also discovered fishing and the wonderful books of these two Loch Lomond angling legends, Ian Wood and Bill McEwan.

Chris used to go out from Balmaha at the south-east corner of the loch. He told me, "We would get a boat from Sandy Macfarlane at the Marina and troll for salmon and, I suppose, anything else that might come along. All I knew about fishing was taught to me by the old worthies I fished with. They were always generous with their time and advice." Macfarlane's boatyard is synonymous with fishing Loch Lomond. The business was established 150 years ago by Sandy's great-great-grandfather, John Macfarlane and it has thrived ever since. Chris soon expanded his fishing interests to the principal feeder streams, Endrick, Fruin and Luss Waters, and to the River Leven, which drains Loch Lomond into the Firth of Clyde. He found the members of the Vale of Leven & District Angling Club to be every bit as helpful as the men he fished with on the loch. Both the river and loch have formidable runs of sea-trout and salmon and Chris enjoyed sport with both species.

My own first visit to Loch Lomond was with two friends, the late Charles Hodget, a local businessman from Paisley, and Tony Sykes, from Bridge of Weir. Only one thing used to delay their arrival at loch or river: the necessity for substantial pre-fishing refreshment along the way – a fact I discovered, much to my cost, when they invited me to join them for a day on Lomond. After several 'pit-stops' we eventually made it to Balmaha, launched our boat and set off towards the islands where salmon lie, or – and perhaps more accurately – are alleged to lie. With fingers crossed and the light of battle glinting in my eye, I thanked my hosts for inviting me.

After trolling, dapping is the next most effective way of luring Lomomd sea-trout and salmon to their doom and I soon discovered why I had been included in the party. As Charles set up the boat for a drift down the south shore of Inchcruin Island, he handed me the dapping rod.

"Now, Bruce," he said, "you sit in the middle with the dapping rod and keep the fly dancing on the surface. When you see a salmon making towards it, lift the fly off the surface."

"And what will you pair be doing?" I inquired suspiciously.

"Tony will fish from the bow and I'll be in the stern. When the dapping fly is lifted from the water the salmon should turn and take one of our flies. Got it?"

I had, and did, but the salmon didn't. Eventually, in exasperation, I had a few casts with my wet flies and immediately hooked and landed a sea-trout. Believe me, I loved that fish.

Chris McManus rapidly expanded his fishing horizons to Loch Tay where he quickly earned an enviable reputation for his skill as a boatman and gillie and being able to produce results even in the most daunting of weather conditions. In January 1988 he featured in Silver Wilkie's angling column in the *Daily Record* newspaper for taking not one, but two salmon on the opening day of the season:

> Chris McManus's feat on Loch Tay on Wednesday's opening day was incredible. He caught two salmon at the same time! Chris, from Killin in Perthshire, was trolling four rods in a boat out of the Highland Lodges when two springers took simultaneously as he neared Ardeonaig. Goodness knows how Chris managed to do it, but he did, and successfully played both fish and landed them, one after the other – two beauties of 18 and 16lbs. There was only one other fish caught on the loch, a nine pounder, out of Clachaig. For most anglers, however, the grand gala opening day of the River Tay, Loch Tay and all the other rivers in the system, is a bleak one.

The following story, which Chris told me, exemplifies his trolling skills and is one of the most amusing fishing tales that I have ever heard.

"Davy Reid was one of the nicest guys on Planet Earth; his brand of humour was almost as legendary as his love of fishing. Dave's other great love in life was good food; it would not be unfair to say that because of this last love, Dave was a bit on the large side, which tended to restrict his movements. But what Dave lacked in gymnastic prowess was more than made up for by his enthusiasm for fishing, and his side-splitting stories. So, with your permission, let me tell you a story about Big Davy.

"Many years ago I gillied for Davy on opening day on Loch Tay when we were fishing from the Ardeonaig Hotel at the west end of the loch, and it was to this hotel that we returned in triumph later that day with the splendid silver bar of a 21lb salmon. It was the start of a very good season for the hotel and I was lucky enough to take several springers in the mid-20lbs and three fish of over 30lbs in weight. It therefore came as no surprise to me, as these accounts trickled down the grapevine, that in the middle of March Davy announced that he was determined to have another day on the loch. So, on a cold spring morning Davy duly arrived at the harbour, well armed with his extraordinary enthusiasm for a good day out and a plentiful supply of food to fortify the inner man. In truth, a lesser man might have been less enthusiastic, because although it was a beautiful, crisp morning, there was not a breath of wind and the loch was mirror calm, and as many anglers will confirm, trolling for salmon along the shores of Loch Tay in a flat calm can be hard going. Most fishermen, myself included, would much prefer a good wave and a good wind, or as Bobby, a local worthy would, describes the best conditions, 'Aye, ye could fair dap an ostrich oot there.'

"However, Davy was not one to be dismayed by a mere technicality. 'Ah, bugger it. We will have a good day out anyway, regardless of the weather,' he said. This sentiment was gleefully shared by our other companion for the day, my black Labrador Old Blue; like all Labradors, his main reason for getting up in the morning was food, whether raiding the bins when no one was looking or scrounging from guests with his standard, doleful, 'I'm starving' look. The somersaults and back flips being performed by an excited Labrador that morning suggested to me that Old Blue was glad to see Big Davy. But let's face it, to Old Blue, Davy was, quite simply, a walking food factory – his Barbour jacket pockets were always full of mouth-watering goodies, his bulky game bag stuffed with culinary delights.

"As we sailed out into the loch I could feel the gentle warmth of the sun as it rose steadily. We passed boat after boat of local gillies and their guests, with everyone bemoaning the conditions. Some ever resorted to calling upon divine intervention, trying to whistle up a wind through puckered lips. However, most just settled down and enjoyed the day as best they could. After all, 'a bad day's fishing is still better than a good day in the office'. Personally, I was not too upset. Dave's company more than made up for the conditions and I was soon laughing out loud at his mad sense of humor.

"A certain Labrador, totally indifferent to any weather pattern, was snapping up the frequent half-eaten pie or sandwich that was cast in his direction. My protestations of, 'Please don't feed him,' fell on deaf ears. At this point I should explain that this loopy Labrador, when out on the loch with me, always resided in the bow of the boat, just under the spray deck where under normal conditions he would sleep for most of the day, uninterested in anything to do with fishing. But not when Big Davy was onboard – nope. Old Blue was as wound up as a coiled spring, his every sense geared up for that moment when a half-eaten butty would sail in his direction.

"Thankfully, by midday Davy's seemingly inexhaustible lunchbox was finished. 'All gone,' he said, showing his outstretched hands. Blue uncannily understood the meaning, gave a long, doleful sigh and curled up on his blanket and was soon asleep, no doubt dreaming of dinner. It really was a picture-perfect day, snowcapped Ben More and Stobinian in the distance, and the graceful shape of Ben Lawers reflected in the deep waters of the loch. Maybe not the best of fishing conditions but, boy, it was good to be out. One hour later, as we swung round from the Ardeonaig rocks to head over to the north shore, a somewhat peckish Dave reached into his magical game bag and produced a small camping stove and a large catering tin of ravioli.

"'Davy,' I said, 'you have got to be kidding!'

"'Oh,' he replied, just a wee snack till we get back for lunch.' I looked on in total disbelief as he proceeded to open the tin and sit it on the small gas stove. 'Nae bother,' laughed Dave as the stove roared into life. As he bent over, stirring his bubbling ravioli, another apparition appeared from behind Davy's ample frame, a large dog, drooling uncontrollably.

"We were by now about 200 yards into our journey across the loch and everything was normal, expect for this big guy heating a catering tin of ravioli, closely watched by an over-excited dog. However, the tranquility of the scene was not to last. The steady hiss of the gas stove complimented by the gentle bubbling of superheated ravioli was suddenly replaced by the scream of Davy's Alvey reel as it roared into life. The hardy fly rod bent round in the rod rest as we hooked into a fish. We had hit a running fish in the middle of the loch. You often see them leaping headlong out of the depths but the chances of connecting with them are very remote. Overjoyed and thinking that you just never know the minute when something will take, I turned and adjusted the engine throttle to a steadier pace and shouted, 'Fish on!'

"I turned to assess Davy's reaction, just in time to see him make a huge lunge for the rod. 'No!' I cried, 'leave it and get the other rods in. Quick.' But Dave was beyond that. With a mighty sweep he struck into the fish. But unfortunately for Davy, who was still sitting, the momentum toppled him backwards. Over he went into the bow, his hands still firmly grasping the rod. I thought for a fleeting second that things could not get any worse, and I was wrong. As Dave went floundering backwards his left foot booted the tin of bubbling ravioli into the air and also knocked over the flaming stove. The tin of ravioli landed upside-down and its gooey contents were rapidly spreading all over the floorboards. The one thought in my mind, however, was to get to the bloody stove and turn it off, as I was by now stamping out flames with my non-fire retardant wellies and slipping all over the place on mountains of ravioli.

"With the stove switched off and my legs recovering from my impromptu Torvill and Dean impression, I gave a sigh of relief and tried to take stock of the situation. Meanwhile, a deranged Labrador that had decided that all his Christmases had come at once, had leaped over the incapacitated Davy, who was still holding onto the buckled fishing rod as though his very life depended on it, joined me at the rear of the boat and proceeded to devour as much ravioli as he could comfortably reach. Old Blue, who had never been the sharpest tool in the box, discovered that still bubbling ravioli was just a tad hot. He was howling in pain and busily engaged in trying to regurgitate that which he had eaten.

"Once again my bewildered brain tried to take stock of the situation. I cast my eyes over the disastrous scene: Dave lying on his back with the bent fishing rod, a bewildered dog hanging over the side trying to cool its tongue in the loch, smoke gently rising from the soles my wellies and ravioli parcels everywhere. In this dream-like state, I honestly wondered for a moment if we had been shelled from the shore. Thankfully, reality quickly kicked in. I cleaned the mess as best I could, ordered a very sheepish dog back to his blanket, and helped a large, helpless fisherman back onto his seat. And the fish was still on. Yes, it was by now miles from the boat but, joy of joys, it was still on. A short time later a relieved and overwrought gillie slipped the net under a very confused small fish for a very large happy fisherman.

"'Jings,' roared Davy, 'that's one for the book!' A much-needed dram was raised in salute to a 12lb 8oz salmon – not necessarily the largest fish that I have seen, but certainly one of the most memorable.

"Yet again, Big Davy and I returned to the Ardeoniag Hotel in triumph. Dave was in excellent form as he entertained his fellow guests with his unique account of the one that didn't get away. Sadly, neither Old Blue nor Big Davy are with us now but, just occasionally, especially on a flat, calm spring mornings, I find myself laughing out loud as I remember that mad ravioli day on Loch Tay."

Chris has had many 'day jobs' during his life, in sales and marketing, but nothing that he ever seemed to want to turn into a career. I suppose that he could be described as a rolling stone, never to be coated with the moss of conformity, but quietly determined to do that which he loved best, which was fishing, shooting and stalking. In many ways I followed a similar pattern to Chris, and was once described by a heavily be-suited senior executive interviewing me for job as a 'rolling stone'. Well, my stone stopped rolling when I decided that all I really wanted to do with my life was to write – about fishing, Scotland's history and amazing landscape and the people I met along the way. I was able to do this because my wife Ann encouraged me to do so and was able to carry the financial burden that my decision entailed.

Chris, who lives with his partner Shirley, found his neuk and he worked hard to protect, develop and preserve it. At one stage Chris spent a year in Holland learning the skills required to trap eels, then returned to Scotland and trapped eels professionally; whenever and wherever, a riparian owner gave him permission to do so.

Chris also became acquainted with Mervin Browne, who owned an estate at Midtown on Ardtalnaig on the south shore of Loch Tay. Chris used to help out with estate work, take guests grouse-shooting and stalking. He also reared pheasants for the estate shoot as well as helped with the lambing and haymaking.

Ann and I have walked over a large part of this area. On a sharp April morning a few years ago we parked our car at the gate at the end of the road up from Ardtalnaig. During a memorable day we climbed Tullich Hill (2,238ft) and followed the ridge over to Meall nan Oighreag (2,684ft) then on to the highest peak of the day, Creag Uchdag (2,884ft), 'the crag of the hollows'. The tops were still widely patched with snow and we were rewarded with the fine sight of mountain hares going about their hare-like affairs. On our return journey, crossing the streams of the infant River Almond, we picked up the excellent track at Dunan and hoofed it back to Claggan, where the estate shepherd was busy with his flock. He asked me if I had anything to do with sheep and when I replied that I hadn't he said, "Ah, a sensible man."

Whilst helping out on the estate Chris continued his work as a gillie on Loch Tay but also found the time to travel extensively in pursuit of fishing, including regular visits to the Altnaharra Hotel in the days when it was owned by Paul Panchaud to fish Loch Naver. He has also fished in New Zealand, Tasmania and British Columbia, and even discovered excellent trout fishing in Sri Lankra, where, he told me, the initial stock of trout came from Loch Leven. Chris also has fishing on a beat of the River Tay near Grandtully.

When I last spoke to him on the phone, he and Shirley had just returned after a week sailing in the Firth of Clyde, Bute and the Crinan Canal, in the company of one of the friends he had made when learning how to trap eels in Holland. As ever, Chris was bubbling with enthusiasm for fishing. Just speaking to him made me want to be out on river or loch without delay, and I think that this is part of the magic that Chris brings to everything he does.

3
Ian Smart, Ben Loyal Estate, Sutherland

I named my black Labrador puppy Sgeireadh, the Gaelic spelling for the township of Skerray, a small, sea-girt community clustered around a rocky headland in North Sutherland. It lies between Tongue, where my wife Ann and I live, and Bettyhill. Sgeireadh's parents were working dogs from Sutherland sporting estates and she was utterly beautiful. I am an angler and had called my previous dog, a golden retriever, Breac, the Gaelic name for trout. When Breac died, Sgerieadh arrived as a wonderful gift from Ian Smart, head keeper on the Ben Loyal Estate. I had known Ian Smart for a number of years, a countryman through and through, thoroughly wise in the ways of the hill and all that resided therein. However, I came to know Ian much better when he married Jean, my younger daughter.

We adored Sgeireadh, but difficulties arose when I began to try to train her. I had never had any problems with my retrievers; they were good-natured, eminently biddable beasts and always keen to learn. Sgeireadh defeated me. At one stage, having thrown out a dummy on a long string, she picked up the dummy and dived behind a gorse bush. In my efforts to bring her to heel, I ended up essentially tied to the bush by my own string. It was humiliating. Ann and I used to take her for frequent walks, but as far as Sgeireadh was concerned, a few miles a day on the skirts of Ben Loyal was never, ever enough. At that time we were having extensive alterations done to our house and Sgeireadh was all too anxious to help, chewing everything she could lay her teeth into, including walls, doors, chairs, carpets, table legs, shoes, hats – whatever. If she could reach it, she chewed it.

The final straw came one day when Ian called at our cottage. I explained my problem. Ian had a recently shot mallard in his game bag and Sgeireadh was sitting by him, looking at it expectantly and perfectly to heel. Ian removed the bird from his bag and showed it to the dog, and then threw the bird as far as he could, down into the little glen by the side of our house. Sgeireadh never moved an inch, although I saw her body trembling with excitement. Ian pointed in the direction of where the bird had landed, muttered something, and Sgeireadh shot off like a rocket. At some distance, she glanced back at Ian, who pointed to his right. Moments later Sgeireadh was back in front of him, with the mallard in her mouth. Ian took the bird, put it in his game bag, then turned to me and said, "Can't really see what the problem is, Bruce. She seems fine to me."

We realised then that it would be wrong for us to keep Sgeireadh, no matter how much we loved her. Reluctantly, we discussed this with Ian and Jean and it was decided that Sgeireadh should go to a better place, a place where she could do what she was bred to do. One of Ian's brothers, also a keeper, took Sgeireadh, and as far as I am aware, since then she has lived happily ever after. The last time we saw her was when we were in Ian's kitchen at Loyal Lodge and Sgeireadh and her new owner called to say hello. Sgeireadh saw Ann and instantly flew at her, jumping up to her chest, almost knocking her over, whining and licking furiously, and in so doing, sending a considerable array of ornaments various flying in all directions. But when she was called to heel she obeyed. I watched her settle below her master's chair whilst we chatted and drank coffee. I confess, however, that I was gratified to notice a few moments later that she had surreptitiously sequestered her master's best bonnet and was busy tearing the innards out if it. That's my girl, I thought. That's my girl.

Some years later, I reminded Ian about Sgeireadh and the mallard. He said, "You really have to show a dog what it is supposed to do. If they don't understand, they won't do it. I also remember that I once bought a beautiful dog, a big black Labrador – not very expensive, but expensive enough, nothing special and not necessarily well-trained – just to retrieve ducks. It was aggressive and I wasn't very sure about it. When I had it out it didn't seem to do much; the dog wasn't comfortable working in the dark and when I tried him on woodcock, rather than retrieve them he would just stay to heel. All this changed when I went to a pheasant shoot. The dog was with my boss, who was one of the guns, and as I passed on the first drive there were still birds being shot. I saw the dog watching a bird fall and knew that he had marked it, about 150 yards away, behind some trees. I sent the dog out, over the river, in behind the trees and back it came with the pheasant. That is what the dog wanted to do, and he did it all day like a perfect gentleman."

I asked Ian why sheepdogs, highly intelligent animals in their own right, were never used as gun dogs. "A lot of sheepdogs are actually gun shy," he said. "I don't know if it is in their genes but that seems to be the case." He paused and smiled. "When I first came to Loyal, there was a shepherd along the road who had trained his sheepdog – I think its name was Nick – to respond to signals from the horn of his van. He could put the dog out almost a mile away and it would still hear the horn. One New Year's Day, when they normally take the tups in from the hill, he was badly hungover from the night before, a sore heed, and he couldn't whistle. Anyway, I thought that I had mastered using the horn signals so I said that I would help him out. However, I must have given one beep too many because the dog began herding the sheep the wrong way. They were all heading back out onto the hill. After about ten minutes my friend managed to sufficiently compose himself to get the dog under control, and to give me a piece of his mind for causing near disaster."

We were sitting round the kitchen table, talking, with one eye on the clock. Jake, my youngest grandson, was due home from school shortly, meaning peace would soon end. Ann and I have been blessed with ten grandchildren, collectively known to me as 'The Enemy', but not if any of their parents are within earshot. As Ian and I began talking, this is what he told me of his life and experiences as a keeper.

Ian was born in 1962 and he has had dogs since he was twelve years old. The family lived at Boath near Alness in Easter Ross. His father was a keeper on the Novar Estate for some twenty-three years. Ian said, "I remember him telling me that in his whole life, including being in the army during the last war, he had only seven jobs. He was good at lots of things. His own father was a drover in Aberdeenshire, moving hogs about all winter, and I spent the first few years of my life at Killilan, near Kyle of Lochalsh on the Road the Isles in Wester Ross. Father was a stalker there and it was probably the best job in the world. One of his tasks was to catch spring salmon and send them to market in London. That was in the late 1960s, I suppose, because there were hundreds of fish there then, and a lot of poachers as well. Father once ended up in hospital for a few weeks after tackling a gang. But Mother got weary. There was one winter when it rained almost consistently for weeks on end. There were seven children in the house and she had nowhere to hang the washing out to dry. So they moved back Ardross and I went to school in Alness and then to Invergordon."

In those days, before the arrival of the ill-conceived Invergordon Aluminium Smelter and the off-shore oil industry, Easter Ross was a much quieter place than it is today. The smelter, which was supposed to bring long-term security to the community by providing 2,000 jobs, didn't last, leaving the people who had moved north to work unemployed. Ian told me, "School was fine. I quite enjoyed school. Well, up until the big industries moved in. Thousands of people came with them, from all different nationalities. It was a shock to me. There were about twenty-three children in my primary school, suddenly there were three or four hundred. Secondary school was the same, and I just didn't take to all these hoards of people. The change for me came when I was thirteen. I was out shooting rabbits one night with my tame fox; Father had caught it in a trap, and I was smart enough to realise that if I reared the fox it would help me to find more rabbits to shoot. I think I knew then that I wanted to be a stalker."

Ian didn't have the fox long, however, because that same year he acquired a roe deer as well; some well-meaning individual had found the little thing, and thinking quite wrongly that it had been abandoned, brought it to Ian's father, who allowed Ian to keep it. Ian got the fox in April and the roe deer in June, so by September the fox was fully-grown. Ian said, "The fox had got quite wild by then. When I went out after rabbits it would follow me at a distance and when I shot a rabbit it would charge in, take the rabbit and run off with it. It was eventually run down on the road by a car.

"I think I grew up in every boy's dream world, where I could walk out of the house, cross a small, quiet road, follow a track into the woods and immediately start stalking. It was during one of those evenings that I shot my first deer. A roe deer got up, running through a forestry plantation, running hard. I just threw the rifle up, fired a shot and it fell over. When I looked at its head – a buck – I thought it was a good one, but I was scared to tell my father in case he would be angry. One of my brothers was home at the time and I took him to see the deer. He told Father.

"I remember being in my bedroom and hearing Father shouting for me to come down. I thought that's it, my .22 rifle would be confiscated and I wouldn't get it back for days. He weighed in to me, but I could sense his heart wasn't really in it, for eventually he said, 'Son, I am very proud of you. That buck is the finest I have ever seen here. It is almost in the bronze medal class for roe deer.' It remained top beast for that beat on the estate until a few years ago, and I still have the head.

"Part of Father's job was to keep roe deer out of the plantations, where they damaged the new trees, so after that incident Father started taking me with him. He told me, 'Ian, anyone who can stalk a roe deer and then shoot it with a .22 rifle when it was running can shoot anything.' We shot bucks in the summer and the females in winter. Father was a terrific shot and could account at times for four or five deer, no matter whether they were standing or running. If a beast was wounded, then my job was to stalk in and shoot it with my .22 rifle."

Ian, for me, is the epitome of a Highland keeper – determined, confident and always in control. He does not seem to understand the words "can't be done". No matter what the situation – be it recovering a bogged-down Argocat single-handedly, to dealing with a recalcitrant guest on the hill – Ian will cope. He is also a highly competent angler. The first time we were salmon fishing together, on the little River Borgie, I was still struggling into my waders when he was tackled up and ready to go. I asked him to leave me and begin on the first pool. By the time I arrived Ian had an 8lb salmon on the bank. His son, Jake, is now eight years old and is already displaying all the traits and attitudes of his father, including an instinctive love of and appreciation for the wildlife around him. My guess is that Jake is another keeper in the making, and you will meet him again later on in these pages.

There was never any doubt in Ian's mind about what he wanted to do after he left school. When he was fourteen his teacher asked the class to write down where they thought they would be and what they thought they would be doing when they were thirty. Ian wrote that he wanted to be a stalker on an estate, and that is exactly what he became. His father had an enormous influence on Ian and quietly encouraged him in all he did. When his father was getting on a bit and not as agile as he had been, in the winter Ian would skip school to help him out. "I used to be driven four or five miles to the point where I caught the bus that would take us to school, and if it was good hard stalking weather, with snow on the ground, Father would give me a nod before I set off. If the bus was just a minute late, I would run back home and go stalking with him. The school never complained. I think that they knew what was going on, but perhaps they realised that I wasn't getting into trouble and probably learning more by doing that than I would have done sitting miserable in the classroom. So my last years at school worked well for me. I left in the following March, just when the heather burning began."

Ian's first job was with his father on a youth training scheme, and he worked through the summer and winter until the spring. An elder brother was a gillie in Knoydart, and when he came home he told Ian about his work there and that the estate were looking for another gillie, Ian took the job. "I realise now that Knoydart was probably not the best place to go. It is probably the toughest place that I have ever been in all my life. I was turning seventeen when I went there and it took me weeks to get fit enough to tackle all that I was asked to do. I wasn't keen on the owner's attitude. We were all lined up outside the big house by 8am and if it was raining, then we were soaked even before we started the day. It had to be an early start because it could take an hour or more to reach some of the stalking beats. The laird would then come out and pair off his guests with a stalker. 'Right, you go with that stalker, you go with him', and so on. However, that would be the last we would see of him until the following morning."

One of the reasons that Ian had decided to go to Knoydart was to learn more about working with ponies, but because of the rough nature of the terrain, there were many places that even ponies could not reach. Ponies were used to take the stags that guests shot off the hill, but the beat that Ian was assigned to was too wild for the ponies and the gillies had to drag the beasts down the mountainside to the nearest Land Rover track. This was hard, hard work and could sometimes take more than four hours. When Ian had arrived in Knoydart, he weighed 10.5 stone, and within a few months he was 13.5 stone, without an inch of fat on his body. Even then, he found himself dragging animals that were considerably heavier than he was, sometimes stags of up to 18 stone. The heaviest stag Ian recalls dragging weighed more than 21 stone.

Ian stayed at Knoydart until the end of November and then decided to leave. "It was not really for me," he said. "There was a lot of drinking going on and I got fed up with that. And we stayed in a very primitive bothy. You had to light a fire if you wanted to dry your clothes, light a fire if you wanted a bath." So he was not too sad to say goodbye to Knoydart and its Rough Bounds.

After Knoydart, Ian moved round a number of Highland estates, always seeking jobs where he could further expand and develop his knowledge of keepering. He spent the winter after Knoydart helping his father, culling deer for him, then went to nearby Ben Wyvis Estate, and on to the Monar Estate. He also worked at Braemore Junction and Brae Langwell and Glenbeck in Wester Ross and Inverlael, where one of his brothers was a shepherd. Ian told me, "I enjoyed the hill and I also enjoyed shepherding. I thought that this might be a bit of my grandfather's days as a drover coming out in me. A lot of the stalkers were also shepherds and there was a good atmosphere over at Ullapool. I was doing all kinds of different jobs in the summer, but always kept myself free to go back and help my father in the winter."

Ian came to the Ben Loyal Estate in 1987 and I first met him when I was working on a programme for the BBC television series *Landward*. One of the episodes was to be centered round graceful Ben Loyal (2,509ft), the 'Queen' of Scottish mountains. The presenter, Lindsay Cannon, and I planned to walk the high tops, exploring the flora and fauna as we went. In order to facilitate this plan and get the cameraman, sound man and all their gear up the hill, I asked the estate if they could help out, and they kindly provided an Argocat, with Ian Smart in the driving seat. As we were approaching An Caisteal, the highest peak on the ridge, Ian suddenly stopped the Argo, leapt out and set off at a great rate, running across the hill. He had spotted a dotterel, a small summer visitor that is rarely seen below 2,500 feet. I had also spotted it, the first one I had ever seen, but had not been sufficiently confident to mention it. These are beautiful little birds, the upper parts brownish-black, with a brown breast separated by a white band from the chestnut colour of its lower breast and flanks. The tail is black and bordered white.

When Ian returned to the Argo, he explained that he had been watching a dotterel. He was excited and pleased with the sighting and I too was delighted that I had caught a glimpse of the bird. I think it was at that moment I realised Ian was a special sort of person. In my experience, very few would react in such a fashion.

Indeed, I am minded of a time driving down the side of Loch Loyal when I saw a pair of black-throated divers enjoying the waves, much to the dismay of my passenger, another high-powered female BBC television executive. I screeched to a halt to watch the birds. She turned to me and said dismissively, "For God's sake, Bruce. Don't get your knickers in a twist, it's only a bloody bird." The purpose of our journey that morning was to investigate the implications and impact of proposals for a super quarry at Loch Eriboll, designed to excavate Beinn Cannabeinne

(1,257ft), a considerable mountain, and relocate it in bits to various roads and building projects throughout England and Europe. So, I thought, no prizes then for guessing upon which side of the super quarry fence she will be sitting.

Ian also has his own ups and downs with stalking guests. He told me of one incident where it had taken hours to get his guest in position for a shot. When Ian indicated an animal to be shot, the guest complained, "Oh, but that one doesn't have enough points." Ian stood up. "What on earth are you doing?" the guest shouted.

Ian replied, "Well, if you are not going to shoot that stag, we might as well go home because there is not another stag on this hill that you will shoot. I decide which beast is to be shot, not you."

One day, Ian had stalked into a stag that had only one horn and his guest refused to shoot it. A mist had come down, so Ian took him away and walked him about for a while, and then brought him back to the stag. "Oh, look," Ian said. "There's a stag! Let's shoot that one," which the guest did – the one-horned stag. On another occasion, again on a misty day, Ian had stalked in to a six-pointer. The stag was lying down and the guest could see how narrow the horns were. "I don't like that stag," he said. "Its horns are too narrow." They crawled out and did another walk in the mist, and Ian stalked back. The stag was side-on and the horns hardly visible. Ian said, "Just shoot it in the neck." The guest did. Ian said, "If there is a stag on the hill that I don't want shot, I will walk miles round it and put hundreds of deer in front of me so that we can't get to that stag."

Ian also had the pleasure of stalking with one of the world's most famous authorities on deer, the late G. Kenneth Whitehead (1913–2004). Whitehead wrote ten books on the subject, including his monumental work, *The Whitehead Encyclopedia of Deer*. He hunted and photographed deer all over the world and was a founding member of the British Deer Society. Ian was naturally nervous about stalking with the great man and determined that he would follow the book in all regards to avoid attracting criticism. "I met him in the morning, a lovely old man," Ian said. "I think he was about eighty then, white-haired, jolly and smiling, with a dog at his heel. So I said, 'Grab your rifle and we'll go to the target.'

"'Oh no,' he said, 'we don't need to go to the target, I tried it yesterday.'

"I replied, 'Well, if we are not going to the target then we are not going to the hill.' He got his gear and off we went. And he had forgotten the bolt for his rifle. We returned to the lodge and he got it, and he then put three bullets into the centre of the target."

Ian continued, "My problem was keeping him out of sight during the stalk, because he was wearing a dark green coat that stuck out like a sore thumb. His dog, Benji, was fine. It was yellow and blended into the landscape. Once I relaxed, the day got better and I realised that he was not there to find fault, but just an ordinary guy enjoying his stalking. He was really friendly, cracking jokes, a good companion and easy to be with on the hill. It was fun to stalk with somebody who put you on your toes, and I remember that day fondly. He shot two stags with me the first day and a single stag on the second."

Ian also told me a wonderful story about an unhappy guest. "We once we had a guest staying in the lodge who never really had an exciting stalking story to tell at the dinner table. After the second night of his stay, the Count Knuth, the Danish owner of the estate, asked if he could have a word with me in the office. The Count explained that the past couple of evening dinner parties had been a bit dull, so please could I make the stalking a bit more exciting for the guest? I assured him that I would do my best.

"The next morning the sun was shining and the wind was blowing from the north-west, perfect stalking conditions. We set out from Inchkinloch in the Argocat, heading uphill to Loch nan Beiste. Half a mile before the loch, we stopped and went forward on foot. It was rutting time, when the stags collect as many hinds as they can manage for mating. Competition between the stags for control of the hinds is serious business. The sound of stags roaring that day was intense, but after a good long spy with my glass I could see there was the chance of putting in a good stalk over open ground with the deer in full view. We crawled over a ridge into the shadows of Duncan's Corrie and got within 200 metres of two stags, both of which had each gathered thirty to forty hinds. We crawled a further 100 metres through the shadows and onto open ground. The sun was sitting low in the sky behind us, but shining directly onto the stags. As a result it blurred their vision and they weren't able to see us. I sensed that being so close to the roaring stags made my guest nervous, and he said, 'I think we are close enough now.'

"I said, 'No, we will crawl a bit further to that hummock over there as it will make a perfect rest for your rifle.' He was not too happy about this but agreed, and we crawled slowly towards hummock. Once there, with the two stags and their hinds eighty metres in front of us, a third stag suddenly appeared over a ridge about fifty metres to the left, roaring its socks off.

"At that point I thought things were going to get interesting and there was going to be a fight. With all three stags roaring loudly at each other, the new stag and one of the stags holding hinds started moving towards each other, obviously to fight. They walked parallel for twenty metres, roaring at one another, then stopped, put their heads to the ground and started tossing the heather and moss with their antlers, weighing each other up. Once again, they walked parallel, getting closer and closer. There was a crash as they locked horns. The fight came to an end after about three minutes and the new arrival won; he was a bit older and heavier than his rival and had a black horn. He turned round to claim his prize only to find the third stag had rounded up all the hinds whilst the fight was going on.

"So it all started again. The two stags quickly came together and started fighting, slightly up the hill, right in front of us and only about fifty metres away. They pushed each other about, all the time getting closer and closer to where we lay; we could hear their horns clashing, their heavy breathing and angry snorting. I could hardly believe that I was so close to such an amazing spectacle. It was one of those once-in-a-lifetime moments. I looked at the guest and thought, 'Now you will have a story to tell.' But he was lying with his head down and wasn't watching. Why, I don't know. Perhaps he was scared that the stags would charge us. 'Well,' I thought, 'let's have some fun.' I told the guest to get his rifle out before the stags were on top of us and with that he looked up and saw what was going on. However, when he took his rifle out, the hinds saw him and started to move away, with the victorious stag, the beast with the black horn in hot pursuit, determined to make sure that he claimed his rightful prize before further interruptions. He was within 150 metres of the hinds when he paused briefly on a knoll, broad side-on to where we lay – an opportunity not to be missed. The guest aimed and fired and it was over. I took a very happy and excited guest back to the lodge that night. The following morning the Count looked at me, smiled and said, 'Dinner was excellent last night, Ian. Thank you.'"

Before Ian came to the Ben Loyal Estate, he had rarely fly-fished. As there were a number of good trout lochs in his charge, he decided that it was time to rectify that position. In May and June, therefore, he would walk out to various lochs where he soon had 'mastered' the gentle art of casting a fly and catching and landing trout. One of the lochs Ian fished was Loch Fhionnaich, tucked between Sgor Fhionnaich (1,864ft) and Beinn Bheag (2,441ft), two of the five peaks in the crown of Scotland's mountain 'Queen'. The loch is also known as 'The Children's Loch', because it is the ideal place to introduce little ones to fly-fishing; blank days on Fhionnaich are unknown, the record being 140 trout to one rod in a single day. One morning, tramping out to Loch Fhionnaich, Ian glanced down on another of the estate waters, Loch Haluim, and thought he could see rain falling on the surface of the loch, although there was blue sky all around. It wasn't rain but trout rising. He tried to count the rings made by the fish as they rose to take surface flies, but gave it up when he was in the hundreds and still counting. Ian decided to invite his father and brother Bobby, who both fished, to join him for a day on the loch, and also so that he could benefit from watching experienced anglers in action and thus hone his own skills.

They were late starting and didn't arrive at the loch until about 11am. On the first drift, Ian's dad said, "Ian, you must fish as well."

But Ian told me, "Really, there was not time for that, right from the start, because I was busy keeping the boat in position and unhooking all the trout they were catching. My father fished a short line with two flies and caught just as many as Bobby fished with three flies. Father would hook a fish and hesitate whilst playing it to let another trout take his second fly, generally within a few seconds. They had lunch at three, very quickly, as they wanted to be out on the loch again as soon as possible. Towards evening, Dad said to me, 'Ian, the fish have gone down.'

"'What makes you think that?' I asked.

"'Well,' he answered, 'I have had three casts without getting at least a tug.'"

They finished at 7.30pm and Ian told me that his father had said that it was the best day's fishing he ever had in his life. During his final years, Ian's father always spoke about the wonderful day he had enjoyed on Haluim and always hoped to return there. Sadly, he died before this wish could be achieved. Ian said, "For me, the memory of that happy day on Haluim with Dad is always with me and I often use the flies he used then, Blue Zulu on the bob and a Goat's Toe on the tail."

When Ian arrived on Ben Loyal Estate there was no effective deer management plan in place. Ian said, "It has been a privilege to work here. It is a unique experience to manage a herd that's never been managed before. You are aware that you are creating future generations of deer. I guess that by now I am on my third or fourth generation. I think that present deer management practice is too hard and at times I wonder if Scottish Natural Heritage and the Deer Commission Scotland really want deer on the hills; they are ordering so many animals to be culled. Whatever the rights and wrongs might be – and everybody has their own opinion on that subject – I am satisfied that the animals on my ground are a lot better now than they were when I first came here."

Amen to that, I thought as I watched Ian turn to greet my grandson Jake, home from school. Ian set off for the deer larder, with Jake bouncing happily along beside him.

4
Jock Royan, Kinermory, Spey

Jock Royan is every inch an angler. He exudes a deep love of salmon fishing that is instantly recognisable, tangible and entirely captivating. His enthusiasm is boundless. You instinctively know that you are in safe hands and assured of the best possible opportunity of sport when Jock is around. He is head gillie on the Kinermory beat of the River Spey, upstream from the town of Aberlour where the five-year average for the beat has increased to almost 200 fish. On a fine April day I called to see Jock at his fishing hut on the banks of the river. It is not easy to find, but eventually I spotted the rough track and followed it down to the hut. Jock greeted me with a wide smile and a strong handshake, his black Labrador dogs happy at his heels. Over a cup of coffee in a small side room, we settled to talk whilst his fishing guests next door enjoyed their lunch.

Jock was born in 1963 in Turriff. He told me, "I was very lucky, because my uncle was a keen salmon fisherman and on school holidays he soon had me fishing the River Ythan near Methlick. I caught my first fish on a homemade black-and-white Devon minnow there when I was twelve years old. The stream was very narrow at Methlick and most fish came out from under the bank to take your lure." I can certainly vouch for it being a narrow stream, because some years ago my son Blair and I fished there and found it to be a challenging business, stalking fish and fighting off the midges.

Jock continued, "At the same time, my father took over as

manager for the British Legion Club in Turriff, and a lot of the local anglers used to gather in the bar to swap fishing stories. One of them was Jock Masson, an enormously experienced and respected angler who had recently retired. He took me under his wing, introduced me to salmon and sea-trout fishing and taught me how to cast more proficiently. Jock and I spent many wonderful hours together, days and nights fishing the Deveron's private beats, sometimes with permission, sometimes without. As a teenager he used to fish the Forglen beat throughout the summer months for sea-trout and, of course, the best time to catch them is when the bats appear.

"I used to cycle along the drive to Forglen house in the dark, peddling like there was no tomorrow on the way there through the sheer anticipation of fishing, and on the way home, as fast as I could because of fear of the dark. I was fishing alone one evening in a pool called the Stable Flats, just as the light was fading. For some strange reason, I turned to look up river just as a scraggy heron was about to land on my head. To this day I don't know which of us got the biggest fright, but the smell when it deposited its stomach contents all over me was disgusting. My only solace was the thought that, in future, that heron would think very carefully before landing on what it thought was a fence post in the middle of a river. My cycle journey home that night broke all existing records."

Another great influence on Jock then was Jonathan Taylor, a well-known gillie on the Deveron's finest beat, Forglen. Jock said, "He was still fully employed at eighty-four years old when I first met him. He was such an inspiration that I couldn't wait to leave school and become a gillie. When I did, after passing my standard grades in 1980, I had a great year on Forglen under Jonathan's watchful eye. Not only did he and Jock Masson teach me about salmon, their life cycle and habits, but also many other lessons about life in general. They were remarkable men in the great tradition of distinguished Scottish salmon anglers and wonderful role models for a young lad.

"Forglen was a fantastic beat," Jock said. "It used to produce more than 1,000 sea-trout and many hundreds of salmon each season, and even today the beat can take 500 to 600 fish. Jock Masson and Jonathan had both been in the army and having them as mentors was a huge privilege. People remember their younger days in different ways, what sort of childhood they had, but I vividly remember these two men. They had an enormous effect on me and to this day I still value their kindness, patience and good advice."

Jock has been fishing for salmon since the age of twelve and has spent the last thirty years of his life on various rivers throughout the world where he has caught in excess of 1,000 fish. However, following his chosen career did not come easy for Jock. His parents were convinced that being a gillie was not really a proper job for their son, and towards the end of 1980 they marched Jock off to Aberdeen to join the Royal Air Force (RAF). Jock served for twenty-six years, initially in East Anglia, then Lossiemouth, and in Germany for five years. Jock rose through the ranks until he was promoted to work on the Euro fighter aircraft and he told me, "I was doing a great deal of appraisals and engineering reports, which all came with the rank. The hands-on approach had long since gone, and the combination of these various reports, welfare issues and personal appraisals became rather tedious." Apart, that is, Jock said, from when he was serving in the Falkland Islands, where, of course, he went fishing.

"I was fishing on the incoming tide in an area known as the Frying Pan, and was amazed to see such frantic activity. The run of sea-trout was enormous, to the extent that they appeared fearless and entirely unaware of my presence; I even had one swim between my legs. It seemed bizarre behaviour and I was at a loss to understand why the fish should behave in such a fashion. However, all was quickly revealed when no more than ten feet from where I stood, an enormous elephant seal broke the surface and roared. It would have been a moment of complete comedy today if it had been captured on YouTube, and a delight to millions of viewers. But I can assure you it would have been a very short clip. For the first and last time in my life, I walked on water and was on dry land in seconds. As I looked back at the huge animal, I am convinced it had a wry, satisfied smile on its face.

"I remember reading about an incident in the Falklands shortly after the end of hostilities, when an RAF officer had a similar fright, although it came from behind him rather than the sea, in front of where he was fishing. Even for these remote islands, he was fishing in a remote area. In fact, if I remember correctly, he had been helicoptered in. The sea-trout were more than accommodating and he was enjoying marvellous sport. Suddenly, he heard a voice behind him and almost fell over in fright. 'Can I have a word with you, sir, please?' it said. Our angler turned round to find a local man on the shore gesticulating wildly. Recovering, he asked what the matter was, had there been some disaster, another outbreak of war? 'Oh, no,' came the reply, 'I just wanted to see your permit. I presume that you do have permission to fish here?"'

When Jock found that he was spending about nine months a year away from home and family, he was concerned. He had a daughter aged fourteen and a son of nine. "I knew that they really needed their dad at home." But Jock still retained his dream of becoming a gillie and was determined that somehow, some day he would become one. That day came in 1995 when he noticed an advert in his local Morayshire paper, *The Northern Scot*, for a gillie's job on the Kinermory beat of the Spey. He discussed the situation with his wife, who knew that that was what Jock really wanted to do, and he applied for the position. He told me, "I didn't think that I had much of a chance getting it, but much to my surprise, I did. Now I go to work in the morning with a spring in my step. Although I am earning but a fraction of the money I used to earn in the RAF, it doesn't really matter. Every day on the river is a pleasure. This is my seventh season now, and as a family, we could not be happier. I think that when you have a high level of enthusiasm it impacts on the guests as well. It becomes a buzz. We are fully-booked throughout the season and have a long reserve list of clients who would like to fish our water."

Jock has no regrets about the years he spent in the RAF. The people skills he acquired there have ideally equipped him for establishing excellent working relationships with his guests. Having spent eight years myself in the army and the Territorial Army, I could empathise with Jock. Over the years I also got to know a number of anglers who were former RAF officers. One lunchtime at Loch Hope, a member of our party was a very senior officer in the RAF. He was also an excellent rod and as we blethered, I asked if he had ever served in Southern Arabia, where I had done a tour of duty. I mentioned the problems we always had trying to contact the Meteor fighter jets that provided air cover at difficult sections of our convoy journeys. We always had an air liaison officer with us, but no matter how much he twirled knobs and pressed buttons, I can't remember ever hearing any response from the aircraft that screamed overhead. My companion smiled and said, "Funny you should mention that, Bruce. I used to fly one of these planes."

The other RAF couple I knew were the late Air Vice-Marshall Ron Morris and his wife Mary. They fished with me for many, many years and were wonderful company and great friends. Their first visit to the far north was on a trout-fishing expedition to a number of Caithness lochs, beginning with Loch Watten. When I arrived at the boat-mooring bay, they were ready for the off and we launched the boat and got down to business. However, there was a problem when I decided that we should lunch on the shore opposite the island in Factor's Bay: neither Ron nor Mary were wearing Wellington boots. Not daunted, I suggested that I piggyback them ashore. I did so, without mishap I am pleased to say, and after lunch carried them back to the boat. I think that sort of sealed our friendship. They were splendid company and are sadly missed.

None of the people that I introduced you to above suffered fools gladly, which I suppose is a consequence of military service. Neither does Jock. Whilst the vast majority of his guests are decent and friendly – as indeed most anglers are – there is always the odd one who needs 'special guidance'. The conservation code on the Spey is that anglers may keep every second fish; however at Kinermony, Jock likes his guests to keep only one for the week. The first, middle or last fish they catch so that they go home with a fish at the end of their week. Jock clearly explains all this on day one. However, on a couple of occasions after the guest has killed his/her fish for the week, a larger fish is caught and the angler will argue that because the code is voluntary, they are minded to kill it. Jock suggests that, of course the rules are voluntary, and they are entitled to keep every fish if they so wish; however, if they do, then they needn't think about coming back the following year. The fish is quickly returned to fight again another day.

Jock also tries to maintain a balance within his fishing parties. Even though the group are all the best of friends, the occasional guest, the one who generally thinks he knows the river better than anyone else, invariable wants to be first in the best pool on the Monday morning, even if he is not down to do so on the prearranged rotation. Jock said, "It can be a bit tricky, but if this happens, I concentrate all my efforts on the other rods and try to make sure, as far as I possibly can, that by the end of the week they have had more fish than their 'troublesome' companion."

Personally, I have always puzzled over why otherwise decent and considerate people suddenly behave like that. Is this something exclusive to salmon fishing? I remember two men, old friends who had been fishing together on the Thurso River. You could not hope to meet more charming and considerate companions. Politeness personified. There is one pool on the river where, if there is fish about, then the first rod down the pool catches it. When it came to getting this pool ahead of the other, these men would stoop to the most dastardly deeds to delay each other in tackling up and tying on flies. They would suddenly develop an aggressive personality akin to Robert Louis Stevenson's character, Mr Hyde; I have even seen a spool of nylon being 'accidentally' dropped and kicked under the car. However, once they were in the river, sweetness and light returned as though nothing untoward had taken place.

Of course, the opposite can also true. John Ashley Cooper, fishing with Jimmy Ross at Rothes, said, "Right, Jimmy, you go down the pool first."

"Oh, no, Major, that would never do."

"Yes it will, Jimmy, you and I have been fishing together for more than twenty years so it is about time you went first."

I remember last year fishing with the late Lord Matthew Ridley on the little Forss in Caithness. He had enjoyed reading my books and invited me for lunch and a cast on the river. After lunch we went over the Falls Pool. There is a very accommodating seat by the falls. It was a splendid afternoon, full of birdsong and light as we sat talking for a while and listening to the song of the river. Eventually, Matthew said, "Come on, Bruce, let me see how it should be done." I insisted that he should fish the pool first, but to no avail. Matthew died a few months later, in March 2012, but I will always remember his courtesy and gentle humour.

Jock Royan remembered his first year at Kinermony, "One of my guests turned up with a line on his reel fitted back to front. From his demeanour and attitude, it was obvious that what he didn't know about tackle wasn't worth knowing, and he was also less than unimpressed by the new gillie. So, rather than giving him a clue about the line, I let him fish on with it until the Thursday, even though he was having casting problems because of it. After all, who was I to tell anything to such an expert angler? When I did explain the situation and had sorted it out, he had the grace to be embarrassed, but relieved when he found that his casting skills had not entirely deserted him. I was bribed and sworn to secrecy – until now."

"Last July," Jock continued, "we had a guest who, as well as being a menace, wanted answers to every daft question he could ask me. His *pièce de résistance*, however, was undoubtedly at lunch on the Friday when he said, 'Jock, has anyone ever asked you a stupid question?' I replied without drawing breath, 'Not until this week.'"

I can't think of any situation that would find Jock Royan at a loss, and I am quite certain that his innate courtesy and sense of humour would always find the best way forward. He told me, "Of course, the gillie's role is to get to know his water thoroughly and to know which flies and lines to suggest that his guests use, but fundamentally, it is the way in which you interact with people that counts most. My first couple of seasons were challenging, purely due to the slower pace of life after such a busy career in the RAF. Fortunately, the previous gillie on the beat, who had been there for eighteen years – a lovely man, Geoff Harris – was always a great support and ready to stand in for me and help out whenever I asked. My real aim is not to worry about the number of fish my guests catch, but to see the look on their faces when they leave of a Saturday afternoon, secure in the knowledge that they are already thinking of coming back the following season. For me, that is the real joy of the job, along with being involved in the capture of someone's first ever salmon."

Jock is on the Spey Foundation committee, representing Spey Rods and Gillies. The Foundation has been recently re-established out of the previous Spey Research Trust, formed in the mid-1970s to advance the study of salmon and other freshwater species within the Spey catchment. The Foundation plays an important part in informing the Spey Fishery Board of developments within the river and helps to determine the board's approach to fishery management. Jock avoided being the official representative solely for the gillies because he was aware that there were gillies on the river who have been there far, far longer than he has. Nevertheless, he has a first-class website (www.speyghillie. co.uk) where he can freely express his personal opinions; and he does, although the Spey Board are sometimes not always entirely happy with his frankness.

Jock also has serious reservations about the impact that fish farming is having on wild salmon and told me that he recently had Dave Gordon (Diver Dave) from Aberdeen at Kinermory. Dave and he were talking about fish farming and Dave described to Jock the scene of desolation that he had found when he dived below fish farm cages in Loch Eriboll in North Sutherland. I could confirm the validity of this statement because I had persuaded Dave to undertake the dive for inclusion in a film I was making about fish farm disease and pollution. Jock, as ever, is not content to just inwardly seethe about the injustice of what is happening to wild salmon and sea-trout because of fish farming; he also spreads his personal message wherever and whenever he can. When Jock was invited to speak to the Methlick Angling Association a few years ago, he explained his views on salmon farming and why he would never buy or eat farm salmon or farmed smoked salmon. The message seemed to get across, because he was then asked to repeat his talk to the Elgin Baptist Church congregation. He said,

"I think my presentation was well received, as not many of the people I spoke to now buy farmed salmon. Word has finally got round. Anything I can do, either by word of mouth of through my website, I will. The government has to get its head out of the sand and do something to stop this madness."

Jock's passion for fishing is as remarkable as it is invigorating, and I asked him if he could explain it. "I really don't know," he replied. "Maybe it is just in your blood? Every boy should learn to fish for trout in a burn with a worm. I used to be quite happy just standing watching other people fish, and puzzled why a trout would take a fly or worm in a particular manner. If I was fishing a burn, it never mattered if I didn't catch anything. I think that it was just the excitement and pleasure of being so close to nature. There are always so many mysterious things to see when you are fishing. The day goes by so quickly. Looking back, it was wonderful to fish the small burns around Turriff. I experienced a sense of freedom that few boys experience today. I spent hours there and knew every inch of the Turriff Burn, a tributary of the Deveron, which was just outside our family home. I only had to cross the road and could fish down to where the burn met the Deveron, a distance of around a mile or so. In September and October salmon and sea-trout reached the burn, and in the winter I would see them spawning when I walked the burn."

The rod that Jock started his career with was an old Second World War tank aerial, and in the narrow confines of the burn, which was frequently bounded on either bank by trees and bushes, he quickly developed his casting skills. It was the only way to reach where the fish lay.

I also used a tank aerial in my youth, a one-piece affair, and very, very heavy. I can't remember if I ever caught anything with it – probably not – but I remember mightily thrashing the Water of Leith near Powderhall in Edinburgh trying to do so. Ann also began her fishing days in 1952 using an old tank aerial and a worm on Lyne Water, a tributary of the River Tweed, which I also fished. She was with her father and one of his friends, and still talks happily about cooking trout on an open fire by the riverbank. By that time, I had graduated to an eighty-year-old twelve-foot Greenheart rod and a cast of flies; although Ann and I were barely one mile apart, it was to be another eight years before we met and married. These heavy old aerial rods might have been awkward to use, but by the time we had finished with them and moved on to superior tackle, you could cast with any rod without thinking. Jock said the same. "Some of my guests will compliment me on my casting skills, but the truth of the matter is that they were learned out of necessity by trying to cast effectively with these unforgiving old aerials."

Jock Royan is also a trout angler of considerable skill. He was captain of the RAF Fly-Fishing Team for a many years, when their 'arch enemy' was the Army Team, now all friends together. The main event of the year was an inter-services competition between Army, Navy and RAF, with the Royal Marines along to make up the numbers. There were also competitions with the English Federation of Anglers, and most of these events were held on Rutland Water because the majority of the teams were based in England.

Jock also fished in the Scottish International Team recently at Chew Valley in England and Llyn Trawsfynedd in Wales. He told me, "I haven't won a gold medal yet, but last year the Alba six-man team, of which I was captain, won the Lexus Team Championship, an international competition, and the largest such event in Europe, known as the 'friendly fly-fishing championships.'" These competitions are exceptionally well supported and well run, and although competition fishing isn't to everyone's pleasure, you can learn a hell of a lot from a guy after eight hours in a boat together.

I could hear Jock's guests finishing lunch, so asked Jock a final question: What did fishing mean to him? Jock hesitated, thinking, a smile on his face. Finally, he replied, "Outwith my family, fishing to me is why I get out of bed in the morning. Let's face it, Bruce. If I didn't, I'd be late for work. You know, when I was in Germany, I was walking along the banks of the River Mosel one day with my new wife, actually on a wine-tasting trip, when I saw this young lad trying to catch Chub with a piece of bread on a hook. But he wasn't getting far enough out. I took the rod and showed him how to cast a greater distance, even hooked a fish and handed the rod back. I don't think that I could ever pass a river without wanting to fish it. I think my wife could verify that, as she was heavily pregnant on our wedding anniversary – afloat with me fishing on Rutland water. When I have a rod in my hand – salmon fishing, trout fishing or sea fishing – I feel the rod is part of me. I would like other people to find the same passion and pleasure in fishing as I do."

I remembered once being at the fish mart in Puerto Montt in southern Chile. A young boy had been fishing in the harbour for I don't know what, but his line was in a furious tangle – a huge bird's nest of nylon – and he was patiently trying to sort it out. I sat down beside him, and having been in a similar situation many times, soon had it back in order. I made up another cast for him, and the boy smiled at me and said, "Bueno."

As I said goodbye to Jock, I grinned at him and said, "Thank you." I stopped on the hill above the beat and looked back. Jock, like a mother hen, was carefully herding his guests to the river, his black Labrador dogs' tails wagging happily at his heels.

5

George Ross, Steven Mackenzie, Ronnie Ross, River Oykel

I committed a cardinal angling sin when I first fished the River Oykel. I was staying at the Inver Lodge Hotel in Lochinver and had booked a beat on the upper river. The river there is narrow and bordered by forestry, and I inadvertently strayed on to the adjacent beat, the top beat of the Lower Oykel. When the angler whose beat it was came up to explain my mistake, I was mortified and apologised profusely. But he was the perfect gentleman and invited me to continue fishing. That is how I met the late Peter Harrison, who became a good friend. I discovered later that Peter was an architect and subsequently asked him to design and manage the alterations to our cottage on a hill near Tongue. He did so with similar courtesy.

The River Oykel is one of the finest salmon streams in Scotland and can produce upwards of 1,500 fish during a season. The Oykel rises on the southern skirts of Ben More Assynt (3,274ft), the highest peak in Sutherland, and flows east for thirty-five miles through a rugged glen and the fertile lowlands of Strath Oykel to join the tidal waters of Kyle of Sutherland. I visited the source of the river some years ago when Ann and I, along with the then Assynt Estate factor, Peter Voy, fished the remote hill lochans that feed the river. I also fished Loch Ailsh, a wonderful loch into which the infant Oykel flows and pauses, before hurrying on down through Glen Oykel.

Colin Pringle at Makerstoun with dog Tweed

Chris McManus with his two opening day salmon

Dave Reid and Blue on Loch Tay

Chris McManus
with Loch Tay
salmon

Ben Loyal Estate

Woodcock Shooting on Ben Loyal Estate

© RICHARD ELSE

Ian Smart

© MIKE BROOKES ROPER

High bird

Jock Royan
casting

Bruce Sandison on Loch Ailsh

Steven Mackenzie, River Oykel

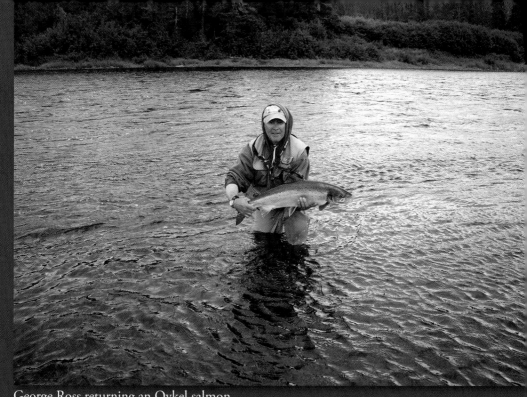

George Ross returning an Oykel salmon

George Ross with son Michael with Loch Damh brown trout

Dickie Graham

Kenny Wilson
repairing a
grouse butt

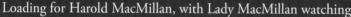

Loading for Harold MacMillan, with Lady MacMillan watching

One of the best-known characters associated with the Oykel is George R. Ross, MBE. George retired recently after spending many years caring for the river. When preparing updated editions for my book, *The River and Lochs of Scotland*, I always telephoned George so that he could check the Oykel entry. George had agreed to talk to me in connection with my new book about Scottish keepers, stalkers and gillies, so I was very much looking forward to meeting him. I had also arranged to meet George's successor, Steven MacKenzie, the current manager of the Lower Oykel Fishings, and Steve's stepfather, Ronnie Ross, who also used to gillie for guests on the Oykel.

I found George at his cottage in the small village of Rosehall and we settled in his Aladdin's Cave of a study to talk, surrounded by books and photographs most of which were, not unsurprisingly, about fishing and fishery management. Three generations of his family have worked on the Oykel – grandfather, father and George. He told me that his father had been forty-five years on the river and that he himself had served fifty years. When he was at school, his class were once asked by a visitor what they wanted to do in life. One said that he would like to become a joiner, another wanted to work on his father's farm, but George said that he wanted to be a gillie. The visitor asked what a gillie did and George told him. The man, who clearly had no idea about keepering, replied, 'Oh, I suppose it's better than nothing.'

George left school when he was fifteen and became a gillie. He said, "I simply could not see anything else to do, other than go to the river. In those days there weren't many alternatives and people tended to follow in their father's footsteps. I'm not making excuses, but that is what it was like then, either shepherding or salmon fishing. I would have liked to have been involved in stalking, but the Oykel season is quite long, starting on 1 February and going on until the end of September, by which time the stalking was well under way."

A catch and release policy is now common on most of Scotland's salmon rivers and the Oykel is no exception. Personally, I have reservations about this dictate. For me, the whole point of fishing is to catch a fish, kill it and eat it. I agree entirely that not every fish caught should be killed – unlike the havoc still caused by indiscriminate interceptory netting of salmon in our coastal waters – and most anglers that I know return the majority of the fish they catch to fight another day. But it seems to me inappropriate to demand that every fish should be returned. I don't think that I would fish a river that was one hundred per cent catch and release. As such, I wanted to hear George's views on the subject and asked him what he thought about it.

George said, "I am not far away from your point of view, because I agree with what you say, and yeah, it is very much catch and release here. From the start of the season until June it is one hundred per cent catch and release. I don't fully agree with this. I think that it is too stringent and I question the validity of that policy. I know it is supposed to protect stocks, particularly of spring fish. But if stocks are so low, then surely we shouldn't be on the river anyway, torturing the fish? As far as I am concerned, it is simple, as it is with all game sports – whether it's pheasant, grouse, woodcock, stags, trout or salmon, whatever – we are killers. Either you do it or you don't do it. And as far as salmonids are concerned my view is that the real problems these fish face are not in our rivers, but at sea.

"When catch and release was first introduced here in the 1990s it did worry me quite a bit. I thought it was going to be a nightmare, you know, taking a lot of money from people and having to tell them that in the interests of conservation they must put their fish back. I thought this was not going to work, my life would be terrible. But it was amazing how guests reacted, and nobody has ever made me feel uncomfortable about it. However, that being said, I know a lot of people would really like to keep the odd fish, and that they only put them back out of respect and politeness. I wonder what our fathers and forefathers would have made of it all."

Over the years, George has looked after a wide range of people. In the old days they were mostly former serving officers in the forces, judges, doctors, dentists, farmers and, of course, other river owners, but today the spectrum is much wider and includes financiers, bankers, industrialists, media people, journalists and actors, electricians and joiners. But George himself is as keen as ever to fish. His son and daughter fish and George always treasures any days he manages to spend with them. Most recently he and his son Mike, who works as a chef in Pitlochry, had tremendous sport with brown trout in Loch Damh in Torridon. George showed me a marvellous photograph of a 13lb trout he took from the loch, and said they also had fish of 4lbs, 5lbs, 6lbs and 8lbs. His eyes sparkled as he told me they planned a return visit this year.

George also has happy memories of his fishing guests, many of whom became close friends. He fished with Geoffrey Palmer, the actor and television personality, most famous, as far as I am concerned, for the brilliant role he played in the comedy *Butterflies*.

George said, "He has fished here for about twenty years now, and he is the same on the river as he was on television. He is a lovely person, very funny, considerate and kind. Last year I had the great privilege of introducing his grandchildren to salmon fishing, when, I am delighted to say, one of them caught his first salmon. I don't know who was more thrilled and pleased, the grandfather or the grandson."

George also fondly recalled two elderly judges, Lord Salmon, who was Lord Justice of Appeal from 1964 to 1972 and his friend, Judge Cohen. "They were a priceless pair," George said, "always chaffing each other and great fun to be with. By that time, however, Lord Salmon was getting a bit forgetful, losing his car keys and the like, and falling in and so on. A gillie had to be with him all the time in case of accidents. Mrs Cohen also fished, but she rarely saw a gillie because they were busy keeping an eye on Lord Salmon and her husband. One evening she said to me, 'Tomorrow, George, whatever happens would you please spend the first hour of the morning with me.' I was delighted to agree and the following day found myself at the head of a pool with Mrs Cohen, whilst the two men were about 200 or 300 yards away downstream, but round a bend in the river and out of sight.

"We had hardly been fishing for ten minutes when I heard an awful noise coming from where the men were fishing. It was Judge Cohen, shouting for me. 'George, George! Come away down here for goodness sake, and hurry!'

"I thought, 'Oh, my God. What has happened?' So I looked at Mrs Cohen and said, 'I'm sorry, but I have to go.' Judge Cohen was still waving his arms and shouting when I got there. 'Come and look at this!' he said. Lord Salmon had fallen in again, and there he was, in all his glory, standing stark naked by the hut. He had taken his clothes off, wrung them out and hung them up to dry and couldn't understand why we were laughing. We laughed until we could laugh no more and I can assure you, Lord Salmon was never allowed to forget that incident."

George has had a busy life, not only on the river, managing the bookings and organising the fishing roster, but also arranging the overall care and maintenance of the huts, riverbanks, access points and paths. George also runs a small business, consulting on salmon fishery matters and supplying excellent salmon flies and tried and tested fishing tackle (www.oykelsalmonfliesandtackle. com). In the evenings he told me that sometimes the telephone never stops ringing. He was happy to retire and hand over the reins to his young colleague, Steven MacKenzine. "I am enjoying retirement," he said. "I can go to the river by myself now without another thought in my mind other than to enjoy my fishing." George's retirement brings to a close a momentous era on the river stretching back for almost a century, during which time members of his family devoted their lives to the stewardship of the Oykel. They will not be forgotten.

Steven MacKenzie, manager of the Lower Oykel Fishings (mackenzine671@btinternet.com) also lives in Rosehall, a stone's throw from where George lives. He came out to meet me as I parked. A tall, fit man with a winning smile, a firm handshake and a friendly Labrador at his heel. Steven never knew his father; he had been a postman in Ardgay and died in a traffic accident when Steven was three months old. Four years later, Steven's mother married Ronnie Ross, from Gruinards, and Steven has an older sister, a younger half-brother and a half-sister. I asked Steven where he went to school and he replied, "I went, occasionally, to primary school near Ardgay and then to senior school in Tain."

"Why 'occasionally'?" I said.

"Well," Steven told me, "I didn't do much when I was there, only just enough to keep me out of trouble. My whole family have Honour Degrees in something or other – Granny, Mother, aunts and both my sisters – but the day I was sixteen I couldn't get out of school fast enough. I never went back. But I was always good with my hands and will never be beaten by anything – mechanical, building or joinery work – whatever it is, I will do it." Steven's house is a substantial, attractive building standing in its own grounds surrounded by a well laid-out and maintained garden. He built it himself.

Steven's first job was on the River Carron at Amat, but after four years, when the owner of the estate, Admiral Robson, died, he was made redundant. Other job offers flowed in from the River Naver in North Sutherland, but George Ross offered him a job on the Oykel, which he took. "It was the best thing that ever happened to me," Steven said. "He is such a good guy, easy-going, and what he doesn't know about fishing isn't worth knowing. I have worked with George for twenty years and though he is officially retired, I know that I can always rely on him to help me out if I am in a jam or short of a gillie."

As a young man, Steven was more interested in shooting than fishing. He preferred his gun and his motorbike to a fishing rod then. "Sometimes," he said, "I would fish the hill lochs for trout, but that was as much for the sake of getting to them on the bike as it was for the fishing. I also used to enjoy stalking, but I don't have time for that now, and I miss it. I used to do a lot of competition shooting as well, with my stepfather Ronnie, and my little brother Adam. We used full-bore stalking rifles. Two of the other gillies here, Ally and Foggy, are also really good shots and we used to represent the Highland Branch and travel all over the country to take part in competitions."

Steven caught his first salmon when he was eight years old, on a worm, in the River Carron. By the time he was eleven, he was fly-fishing and had his first fish on the fly, again on the Carron, following his stepfather Ronnie down a pool. The salmon weighed 12lbs and Steven still remembers the excitement of that moment. "It was an absolute cracker," he said. "I don't get much chance to go fishing now, but at least I can choose a moment when there is a good chance of a fish. I sometimes take my wife, Lisa, to the river; her grandfather used to gillie on the Carron, and Lisa has a natural talent for fishing. One of our proprietors, Mrs Lilla Rowcliffe, an expert angler and fishing legend – who still fishes in Tierra del Fuego and Iceland and is well into her ninth decade – bought a new rod and had it delivered to the school where Lisa is a teacher. Mrs Rowcliffe asked me to try the rod out, but it was a light rod so I thought that it would be better if Lisa did the testing. That evening on the river the midges suddenly came out in droves, and as we were scurrying from the river, I asked Lisa to have a quick cast by a stone at the end of one of the runs in the gorge. The instant the fly landed, a fish rose and took it. Lisa quickly brought in the fish; we released it and were back in the kitchen within half an hour of leaving the house. Job done, rod tested."

Steven and his Oykel team work well together, and with their fishing guests. There is invariably laughter and humour throughout the day and not a little amount of leg-pulling. There is one section of the river – the gorge – where the only way of crossing to gain access for the repair paths on the other side is by an overhead cable. Repairs are carried out every five to ten years. Recently, to get the concrete across, a steel wire had been set up, securely anchored on either side to telegraph poles. One of the angling guests' ladies was watching the procedure and asked what we they doing. Straight-faced, Steven explained that under new European Regulations they had to provide disabled access to all parts of the river. The structure was so that anybody in a wheelchair could be hooked on and transported over the gorge. That evening, in the hotel, the story was recounted faithfully, much to the amusement of the other guests.

Similarly, when a hatchery was in operation rearing eggs taken from spring salmon, keep nets were placed in the river to trap fish. In the late afternoon the gillies used to go round and collect any salmon from the traps; the traps were quite visible, with two or three inches showing above the surface. One day as they were being inspected, a group of ladies whose husbands were busy fishing passed by and asked them what was going on. Atty, the gillie clearing the trap, told them that every afternoon at 4pm the salmon moved into the shallow water and swam straight into the traps, and just to prove that this was the case, and knowing full well that there was already a fish in the trap, he pulled it up to let them see the fish. The ladies were convinced.

The river is in excellent health and has been fishing wonderfully well in recent years. The whole of the system is now under single management and even Loch Ailsh, which used to be renowned as a sea-trout fishery, is again producing good numbers of that most sporting of fish. Last August a party on the loch had some forty sea-trout of up to 4lbs in weight. Sea-trout appear to be in the doldrums round Moray Firth streams, but numbers on the Oykel are increasing. The largest salmon caught last year was estimated to be 28lbs 8oz, a pound less in weight than the biggest salmon ever taken from river back in the 1960s. Last season produced twenty-five salmon of over 18lbs, fourteen of them over 20lbs, and, significantly, some of these fish were being caught in March. The 2011 season was exceptional, with 732 fish caught in the month of July.

Steven MacKenzie is essentially a pragmatic, practical man, and like so many of his breed, exudes an air of confidence that is palpable and exhilarating. As manager of the river, he has to spend a lot of his time attending to administrative details, which he does efficiently. However, as I said goodbye, I recalled what he had told me about going, or as was sometimes the case, not going to school and being good with his hands. "I don't mind the administration, although by the time I have put five hundred sheets of paper through the printer, which I do most days when dealing with the lettings, I am more than ready to get outside, to go and grease the tractor, to get my hands a bit dirty, to be in the fresh air." The Oykel is indeed in excellent health, and I know exactly who will keep it that way, grease on his hands et al.

I left Steven and drove back through Invershin to Bonar Bridge and Ardgay, then followed the River Carron to where Ronnie Ross, Steven's stepfather, and his wife live in a pleasant bungalow by the river. Fortified with coffee and home baking from Mrs Ross, Ronnie and I were left to talk. I confess that it was easy to do so, because Ronnie and I found that we shared many mutual acquaintances and had visited many of the same places, not the least of which was Southern Arabia, where Ronnie and I both dutifully served Queen and Country. Ronnie was born in 1936 and spent his early years at Kinlochewe by Loch Maree in Wester Ross, where his father was employed as a keeper from 1934 until 1954.

His family on his father's side were from Glencalvie and were cleared from their glen to make way for more profitable sheep. James Gillanders, factor to the Robertsons of Kindeace, ordered their removal on 24 May 1845. Eighteen families, amounting to some ninety people – men, women and children – were cleared from their homes. They gathered at Croick Church in Strath Cuileannach and famously scratched on the diamond window panes of the church their pitiful messages: *Glencalvie people was in the church here 24 May 1845; Glencalvie people, the wicked generation; John Ross shepherd; Glencalvie people was here; Amy Ross; Glencalvie is a wilderness blow ship them to the colony; The Glencalvie Rosses.* These messages can still be seen at Croik Church today.

Ronnie said, "Two of the family crossed over into the Alladale Glen, which was not cleared, and my grandfather, who was born in 1848, and his brother were stalkers there. My father was born in 1894 and was also a keeper. I suppose we have all been deerstalkers and keepers ever since. But growing up at Kinlochewe was paradise. There was always plenty of sport, grouse, ptarmigan and deer, and the fishing was absolutely unbelievable. The Coulin Forest lochs, Loch Clair and Loch Coulin which drained into Loch Maree through the A'Ghairbhe burn and the Kinlochewe

River, were not so well known as Loch Maree, but in many ways much better because they were more private and reserved for estate guests.

"When my father went there the estate was owned by Lord David Davies, a friend and colleague of David Lloyd George, prime minister during the Great War (1914–1918). I remember seeing Lloyd George there once with Lord Davies, when I was about seven or eight years old. I thought that he looked like Winston Churchill. My father told me that in 1934 Lord Davies decided that he would try to beat an old record for the largest number of sea-trout taken from the Coulin lochs in a single day. Nobody could remember who had set the record in the first place, but Lord Davies was determined to better it. Charlie McLaren's father used to come up and give him casting lessons. Anyway, Lord Davies achieved what he set out to do, taking from Loch Clair in one day seventy-two sea-trout averaging just short of 4lbs in weight, and two salmon.

When Ronnie came out of the forces, after National Service, he was looking forward to going back to Kinlochewe, but by that time his father, after so many years, was finding the hills a bit much for him, so they moved back to Gruinards in Strath Carron, where the hills were less taxing. He hoped to retire there after four of five years. In fact, his father spent the next twelve years on the estate. Ronnie was asked to give a hand with the heather burning for a few days, which somehow stretched into fifteen years. Their beat on the River Carron was very lightly fished, so he enjoyed excellent sport. Ronnie told me, "I rarely ever saw more than two rods on the river and the rule then was that you had to be off the river by four in the afternoon. It was great for sea-trout, so I asked my boss, old Commander Kemmis, if it would be all right if I fished on for sea-trout. He had no objection, provided he didn't hear about it; like many proprietors of salmon rivers then, he considered sea-trout to be little other than vermin which should be killed. As a result, I had far more fishing than he had and enjoyed every moment doing so."

During that time Ronnie met a lot of people, many of whom became firm friends. "I remember I was with a couple at Amat, Rodger and his wife Cecilia were their names, and we were talking about painting and artists, Barrington Brown and Frank Wallace, both of whom fished. I mentioned one of my favourite wildlife artists, Rodger McPhail." Personally, I have always admired Rodger McPhail's work. At the age of nineteen, one of his works graced the front cover of *Shooting Times* and is considered by many to the natural successor to the Scottish-born artist Archibald Thorburn. Ronnie continued, "I asked my guest if Mr McPhail was still around and he said that he thought he was, although he had heard that he was getting a bit decrepit these days. Then he suddenly leapt in the air, throwing his arms above his head and shouted, 'It's me!' I thought, 'How stupid of me.' I had been given four of his books over the years and should have recognised him. But he and his wife were grand company and good rods."

Ronnie also met Brian Franks, a formidable and famous commanding officer in the Special Air Service, and ultimately the honorary colonel of the regiment. "He was a good-looking guy, big and powerful, and I was amazed to discover later that he was in his eighties. I was told this when the son of the owner of the estate came up the following week and asked I how I got on with Brian Franks, and if he talked about the war. He didn't. But he was a fascinating companion, endlessly polite and an excellent angler. He was fluent in five or six languages and fished the River Awe and Loch Awe for many years, where he had great sport. I was sorry to hear that he had died."

I asked Ronnie if he agreed with me that one woman angler was invariably more successful than any ten men. "Never mind one," he said. "When there are two they become an unstoppable force, like Mrs Rowcliffe and her friend Mrs McAndrew. They have been fishing together for years. Mrs Rowcliffe's biggest salmon was caught on the Spey when she was eighteen years old and the fish weighed 47lbs 8oz. She is nearly ninety now, still going strong and frightened of nothing. In Tierra del Fuego she has had sea-trout of near 38lbs. I didn't see her last year, but when she was here the year before it was business as usual. Mrs Rowcliffe arrives on the river at 9am and fishes until about 6pm. She told me that she had been invited to Iceland and wondered if it was just to make up the party. She has a wonderful sense of humour and laughed when I suggested that they were planning to drown her." Ronnie also fished with Geoffrey Palmer. "He is a terribly nice man, a shareholder on the river, full of common sense and always prepared to listen to your point of view."

Ronnie was less impressed with the goings on at Alladale, a neighbouring estate that aroused controversy when the owner announced that he was going to introduce wolves to his ground. "He told me that he was going to bring in helicopters to help seriously cull deer and I reminded him that Alladale had been a deer forest for more than three hundred years and that he should look after it. I remember that he told me this was nonsense and I would soon change my mind when 40,000 visitors began passing my door to see the wildlife reserve that he planned to create. 'Well,' I told him, 'I don't want 40,000 people passing my door, it is just fine the way it is.' He has never spoken to me since."

Glenfeshie on Speyside is another estate that aroused great controversy over the extent of their deer culls. Ronnie, who is never far from humour, told me that he had been there about three times over the past fifteen years. "The last time was with the Deer Society and we climbed to over 3,000 feet. It was cold and windy and we searched around for some sort of shelter in which to have our lunch. We found this little hollow and as we ate a plane flew overhead at about 30,000 feet. One of the keepers said, 'My God, if it's cold here what must it be like up there.'

"Another shouted, 'Aye, right enough, but at least they will all be inside!'"

Finally, I asked Ronnie if he would choose the same path again. "Well," he replied, "you don't make a fortune, that's for sure. It is very hard work, physically, and you are on the go all the time. I always worked single-handed. On one estate where I worked thirty stags and about forty hinds were shot each year, and as the years went on the hind cull increased to one hundred and fifty. I dragged most of them off the hill, as my hips and shoulders frequently remind me today. Then there were riverbanks to attend to, firewood chopped for the lodge, maintaining the vehicles – there was always something that had to be done. Would I have been any better off today if I hadn't had such a life? I don't know. But what I do know is that there have been great times as well. No doubt about that, great times."

Ronnie saw me off with a wave and a cheery smile, and I thought as we parted, 'Yes indeed. A glorious gentleman.'

6

Dickie Graham, Hoddom, River Annan

All in an April morning I drove west from Ecclefechan in Dumfriesshire to Hoddom and the River Annan. On either side of the road, strengthening hedges full of summer promise, bordered spring-bright fields. Shy primroses peeped from shady corners. Buoyant daffodils bobbed and danced in cottage gardens. Then, suddenly, the winding, silver-blue river flowing serenely under the arches of an old bridge, built two hundred and fifty years ago to replace a ferry. My destination that morning was The Meeting Place, a Hoddom and Kinmount Estate gate-house immediately on the right after crossing the bridge. As I parked my car, the scent of wood-smoke, drifting from its chimney, filled the air.

George Birkbeck, the owner of the estate, a tall, weather-beaten man with the reputation of being a fine angler who casts a beautiful line, greeted me with welcoming smile. He took me through to a stone-floored room with a brightly burning log fire to meet Dick Graham, the recently retired head bailiff on the Hoddom and Kinmount beat, two and a half miles of splendid double-bank fishing with nine named pools. The upstream limit of the beat is Milk Foot Pool, where Water of Milk, a major tributary of the Annan, joins the flow. The downstream pools are Horse, Goats, Bridge, Churchyard, Dukes and Banks, with the fishery boundary at Scales Pool, where another tributary, Mein Water, enters the river.

The Solway's rivers Nith, Annan and Border Esk were renowned for the size of their late-running salmon, known as greybacks, the main runs of which appeared from September through until the end of the season on 15 November. Today these huge fish are most noticeable by their scarcity and the average weight of salmon is in the order of 10.5lbs. Nevertheless, opening day in 2012 produced two splendid fish weighing 20lbs and 17lbs, respectively, and the current beat average for salmon and grilse is about 130 fish a season.

The Annan is perhaps more famous as an outstanding sea-trout fishery than it is for salmon, and enormous runs of these most sporting of game fish once were taken during the season. Although they are not so prolific today, Hoddom and Kinmount can still produce over 400 sea-trout which average 2.5lbs in weight. Indeed, fishing for sea-trout in the gloaming and during the night is one of the great joys of being on this lovely part of the river.

The Meeting Place used to be the 'control room' of the Hoddom fishings, where anglers collected their tickets, met their gillies and caught up on recent events – ones that got away, the few that didn't, the most successful flies and reported catches. Bookings for the beat are now handled by James Leeming's Berwickshire-based organisation, Fish Pal, but the lodge is still a happy meeting place where anglers and river staff gather on Saturday mornings, both during the season and when the river is closed, to drink coffee, swap yarns and tell tall tales, all of which are true and some even truer.

Dick, who is in his ninth decade, is a well-built, white-haired man with a ready smile and a huge personality. He rose to make me a cup of coffee and we settled to talk. He was born near Hoddom and used to walk to school in Ecclefechan, a distance of eight miles there and back every day. "My granny, my father's mother, gave me lunch and looked after me very well."

I asked Dick how he became interested in fishing. "Oh," he said, "I have always been keen on the fishing, even as a wee boy I used to go to the Annan to watch the anglers. A water bailiff lived across the road from us and I could fish anytime I wanted and he never said a thing.

"The head bailiff, Ian Earsman, lived about two miles away, and his daughter and my mother were very friendly because they had worked together on Hoddom Farm as housemaids when they were younger. That's how I got to know Ian. I used to go with him to the river and carry his bag. He was a good fisherman. I saw him catch his largest fish – 53lbs it was – just below Hoddom Bridge in big water, spinning water. There were no trees along the bank then and he was up and down the beat a good few times before he got it. In fact, I held the rod whilst he went down and netted it with a large net on the end of a long pole. Two or three days later a Mrs Lumsden got a fish in the same pool weighing 53.5lbs, the biggest salmon ever to come from Hoddom water. These big fish were caught just before the outbreak of war. I think it was in 1938 or 1939."

Dick also remembered another specimen fish, "Not long after the two we had at Hoddom, a fish of over 50lbs was caught up at Lockerbie, also by a woman. The fish was mounted and displayed in the Lockerbie library for many a year. I don't know where it is now. Ian Earsman's fish used to be up at Hoddom Castle, but when the war started troops took over the castle and when they left the fish had gone. When the army moved out, Hoddom Castle was a wreck."

I asked Dick about his first salmon. "It was 10.5lbs and I caught it in the Dukes Pool, near where Willie McLellan's ashes are. Willie and I were mates and for a long time and he helped me on the water. He died a couple of years ago and his ashes are buried at the Dukes Pool. George Birkbeck put a big seat there, all framed off, with Willie's name on the back. When my time comes, I'm going next to him. Willie was born in Ecclefechan and I can mind the first night he came fishing with me. He was still a schoolboy when he landed at Hoddom. The banks at Hoddom then used to have two streams, one either side, or you could fish one side then walk up the gravel to fish down the other side. Willie called to me, 'Are you getting any?' I had four or five by then. So I said I would take him to a better place. We went up to the Dukes and he was soon into a good fish. It was a long time ago. I was maybe twenty, so it has to be sixty years since."

The Dukes Pool is downstream from Hoddom Bridge. Dick said, "You can get right down to the pool with your car. About half a mile before you come to the bridge there is a rough track on your left. You just go down there and that takes you to the Dukes Pool. People sit and have their sandwiches there as well. Our fishing gets booked from about the end of July onwards. It used to be busy right through from May until the end of the season, but lately because of a dearth of sea-trout, that doesn't happen. I'm sure if the sea-trout come back things will change, and it does seem that this might be happening. I have better reports of sea-trout in the River Eden and other Solway streams."

Sea-trout fishing was always Dick's special delight. "I liked the fly-fishing when it was good for sea-trout and, oh, you got a lot of them in the Dukes. I would go in at the head of the pool – it's a long pool, all of 120 yards long – and it was good fishing throughout its length.

"I remember I had twenty sea-trout one night. There were a lot of good sea-trout, 4lbs or 5lbs and heavier. When you were fishing at night you usually got one or something near like that weight. Oh, yes, they fought like mad when they got hooked, splashing everywhere, although I think that the smaller fish fought harder that the bigger ones. The first fish arrived in May and I fished for them using a black Stoat's Tail, a Teal Blue and Silver, and a Dunkeld. The Dunkeld was one of my favourite flies, and, oh, I always had a Brown Turkey on the tail."

Dick recalled the days when the Annan sea-trout fishing was still outstanding. "After a flood you could maybe get a hundred sea-trout, you have no idea what it was like then. I used to fish with two hooks, one maybe a foot above the other, for fishing at different levels. I guarantee you didn't need to move five yards before you got one; it was great fishing. A lot of people would come fishing then, from all over the country, from as far away as Cornwall."

To the best of my knowledge, the only satisfactory explanation for the sudden decline in sea-trout stocks, and indeed salmon, in the Solway streams was provided by research carried out by Alistair Stephen, then the biologist for the West Galloway Rivers Trust. The decline seemed to be associated with the massive tree planting that occurred during the 1970s and 1980s in the headwater reaches of many of the rivers; tens of thousands of acres of foreign conifers, lodge pole pine and Sitka spruce were planted and they starved the rivers of their natural water flow and made them more acidic. Although good numbers returned to spawn, the number of fish that survived spawning diminished. The research suggested that this was caused by acidity: when the pH of the water falls below 4.5, fish die.

However, Dick had another reason that might have contributed to the problem: illegal netting at sea by Irish vessels. He said, "They were fishing with eighteen-yard-long nets, and they had sonar equipment as well to tell them where the fish were. They would go ahead of a shoal, turn and then sweep them up as they came back. Cranes were fixed on their boats to lift in the nets. The decline was quite sudden; the year before we were getting plenty, then the following year there were very few. I have always thought that it was because the Irish boats were targeting returning fish at sea. The Irish government has stopped that fishing now, but it will take a long time for the stocks to recover."

Dick was also unhappy with haaf nets, a fishing method used for hundreds of years, the right to do so being granted in a Royal Charter issued in 1538 by King James V of Scotland saying, 'that citizens of the Burgh of Annan have the right to fish the river and the Solway'. The net is placed on a large wooden frame approximately eighteen feet long and supported on three legs. The fisherman carries the structure into a channel where salmon are known to run and holds it in position. Dick said, "I think it's cruel, these fishermen standing in a line with their long nets make a complete barrier so that no fish can escape as long as the haaf nets are there. But the stake nets were worse – they had to haul in their nets with a tractor, such was the weight of fish that they might catch, and they had a trailer handy in which to cart them away."

Declared haaf net catches seem to be in the order of 2,000 to 3,000 fish taken each year and it is hard to escape the conclusion that these activities, along with stake nets and the intervention of Irish boats fishing at sea, may have be responsible for contributing to the decline of salmon and sea-trout in the Solway river over the last twenty years. Figures indicate that numbers of salmon have fallen by fifty per cent and sea-trout by eighty per cent during that period. If I believed in reincarnation, then the last thing that I would like is to return as a salmon; these magnificent fish are probably the most pursued creatures, by man and beast alike, in the history of planet Earth.

One of the most onerous tasks a water bailiff faces is to protect his fishery from the less than gentle administration of poachers. And we are not talking about 'one for the pot', but the deliberate wholesale slaughter of every fish upon which they can lay hands. Dick has had more than his fair share of run-ins with poachers. "I have been down there at nights and when I saw someone coming I would phone the police, but the poachers would see them approaching, you know, the police cars would have their headlights on and off the culprits went, and you didn't know where. I discovered that they were going through the churchyard at Annan to where their car was parked, but they were always away before the police got there. One poacher, a man from Annan, used to carry a baton, and if anyone went near, he just hit him. They used to do the Nith and the Esk as well.

"Aye," Dick said, "they got a lot of fish up there, but they couldn't keep their mouths shut and were always bumming about how much money they could make and all the rest of it and word soon gets round. We were lucky at Hoddom. It didn't get poached often. I used to phone a few people and they were very quick to come out. I remember one night, fishing with a friend from Carlisle, when I saw the poachers coming. I could see their lights. It was a steep bank from which you could easily fall in, so I said that we should hide ourselves in the long grass just where they would come by as they worked down the pool. Although you couldn't tell who they were, you could see them. One swam across the river with the rope for the net, and they were soon dragging the net, working it down the pool, with another man as a lookout keeping watch on the banking.

"I said to my pal, 'We'll no say a word till they come by and just as they come by we will jump up and shout – and that one will get such a fright that he will leap straight into the river, clothes on and everything.' So, at the right moment we jumped up and shone the torches on them and I yelled, 'Harry, the poachers are here! They are down at the bottom of the Dukes!' The fellow on our side went into the river, as did the lookout, and both swam across to the other side. They went off into the big wood and we could hear them crashing through the undergrowth and they would be in a mess because it's full of briars. I pulled the net in and found one salmon. I killed it and gave it to my friend because he had helped me. I then cut up the poachers' net and hung the bits on a post. When I went back there the next morning, the bits of net had gone."

Our talk turned to fishing rods, and Dick told me that he used to have a Hardy Viking Grey rod for salmon and a ten-foot Hardy Perfection for sea-trout. Apart from my early days, when my fishing rod was an old twelve-foot Greenheart rod, I have always fished with cane rods. It is not a conceit, but because

I prefer their action. If used efficiently their extra weight is not significant. The most common error many people make when casting is not letting the rod do the work for which it is designed. When you understand this, then casting becomes as much a part of the pleasure of angling as is catching fish. Recently, a friend, Derek Fothergill, gave me a rod that I will treasure for the rest of my life, a Hardy fourteen-foot split cane rod, circa 1898. It is a work of utter perfection and a delight to use. However, our talk of rods reminded Dick of an incident that occurred some years ago one morning in The Meeting Place.

I am sure that we have all met the sort of angler who features in this story, the one who catches all the fish, although nobody ever sees him doing so, and he always returns every fish he catches. The man who knows it all and is able to 'top' any story ever told. He used to be a regular at the Saturday morning get-togethers, when he invariably had the last word on any subject under discussion. Dick had decided to sell off some his rods and the 'expert' agreed to buy them. Dick put them all together and delivered them to their new owner. The following Saturday morning, the company listened as the man told Dick how much he had enjoyed using one rod in particular; indeed, that very morning he said that he had landed three salmon with it whilst fishing the Horse Pool, the largest being about 22lbs.

Dick asked him about the rod's action, "Oh, once you are accustomed to it, no problem. I got out forty yards without any trouble,' he replied.

"'And you caught three fish with it, did you?'

"'Yes, mind you the conditions were not perfect, but I knew what I was doing, that's the secret, isn't it,'" he said beaming with pleasure. Dick did not respond, but left the room and went to his car. When he came back he was holding the middle section of the rod which he had inadvertently omitted to include in the bundle of rods that he had sold to the man. "'Now then,'" said Dick, continuing his story. "'You must have completed a miracle this morning, catching these three fine fish with only a bottom and top section to your rod.'" That was the last time the man was ever seen at The Meeting Place.

Many of the gillies, stalkers and keepers that I have met surprised me by the breadth of their knowledge and experience, not only on river, hill or moor, but also by the other activities that they engaged in outside their work; artists, authors, pipers, musicians and athletes. In this regard, Dick was no different, and I discovered that as a young man he had been an outstanding cyclist and I asked him how he became involved in competitive racing. "It was my father," Dick told me. "He used to ride, on grass tracks, and I just carried on and did the same. I rode in road races as well, but I was better on a grass track than on the road."

"You must have been very fit, Dick," I said.

"As I say, my father was a very keen cyclist and he encouraged me to race. I used to cycle to Hawick and race there, five races, and then cycle back home again – Galashiels as well. I cycled to Berwick on a Friday afternoon, raced on the Saturday and cycled back home when the meet was finished." However, Dick's longest journey was when he cycled to Edinburgh to compete at Meadowbank, a round trip of 160 miles.

Dick did his National Service with the KOSBs (Kings Own Scottish Borderers), and when he was training at Gillingham in England rode for the army cycling team. "Once I came out of the army there were a lot of track meetings here in Scotland. I was six times second and five times third in the Scottish Championships. I wasn't beaten by much really, but I was beat and there it was. Then one day, when the Annan Common Riding started again, John Matthews, a hairdresser I used to go to and a committee member of the Common Ridings said, 'You used to cycle on grass tracks, didn't you? If I were to arrange for cycle races at Annan during the Riding's week, do you think that you could get some cyclists to come?'

"I said that I could get any amount of cyclists to come and distributed leaflets round the meets that I went to. When the day came, we had sixty-two riders at Annan, including the Scottish Champion. The first race was a short quarter of a mile event, which I won. The next race was half a mile, and I won that as well. The last race was two miles, with everyone off the same mark. With three laps to go, I moved up, sitting third. Then I moved up another place so that I couldn't get blocked in. It's all tactics, you're going so fast you have to keep your brain clear and get in the right position. The Scottish Champion was in the lead, so I sat on his wheel for a bit and then with barely half a lap to go I moved up again so that we were riding together, then I just shot away and left him. I won three races that day."

Dick's eyes sparkled as he talked and remembered that day so many years ago, sparkled with the same enthusiasm that I saw when he talked about Ian Earsman's 53lbs salmon and about his mate, Willie McLellan, at rest by the Dukes Pool.

Dick Graham is a gentle, courteous man and I felt honoured to be in his company and to share with him his stories of a memorable and happy race well run.

7

Kenny Wilson, Biggar

Kenny Wilson is a remarkable man, not only for his understanding and knowledge of countryside pursuits, which he honed as head keeper on the Leadhills Estate, but also for his excellence in other fields. He is one of the best-known and most admired exponents of Scottish fiddle music. He has played alongside such legends of the art as Jimmy Shand, Ian Holmes and Bobby MacLeod, and still plays regularly with Allan Mackintosh, Bill Richardson and John Renton's bands. Kenny also served as a special constable for twenty-five years and as a Magistrate who sat on the bench at Lanark Sheriff Court for twenty-three years.

Kenny was born in 1930 near Leadhills in South Lanarkshire where his father was tenant farmer. The family lived a mile to the west of the village at Hass, where the narrow B7040 road twists and turns through heather moorlands from Elvanfoot in the east, by Elvan Water, a tributary of the infant River Clyde, to Leadhills in the west. Leadhills is Scotland's second highest village, second only in that regard to nearby Wanlockhead. However, Leadhills does have Scotland's highest golf course, a nine-hole course at 1,500 feet, which is described as being 'not for the faint-hearted'. For more than eight hundred years, until 1928, Leadhills was busy with lead mining, and from about 1500, gold as well. It is also renowned for opening the first subscription library in Britain in 1741, when twenty-three miners set up the Leadhills Reading Society. Leadhills' other great claim to fame is being the birthplace of William Symington, the designer of the world's first boat to be powered by a steam engine.

I have had the privilege of knowing Kenny Wilson for a number of years, and I called recently to see him in Biggar where he now lives with his partner, Pat, a graduate of Glasgow University who studied languages and, until retirement, worked as a linguist for the North Atlantic Treaty Organisation in Paris and Brussels. Another remarkable aspect of Kenny Wilson's character is that although he has achieved so much during his long life, he remains an essentially self-effacing man, patient and courteous, with wide a range of interests, a ready smile and full of humour. He is also an excellent listener, always curious to learn what others have to say about whatever subject is under discussion. Kenny is as fit and bright as his fiddle and good company. Pat is warm and welcoming and shares the same laconic sense of humour as her husband. Being with them is always a delight.

Kenny could have had a successful career as a musician – indeed, he had many opportunities along the way to do so. Kenny told me of one such invitation. "Roy Laing, a talent scout for the Royal Philharmonic Orchestra in London, then under its conductor Sir Thomas Beecham, invited me to join a training course that would lead to a full-time position with the orchestra as a violinist. Well, tempting though it was, I didn't really want to spend the rest of my life living out of a suitcase and travelling the world, but not seeing much of it other than airports and concert hall platforms." At an early age Kenny discovered "the large religion of hills", and his innate love of the moors, lochs and rivers of his native land proved to be stronger than life as a wandering minstrel. Given his early years, this is hardly surprising. A little stream, Shortcleuch

Burn, full of small trout, tumbles down from the skirts of Green Lowther (2,401ft) close to where he was born. To the north, scattered with old, disused mines, towers Wellgrain Dod (1,814ft). These wild hills where he tended his father's flock were his home. He knew them and their changing faces throughout all the seasons of his childhood.

Back in the 1980s, when I was researching my first book on Scotland's keepers, stalkers and gillies, I met another gifted musician in the south west, Walter Maxwell, who lived in Thornhill and was a gillie on the River Nith. Walter farmed the land to the south of Morton Castle near Drumlanrig until the laird, the Duke of Buccleuch, invited him to take the job as head gillie on the river. I remember seeing in pride of place amongst the many agricultural trophies in his living room, a violin. When I asked if there was anything that he would rather have been than a farmer, shepherd or gillie, he replied, "Probably a musician." His mother had been a professional pianist and he had been playing the violin since the age of four. Walter was still in great demand for his skills as a fiddler at weddings and dances and other local events. It seems to me to be a truism that you can go into virtually any small community, anywhere in rural Scotland and find a band – violin, piano, piano accordion –ready to play.

At the age of ten, because his father was ill, Kenny did that year's lambing for him, a flock of 500 black-faced ewes, all in the hills. He was at school at the time and was given leave of absence to do so. In those days, in rural communities many schools were still run by local farmers, known as 'The Board', and they would descend at various times during the year and take a dozen or so boys to help with farm work – turnip-thinning or tattie lifting.

Of course, the boys would be delighted for any excuse to be out of school, so it was not unusual to give boys leave of absence when necessary.

But Kenny did not like farm work and he was making good progress at school. When he finished at primary school in Leadhills, he had to attend senior school in Biggar in Lanarkshire, a considerable distance away. To get to school, Kenny left home before 7am each day and walked down to Leadhills to catch the bus to Abington, then a train connection to Symington, where he changed to another train which took him to Biggar. On arrival at Biggar Station, there was still another mile to walk before reaching the school. It was situated to the north of the town. Kenny remembers these journeys, particularly during the winter months. "The bus was slow, cold and the road bumpy. At Abington, the train on the main line between Carlisle and Glasgow was always lovely and warm. Then at Symington, on the branch line that ran down the Tweed Valley, it was back to the cold again. The windows steamed up and we saw little till we reached Biggar. It was unusual to get back home before 7pm."

However, his father was getting older and needed more help on the farm, so, much to his teacher's dismay, he was taken out of school at the age of fourteen to work at home. "Of course, I did the lambing again," Kenny said, "and then a job came up on the Marquis of Linlithgow's Leadhills Estate as a trainee gamekeeper, so I took it." Kenny served five years as a kennel boy, learning as he went, looking after the dogs and horses, setting traps for vermin, loading guns for guests at the grouse butts, cleaning guns, tending to the rearing of pheasants and the multitude of other tasks that form the daily life of a keeper. In 1950, his apprenticeship completed, he was promoted to under-keeper and given a beat of his own to look after.

Fourteen years later, Kenny was appointed head keeper. In all, Kenny served the estate for a period on forty-seven years, twenty-eight of them as head keeper until he resigned from that position in 1992. During that period he was responsible for enormously improving the grouse moor, and, in doing so, became renowned for achieving impressive results. Kenny told me, "My average bag on the moor during the twenty-eight years that I was head keeper was over 3,150 brace of grouse each season, which was considered to be an astronomical figure." It was indeed, and the success of the moor and the man responsible for it was widely acknowledged.

Of course, Kenny's years at Leadhills were not without incident, both humorous and not so humorous, and Kenny recounted to me one incident during the grouse-shooting season that could have ended in disaster. Leadhills is driven moor, when men walking in the form of a horseshoe quietly drive the birds towards where the shooters are in the butts, carefully constructed and camouflaged hollows dug in the moor. The shooters, who are guests, are in the butts, along with an estate worker who loads the shooters' guns. The birds fly low and fast and the shooter has two guns, one of which he fires, whilst the second gun is being loaded by the man with him. When the second gun is being used, the loader takes the first gun and reloads it. This is easier to say than it is to do, and skilful and experienced loaders can make all the difference to the success of the drive.

The butts, which conceal the shooters from the approaching grouse, should be as invisible as possible, and are generally situated downhill from the crest of a ridge on a forward-facing slope. The beaters stop a good distance from the butts when the guns are firing and wait there until all the grouse have been picked up by the keepers and their dogs. Deciding where to build the butts in which only the upper part of the shooter's body is exposed above a turf rampart, and how close to each other they should be is an art in itself and determined by the head keeper, depending on topography of the moor. The closer the butts are to each other, the higher the risk of an accident, because although the shooter should know only to aim his gun at the sky and never to left or right, accidents can happen if the shooter is inexperienced or becomes over-excited. If his loader is concerned about his shooter's actions, that he might not be safe, then it is the loader's duty to report this to the head keeper at the earliest opportunity. Kenny's story demonstrated this fact.

"The shoot was let one year to Charles, Lord Hambro, chairman of Hambros bank, head of a leading financial institution, and one of his guests was a Mr Theodoracopulus, a Greek shipping magnate who caused us considerable anxiety. I provided all the men for loading the guns and one of them, Bob Badger Smith, was very experienced, so I put him with the Mr Theodoracopulos. The Monday went by without a hitch and everybody enjoyed themselves, but on the Tuesday Bob came to me and told me that he didn't think that his gun was safe and that he thought that his shooter was just an accident waiting to happen. So I told Lord Hambro what Bob had said and he promised to have a word with the guest. The afternoon went well, but on the Wednesday, Bob came to me again and said that Mr Theodracopulus had fired a couple of dangerous shots and that unless someone spoke to him, then somebody was going to get hurt. I told Lord Hambro again, and he asked how may drives were left in the day. I replied, 'Three,' and the Lord Hambro said, 'Well, nothing has happened yet, so we will just have to hope that nothing happens during the next three drives. Apparently, there was a business deal in the making and it was essential that the deal went through. Perhaps this was the reason that nobody seemed anxious to upset the man Mr Theodoracopulus.

"After lunch, the first and second drives passed without incident. On the last drive, the beaters were coming in and were about thirty yards in front of us, so there was no shooting. Suddenly, two grouse rose up between Lord Hambro and Mr Theodoracopulus, who simply pulled the trigger, and Lord Hambro and his loader just disappeared. One of the under-keepers, Tommy Murray, ran forward and yelled to me, 'Come here, quick. The laird and his loader have been shot!' When I got there, everybody was standing round looking down at the wounded men, panicking. The loader got to his feet and he was as white as a sheet, didn't know where he was and bleeding all over the Lord Hambro, who was lying at the bottom of the butt with blood coming from the side of his mouth. We got the Lord Hambro out of the butt and laid him on his side and he eventually came round.

"In the meantime, I ran down the hill to the get the Range Rover, because I was the only one who knew the way to get it up to the butts; it was imperative to get him off the hill and to medical help and all the guests were shouting at me to be quick about it. They seemed to have forgotten about the loader, but I insisted that he come too. My first wife at the time, Elizabeth, was the district nurse and health visitor in the area, and I took them to her. She did what she could and telephoned the doctor in

Biggar. It would have been a long time to wait for the ambulance, so the laird's chauffeur brought the Bentley down, and off the invalids went. When the doctor saw them, he sent them on to Monklands Hospital where a helicopter arrived to take them to the King George Hospital in London.

"The Lord Hambro had been hit by thirty-six pellets, in his chest and face. His loader also had quite a few pellets in him, one of which was right on his jugular vein, and it was touch and go for a while until his treatment was safely completed. He had been very lucky. He had been ready to hand Lord Hambro the second gun and he would have been standing upright. But the gun had got stuck in the side of the butt; otherwise the loader would have taken the full blast of the shot and probably been killed. With the Lord Hambro and his loader attended to, I went back to the hill to check that everyone was there and that the beaters were in the bus and the loaders in the Land Rovers and everybody was accounted for. When I got back to the lodge, Mr Theodracopulus handed me his gun, but still holding it by the barrel with the muzzle pressed against his chest. I think he said something like, 'I want you to aim here and pull both barrels.' I took the gun, disabled it and told him not to be ridiculous. He started to vomit and ran into the lodge and disappeared.

"Lord Hambro eventually phoned me from hospital to tell me that he and his loader were fine and were making a full recovery, and to thank me for my help and prompt action. However, I did smile a bit when he also said that the important financial deal with Mr Theodracopulus the Greek was signed, sealed and delivered. I was not too surprised, but wondered if the price paid to secure it had been worthwhile."

Kenny made many good friends whilst at Leadhills and attended to many notable guests, including the former Prime Minister, Harold MacMillan, who had Kenny as his loader when he came to Leadhills Douglas Estate to shoot. The estate was owned by Alec Douglas Home, the former Prime Minister, and he had telephoned Kenny to ask him he would kindly look after Harold MacMillian and his wife during their visit. Another friend was the US Senator Bill Flowers, who invited Kenny over to his ranch in Georgia to shoot quail. Kenny also knew another of my keeper friends from the past, the late Willie Drysdale, who was head keeper on the Marquis of Linlithgow's estate at Hopetoun on the south shore of the Firth of Forth near Edinburgh. I got to know Willie through his son-in-law, Jim Seaton, a former editor of *The Scotsman* newspaper, which I contributed to for twenty years. Jim's wife Maggie was Willie Drysdale's daughter, and I once asked Willie if there was anything he regretted about his time as a keeper. Willie told me that he would like to have been called by his first name, just once, rather than always being referred to as Drysdale. I mentioned this to Kenny and found myself listening to another remarkable aspect of his career.

"When I started work," he said, "everybody was referred to by their surnames, except me because I was just a wee boy. I was always 'Kenny' and it has been that way ever since. Even the Queen called me Kenny."

"How did that came about, Kenny?" I asked.

"Well, when the laird went to shoot at Balmoral, I always went with him as his loader. I went to Barmoral every year for ten years and got to know the family well. In fact, I was the only visiting keeper who stayed in the castle, in my own room and with my own valet as well. I dined in the evening with the men and women who ran the various departments at the castle – head chauffer, head butler, head of security and so on. There were nine chefs, and the head chef once gave me a conducted tour of the kitchen, just before dinner was to be served.

"In the morning at 6am the valet would come into my room, open the curtains and give me a cup of tea. Then he would tell me what the weather was like, lay out my clothes and ask what suit I would be wearing that day. I only had the one, but it, along with my shirt and all my underwear, had been neatly ironed. The next thing he always said was, 'Shall I run your bath, sir?' and I would say, 'No thank you. I had a bath last night.' He still ran it. The head butler asked me how I was getting on with my valet, explaining that I had to tell him if he wasn't doing everything correctly, and I mentioned about running the bath. He looked at me for a moment, and then said, quietly, 'Ah, yes. Well, we all have two baths a day here.'"

When Jimmy Gillan, the head keeper at Balmoral, was about to retire Kenny got a phone call from his laird one dark and windy night to tell him that he had had a request from Her Majesty: she wanted Kenny to be her next head keeper. "The laird told me that he didn't want me to go but that he would never stand in my way if I really wanted the job. But I didn't go, even though the Queen might never have spoken to me again. Nevertheless, for staying at Leadhills the laird gave me an immediate increase of £1,000 to my salary. Then the Queen requested that I be appointed a Justice of the Peace, with a recommendation that I studied law. I was a special constable then, so I had to resign from that position and studied criminal law for three years in the evenings at Justice of the Peace training sessions in Hamilton and then found myself as a magistrate, on the bench."

I told Kenny about the day I had two retired pipe majors out with me fishing on Loch Craggie near Tongue and how, during a lean spell, when the trout were not cooperating, the one said to the other, "Now, Sandy, if you had just brought your chanter with you and given them a tune, this would never have happened."

This reminded Kenny of similar incident when he fished Loch Awe in Argyll. "Walter Campbell was his name," Kenny said, "and he lived at Ford at the south end of the loch. He originally came from Tiree and was a retired police inspector, although all his service had been in Luton, in England. He was also a very good piper and he and I always used to fish together when I was up. If nothing was doing, Walter would say that he had to give them a tune. He would go ashore and march up and down the bank for about ten minutes, pipes skirling. It was a joy listening to him, and you know, when we started fishing again, one or other of us would invariably get a fish.

"I also remember that one day Walter had gone off to fish a hill loch on the Ederline Estate. He came home to his wife all smiles and she knew at once that he had had a good day. 'How did you get on, Walter?' she asked. 'I got thirty-seven fish and they are all in my fishing bag,' he replied. Walter hadn't cleaned the fish, so he asked if she would do it whilst he had a bath. When finished, Walter went in to the kitchen and poured himself a none-too-small celebratory dram as his wife set about the trout. However, when she opened it, the bag was empty, the reason being that there was a hole in one corner and Walter had walked two miles down the hill, leaving in his wake a trail of dead trout behind him."

Kenny had a host of tales and stories about his days at Leadhills, incidents he recalls with a smile on his face. One that I particularly enjoyed concerned a shepherd. "Most of the local shepherds worked for us during the shooting season – beating, loading the guest's guns and generally and helping out during the day. They came to us from Monday through until Thursday and then spent from Friday till Monday on the hill, gathering sheep and sorting out lambs for the sale. The lamb sales where always held during the shooting season and the farm managers would sell them on the Monday or Tuesday. Anyway, I was going up the road one day in my Land Rover when I saw Sandy Thomson standing by his house. His dog was driving some forty sheep down the road to put in a field, so I stopped by Sandy. His dog was working well with everything under control, coming nicely down the brae in what was a perfect fetch.

"Suddenly, a car appeared behind them and Sandy began bawling at the dog. 'Look behind you! Look behind you!' he roared. 'Look back, there's a motor car coming!' Of course the poor dog didn't understand. So Sandy turned to me and said in disgust, 'Did you ever in your life see such a stupid bloody dog?'"

In the same vein, he told that one day he was repairing a shooting butt with help of Willie, one of the under-keepers. "He was sawing the wood which I needed to be at different widths to effect the repairs, and he said to me, 'Och, don't worry, Kenny. I will just half them in three for you.'"

I was still fascinated about Kenny's 'other life' as a gifted musician. Like many ham-fisted would-be musicians, I have been trying to play the piano for as long as I can remember, and sadly, without very much success. In fact, such is my reputation as a pianist that I can completely clear Castle Sandison of family and/ or any unsuspecting visitors in a microsecond simply by sitting down at the keyboard, never mind before a single note is struck. As such, I greatly admire those who are more talented than I am, and I wondered how Kenny had got started as a violinist. As always with Kenny, it was a fascinating story.

"I have a brother, Ian, who is five years younger than me, and when we were little he was given a fiddle by a shepherd's wife and he learned to play it. I wanted to, but couldn't, and, as boys do, we fought over who should have it. My father always took Ian's side because the fiddle had been given to him and he could play it. But Ian tired of the fiddle and decided instead to learn to play the piano, which he did, and became very proficient as well. In later life, we often played together. But back then it gave me the chance to get my hands on that coveted fiddle. My mother used to sell milk and eggs, to help make ends meet, and one day an elderly man, Willie Todd, who could play the fiddle, came round to the house to collect his milk and eggs heard me scraping away. 'Is that someone trying to play the fiddle?' he asked mother, and she told him that I was very keen. Mother brought him though to see me and he tuned the fiddle and began to play. I thought how much I would like to play as he did and was determined that I would. So I practised and practised, and eventually I was sufficiently proficient to play with Willie one night at a concert in the village hall."

As chance would have it, the Abington postman, Alex Brown, another fiddler, was at the concert and when he called later at the farm to deliver mail, he persuaded Kenny's mother to arrange lessons for Kenny with him in Abington for £2 a time, teaching him how to hold the fiddle and bow properly and how to read music. Kenny cycled there, for several years, a round trip of fourteen miles. I know the road, and it is tortuous.

"Aye," Kenny said, "it was steep and hard cycling once a week, winter and summer, with my fiddle on my back." Kenny progressed so well that Alex introduced him in two amateur orchestras, the Hamilton Orchestra and the Lanarkshire Municipal Orchestra, conducted then by William McGeechan, and Kenny played with them for about three years. Kenny went on to play on BBC radio and television, performing at Christmas and Hogmanay shows with The White Heather Club, hosted by the singer Andy Stewart, who always ended the shows with the song, 'Haste Ye Back'.

Kenny was also a founder member, in the 1970s, of the Border Strathspey and Reel Society and was their conductor for twelve years. He has two highly prized fiddles, a Jean Werro instrument made in 1926 in Berne, Switzerland, and a beautiful Norwegian-style Hardanger fiddle with eight strings, wonderfully crafted and made as a gift for him in 1980 by David Eunson after David heard Kenny give a solo fiddle performance on one of Max Houliston's BBC Radio broadcasts. The scroll of the instrument ends in the type of dragon's head that appeared on Viking long ships, complete with lemmings' teeth, and the body of the fiddle is decorated with inlaid mother-of-pearl and fine engraving work. It takes a full year to make a Hardanger, six months in the manufacture and six months for engraving and varnishing.

I asked Kenny how he had managed to fit all his musical activities in with his job as head keeper on a major Scottish sporting estate. "There was never any problem," he told me, "although it at times took some organising. Most of my commitments were in the evenings and I arranged others during holiday periods. My first priority was always Leadhills, to my employer and to the people who worked with me and to the estate. But when Elizabeth became seriously ill, I began to consider my position and what I should do."

Kenny and Elizabeth were on holiday in 1982 on the island of Islay when they met another couple, also on holiday, and formed a long-lasting friendship with them. Pat took up the story. "Kenny was busy fishing and helping out with the local estate and my husband, who loved tennis, was glued to the television set, leaving us women to entertain the children. So we got to know each other well." When Pat's husband and Elizabeth died of cancer, Pat and Kenny got together.

It was also around this time that Kenny was approached by one of the world's leading estate agents, Savills, who were established in 1855 and specialise in sporting estate management. With his firmly established reputation for grouse moor management, Savills asked Kenny if he would act as their consultant in these matters, and Kenny agreed to do so. This was followed by a similar approach, which Kenny also accepted, from The Game & Wildlife Conservation Trust, an independent wildlife conservation charity which carries out research into Britain's game and wildlife. He then resigned as head keeper at Leadhills to undertake his new duties, advising estates in Scotland and the North of England on grouse management.

Kenny and Pat are frequent visitors to the village of Tongue in North Sutherland, where Ann and I live. They stay at the Ben Loyal Hotel, and that is where I first met Kenny. One evening before dinner, I had called in for a pint and soon got talking to Kenny. We found that we not only shared common interests in field sports, fishing and music, but also a surprising number of friends and acquaintances. Thereafter, we generally shared time together when Kenny and Pat were in residence; the talk being mostly about fishing and country matters. Kenny is primarily a trout fisher, like me, and our talks ranged over lochs and rivers throughout Scotland, for Kenny has travelled widely on business, and always with a trout rod. Happily for us both, our wives are also similarly inflicted with a love of the hills and a love of wild brown trout fishing.

By coincidence, when Kenny and Pat came north last year, their visit coincided with the arrival of the Troot Tour musicians, Pete Clark, fiddle, and Gregor Lowrey, piano accordion. They arrive at their destination in the morning then fish until about 6pm, and then play in the evening. They perform a programme of largely traditional Scottish music, one moment soul-wrenching in its beauty, the next an outrageous, hilarious jig or reel that defies the listener to keep his feet still. Pete had also met Kenny in the past and admired his playing. Thus it was that Kenny and I enjoyed a memorable evening, listening to Pete and Gregor playing melodies old and new to an appreciative audience. After the concert, I also listened spellbound to these two incomparable violinists reminiscing. Listening to them, I was minded of Peter Milne, a famous nineteenth-century itinerant fiddler. Milne once said he was so fond of his fiddle that he could sit inside of it and look out.

The following evening Pat and Kenny came up to our cottage for supper, when our other guests were my daughter, Jean, who is the manager on the Ben Loyal Estate, and her husband, Ian Smart, the estate head stalker. Guess what we talked about . . .

8

Eddie McCarthy, Thurso River, Caithness

Salmon fishing seriously damaged my mind. Only the River Thurso in Caithness saved me from certain insanity. My relationship with *Salmo salar* up until I cast a fly into the Thurso's peat-stained flow had been fraught with angst. The desire to catch a salmon had become an obsession. But no matter how hard I fished, or where, they eluded me. The Thurso exorcised my internal demons. On an unforgettable day there I caught five fish. For my previously distracted state, I blame the Tweed. As a youth I had my first serious encounter with a salmon in a pool near Innerleithen. I was fishing for trout using a nine foot six inch Alex Martin cane rod when the tail fly on my 3lb breaking-strain nylon cast appeared to be snagged on the bottom. I gave a few tentative tugs to release it and then waded in to get a closer look at the obstruction. The fly was caught in the mouth of huge a salmon, which immediately shot off upstream, breaking my cast and my heart in the process.

I had fished Lower Birgham on Tweed to no avail. I thrashed the Findhorn near Tomatin, the Spey at Craigellachie, and the Tay at Dunkeld, froze one spring day on the River Ayr, but caught nothing. By the time we moved to Caithness in 1975 I had sworn an oath never to go salmon fishing again. But my son Blair was made of sterner stuff, and he was determined to catch himself a salmon. So for his birthday I booked a day on the Thurso. As I cast into the river a few hundred yards downstream from the bridge at Westerdale, all the old feelings of hopelessness flooded back. Still, I reasoned, it was only for a day, and Blair was enjoying himself. When my fly stopped in the middle of the stream, I jerked viciously to free it, which is how I hooked the first fish. Blair ran down to land it for me. We admired the salmon enormously. Blair was halfway back to his rod when I hooked the second fish. He ran back and landed it. Five minutes later, a third. I apologised for keeping him so busy. Two more fish came to my rod after lunch and the five salmon weighed just over 50lbs.

The Thurso also provided me with my first experience of spring salmon. On a snow-filled, cold, blustery March morning I found myself standing on the bridge at the top of the river where it flows out from Loch More, wondering if this was going to be any different from all the other days that I had spent freezing/roasting in pursuit of this particular prize. A cheery voice called hello, and I turned to greet Eddie McCarthy, the Thurso River Superintendent. "Have a cast in the pool below the fish ladder," he advised.

I had not intended to do so, thinking that it might be a waste of time, but decided to take his advice and immediately hooked a fish. It seemed to me that I played that fish for an eternity, trying to prevent it from running under the arch of the bridge. Eventually the fly came loose, and I felt the special agony that every angler knows at these moments. But I will never forget the immense power of the fish, or Eddie's courtesy and good advice. As I got to know him better, I soon discovered that I had found a very special friend.

The ownership and management of the river is now in the care of the Thurso River Company, who have a ninety-eight-year lease of the fishings, factored by Simon Laird, who I also know because my elder brother Ian is married to Simon's father's sister. The river has been much improved under the new management, and Simon has earned the respect and confidence of Eddie McCarthy and his excellent team of gillies. The 2010 season was outstanding, with a total catch, including the Thurso Angling Club Beat, of nearly 3,500 salmon and grilse. The river also saw the highest rod catch in a month since records began in 1896.

Historically, the Thurso has given up some huge fish, particularly during the 1920s when several salmon of between 35lbs and 47lbs were landed. Even today heavy fish are taken, the largest in recent years being a salmon of 28lbs, although the average weight is in the order of a more modest 9lbs or 10lbs. Fishing is strictly fly-only, a practice dear to my heart, and there is no compulsory catch and release policy. Nevertheless, upwards of fifty per cent of the fish are returned to fight another day, and there is currently an ongoing debate about the use of barbless hooks; they cause less damage to the fish and are much easier to remove before returning the salmon to its natural habitat.

On a bright spring morning, I found Eddie McCarthy in his natural habitat, in the house where he was born, close to the river in the small Caithness village of Halkirk. Eddie's grandfather, David Sinclair, owned the house and he was Thurso River Superintendent for fifty-four years. Eddie told me that his cousin David had been groomed to take over from his grandfather, but eventually, that didn't really work out. Consequently, Eddie has now been on the river for thirty-two years. He said, "My first recollection of salmon was when I was about four years old. Grandfather always called me 'Ebard', not Edward, and one Saturday morning he said, 'Ebard, are you coming round the nets with me?' (In those days, the mouth of the Thurso was netted.) So I went round with him and he explained everything that he was doing, and why, just as I do today with my own grandson."

Eddie continued, "One day when I came home from school, Grandfather said, 'I want you to see something.' That evening he took me up to Loch Beg at the head of the river where the salmon smolts were gathering, waiting to migrate to sea. It was on the edge of darkness when it went quiet. Suddenly I saw hundreds of smolts, tiny silver specks, sparkling and splashing in the loch, and I thought I was in a dream world. After that I was involved in everything Grandfather did – even during the winter, working with him at the hatchery, freezing, because that was also part of the job. I was very much my grandfather's shadow and I followed him everywhere.

"I think that I was quite bright at school, but I soon realised that if I carried on like that then after the Eleven Plus exams at senior school, I would have to learn Latin and other subjects that didn't appeal to me. All I really wanted to do was to play football and go fishing. So I suppose, thereafter, I managed, sometimes spectacularly, to fail exams. I was fourteen before Mother finally worked out what had been happening. She was angry initially, but then told me not to worry because it was far more important that I should do whatever it was that made me happy."

I sympathised with Eddie, because I had followed a similar pattern when I was at school, spectacularly failing exams. All

I really wanted to do was to be out in the countryside, fishing and bird watching, walking and writing stories about what I had seen and done. Instead, when I departed the hallowed halls of Edinburgh's Royal High School, I found myself working as a junior salesman-cum-office boy for Messrs. Smith and Wellstood, who made Esse cookers and sold fire surrounds – and in the evenings, twice a week, attending a City and Guilds course on ironmongery. As Eddie escaped to the river, I escaped from my nightmare after a couple miserable years and joined the army. I have never had any regrets about doing so and even managed some respectable trout fishing in England and a marvellous trip to the River Rupengazi in Kenya, all courtesy of Her Majesty.

Both Eddie's sons fish, as does his daughter, Kerrie, who is married to Hugo Ross, 'Mr Caithness Angling' and proprietor of the famous tackle shop on Wick High Street. Hugo often fished the River Thurso and met Kerrie through his friendship with Eddie. Hugo and Kerrie have now fished together for more than twenty years. I remember Hugo telling me, "She is a good fisher and instinctively reads the water. Even in low water conditions she always seems to know where a fish might be, and generally catches it." He told me about fishing Beat 12 on the Thurso one evening with Kerrie. "I didn't catch a thing because I was so busy running about landing her fish! Then the evening suddenly went calm and the midges came out and we had to run for it." Of course, in her father, Kerrie had an exceptional instructor. But it was not all bad news, because a new fly was born that evening: Kerrie's Killer, based upon a combination of a Willie Gunn and a Gold Demon and devised by Hugo.

In 1973 Eddie was offered a job as a keeper/stalker on the River Eilt in Lochaber. This was before the full impact of Scotland's first salmon farm, in sea-Loch Ailort, was beginning to hurt the River Ailort and Loch Eilt, which drain into sea-Loch Ailort. Prior to this disaster, the loch was renowned for the abundance and quality of its sea-trout, with catches of more than 1,000 fish each season, and the river was a useful salmon stream. Eddie warned them that the farm was going to be the death of the river and loch, but he was ignored. They claimed that if this did happen, then they would simply restock the system. Eddie was right, and by the late 1980s the sea-trout and salmon had gone. The company Marine Harvest stocked the river with fish from their hatchery, and for a while catches did improve. However, when they stopped doing so, shortly after Jim Slater's company Salar Properties had acquired the full rights to fish Loch Eilt, within a couple of seasons the system was to all intents fishless. It remains so to this day.

Nevertheless, Eddie enjoyed the tail end of the glory days and some great sport with sea-trout on Loch Eilt. He and his wife Isobel lived in the little cottage on the edge of Lochan Dubh, an extension of the river close to the famous Frying Pan Pool. The setting of the lochan is idyllic and much photographed, as indeed is Loch Eilt itself, admired by passengers enjoying one of the world's most popular railway journeys, The West Highland Line from Fort William via the viaduct at the head of Loch Shiel that featured in the *Harry Potter* films, to Mallaig.

One night, just before dawn, Eddie and Isobel were in bed when Eddie woke up. "Isobel," he said. "I know that I had a couple of drams last night, but am I hearing someone trying to play the bagpipes?" He got up and went to see what was going on. "By the lochan I found a bunch of people doing a photoshoot for the fashion magazine *Vogue*, complete with piper and a few young girls dressed in full Highland dancing gear. The piper couldn't play and the lassies were having problems trying to dance on the broken ground. 'Complete madness,' I thought, but I suppose they managed to make it look good in the magazine."

Eddie loved his time at Loch Eilt, but as his daughter Kerrie grew older, she would have to leave junior school at Glenfinnan and stay during the week at Fort William to attend senior school. The choice was either that or moving. Eddie's grandmother died, and when he returned to Caithness to attend her funeral he met Robin Sinclair, the late Lord Thurso, who asked how he was getting on.

He told me that when he arrived back home, "Lord Thurso had been on the phone and wanted to speak to me. I called him and he told me that my cousin David, who was then River Superintendent, was leaving in two weeks to join the Dounreay police and did I want to come back? I said yes, but I had commitments at Loch Eilt that had to be fulfilled first – seeing out the stalking season, winding up the financial position, that sort of thing. Lord Thurso agreed to that, and on 1 November 1980 I found myself River Superintendent on the Thurso River, again following in my grandfather's footsteps."

There is one part of the river, upstream from Halkrik, which is known as 'No Man's Land' and I asked Eddie how it got its name. "When Grandfather saw boys fishing the river he used to chase them away. When I came back, I remembered this and decided that there should be an area where the boys could fish without let or hindrance. That part of the river is not particularly good for salmon fishing, fine for the grilse running through, so I got together about twenty kids who fished and told them that from now on this was going to be their beat, where they could fish whenever they liked, and asked them what they would like to call it. They had a huddle, then came back to me and said that they would like to call it 'No Man's Land'. Now that ownership of the river has changed hands, Simon Laird agreed that this should be continued and that this right to fish should be retained for the people of Halkirk." Eddie's own grandson Ryan learned to cast on No Man's Land and, fishing with his father, Eddie's oldest son, Clyne, caught his first salmon there on a trout rod. The fish weighed over 6lbs and Eddie told me, "The chuckle in his voice as he played the fish was a lovely sound."

One of the advantages the Thurso enjoys is that the whole system has always been in single ownership. Thus the management of the stream is simplified. Back in the early years of the twentieth century, P. D. Malloch (1853–1921), the founding father of fishery science and author of the book *Life History of the Salmon, Sea-Trout, Trout and Other Freshwater Fish*, published in 1910, supervised the building of a dam at the outlet of Loch More to control water levels in the river and encourage more fish to spawn lower down the system. In 1924, a hatchery was established adjacent to the dam. Prior to the hatchery, just below Brawl, ponds had been dug into which fish were put and fed, and after a year, they were released into the river. I remember in the 1970s when I was involved in agricultural land drainage, visiting the ponds to see if they could be reinstated, although this proposal was not pursued.

Eddie said, "For the first three or four years of my tenure, funding for river improvements was limited. We put up luncheon huts on every beat, but these structures only last for about ten to fifteen years, so Simon Laird's company's arrival on the scene was good news. Between the two hotels and the river, they have invested more the £1.5 million in the past six years. We now have our own freezing unit, excellent drying room, purpose-built rod room and space for hanging waders and jackets. The hotel, the Ulbster Arms, has been wonderfully upgraded and offers anglers a comfortable atmosphere in which to tell endless tales of ones that got away and the few that didn't and other stories each and every one of which is true, and many may be even truer. We meet regularly to plan what to do next to continue improving the facilities we provide for anglers."

A regular visitor to the Ulbster Arms was Colin Leslie, head gillie on the Cargill Beat of the River Tay, who I had met in the 1980s. However, Colin didn't come to fish for salmon, but rather to fish the famous Caithness brown trout lochs, which are some the finest trout fishing in Scotland. Colin always came with a group of friends, including his brother Norman and a Dr Riley and Jim Pirie, all of whom are now fishing that great trout loch in the sky.

Eddie fondly remembers Colin Leslie and his party and, in particular, Jim Pirie. As Jim grew older he found walking increasingly difficult. About ten years or so ago, Dougie Reid, a senior Thurso gillie, decided to take Jim up to the Sauce Pool and had asked Eddie to stand in for him at the netting station at the mouth of the river. So Eddie did, and the crew came in at night devoid of fish, whilst old Jim Pirie and Dougie, on the river, had seven. "And what was the best bit, Dougie?" Eddie asked.

"Well," Dougie replied, "the largest weighed 17lbs and the

smallest 7lbs, and we didn't start fishing until 10am and packed up at 4pm."

When Jim Pirie died, both Eddie and Dougie attended his funeral.

I met Colin Leslie one year in the 1980s, on Loch Toftingall near the village of Watten, and reminded him of the account he gave me of a hilarious incident involving two Dutchmen, father and son, fishing with him at Cargill. Colin told me that he was standing by the boat when he saw the young man hook a fish, his first salmon. The son kept calm and played the fish well, finally leading it to a shingle bank to beach it. That was more than could be said for his father who ran up and down the riverbank shouting endless encouragement and advice at the top of his voice.

Colin said, "Just as the lad went to beach the fish, the father dashed into the shallows and started trying to kick the salmon ashore. The more the son yelled at his father to stop, the more the old man lashed away with his feet. Anything I tried to suggest was completely ignored, so I retired to the steps of the fishing hut to see what would happen. The father fell on the salmon, trying to trap it between his knees. As the fish shot between his legs, one of the hooks from the spinning lure caught in the seat of his pants. The father stood up, still bawling instructions, searching for the fish, which was now dangling behind him.

He must have told his son to kill the salmon, for the boy sprinted to a fishing-bag, grabbed a huge priest and started to belabour his father's backside, who shrieked and yelled as though it was himself being killed rather than the salmon. Eventually, the boy grabbed the fish by the tail and managed to get his father to sit down and keep quiet. One final blow and the salmon was dispatched, detached and photographed. It was the funniest thing I've seen in all my years on the river and I thought I'd die laughing."

Eddie also has memories of similar incidents and, in particular, of one on the Sauce Pool. "I was with this doctor and his wife and suggested that he fish Castle Pool whilst I looked after his wife. Within two minutes she got into a fish and after an hour and a quarter she was still playing it. So she asked me if I would take the rod to give her a rest. But I wouldn't, because it is bad luck to do so. She was furious. I have never seen a woman so angry. She said either I take the rod or she would throw the bloody thing in the river. So I took the rod and played the fish. Just then, I noticed her husband making his way towards us on the other bank when *bang*, the damn fly came loose and the fish was away. Well, the doctor came back to fish the Thurso about twenty years later and asked in the bar, 'Does that little bastard who lost my wife's big salmon still work here?'"

Dougie Reid arrived whilst we were talking. He is a tall, distinguished-looking man with a confident air and has spent most of his life on the river. Dougie told me, "Between Eddie and me, it must be about ninety years! Things have changed, of course, the people who come here today don't have all the airs and graces like the old days. Then it was always 'sir', now its first names. I have been looking after some of them for more than thirty years." Eddie interjected with another tale that involved Dougie. "The swing bridge on Beat 7 had lost some of its decking in a gale of wind. It was early in the year and we were repairing it – Dougie, Maurice Murray and me – with massive ice flows going by underneath. No health and safety regulations in those days. As we were carrying the new decking into place, I saw Dougie begin to sway, and, almost in slow motion, topple over into the river. As he hit the water I could see a shiver run through his entire body. Maurice glanced briefly at Dougie struggling in the water and said, 'That bugger will do anything to get a half day off'."

I have spent many a happy hour over the years in the company of Eddie's team of gillies, and not entirely unsurprisingly, shared a few drams with them at the end of a day on the river. I also remember the old fishing huts, essentially drafty places with few facilities. Indeed, I remember my first encounter with a Thurso hut in the 1970s when Ann and I walked out to fish for trout in Loch Garbh, near Altnabrec. The hut was in its final agonies, as was the flat-bottomed punt beside it, which began seriously leaking when we were 100 yards for shore, but we managed to edge our way back to safety. When we returned the following year, all we found of the hut and boat were shattered bits and pieces scattered across the moor, gone forever. Eddie, however, was assiduous in trying to keep the fishing huts looking respectable. To this end, many years ago, he sent two seriously hungover gillies out to paint the hut on Beat 2. He gave them clear instructions that the door and the flashings were to be painted green and the remainder of the hut red. When they met about two hours later they couldn't understand why passing trains were tooting at them: one half of the hut had been painted green, the other red.

Finally, I asked Eddie if he had any regrets about his job and if he would do the same again. "Well, I told Lord Thurso thirty-five years ago, 'You might have the title deeds to this river, but it belongs to me.' It's mine, that's the way I look at it. If something happens at 3am on a Sunday morning, I go and deal with it

because that is my job. If there is a problem, no matter what it is
– a leak in the dam or somebody poaching – I deal with it. I also
told the new owners, so they know the score. But would I do it
again? Without a moment's hesitation," he answered.

9
Interlude: Three Special People

Grant Mortimer is true a Highland gentleman, unassuming and ineffably courteous. I first met Grant in his famous tackle shop in Grantown-on-Spey High Street more years ago than I care to remember. An elderly angler had asked me for advice about salmon fishing, something that he had never tried before, and I decided that the most obvious place for him, with the best chance of a fish, was on the Association water of the Spey. So I directed him to Grant Mortimer's emporium where I knew that he would receive all the assistance he required.

My angler telephoned me after his visit to the river to let me know how he had fared. Mortimer's had hired him rod, reel and line, provided flies and an expert gillie to guide his virgin efforts into the mysteries of chasing the King of Fish. He had had a wonderful few days and was delighted with the help he had received from Mortimer's and from his gillie – and he had landed his first salmon. I thanked Grant for 'birthing' a new salmon fisher, to which he replied with his customary modesty, "Well, Bruce, we try to do the best we can."

On a bright spring morning last April, over a cup of coffee, I sat in Grant's office and asked him about his life as an angler. His office was, like his shop, an angler's Aladdin's cave; brightly shining angling-association trophies lined a bookcase above Grant's desk, and everywhere I looked were reminders of our well-loved pastime; Grant's casting instructor's certificates, awarded by Tommy Edwards the 1960s when Tommy and

Arthur Oglesby ran a fishing school from the Seafield Hotel in Grantown; wonderful bottles of Mortimer's malt whisky, exclusively produced for the shop (tel: 01479 872684, website: www.mortimersofspeyside.co.uk).

Grant was a friend of Arthur Oglesby, a master angler and writer, and I became acquainted with Arthur some years ago when I was invited down to Grantown to give a slideshow and talk to the local historical society at the Seafield Hotel. Arthur was there at the time, running one of his famous angling courses, and he joined the group and kindly contributed to the debate. I would much rather have talked fishing with him, but our audience were happy with our comments. He was complimentary about my work as an angling writer and journalist, which coming from the great man himself, was high praise indeed. Arthur had fished worldwide and in his time took some splendid salmon, including two at 46lbs and 49lbs from the Vossa River in Norway. The fact that Arthur was born in Scarborough, where his father ran the family pharmaceutical company, also gave us common ground because I had had the good sense to marry a Yorkshire lass who had relatives in Scarborough and whom we often visited.

Grant caught his first salmon when he was nine years old. "I got it on Castle Grant. It was one big beat in those days, now it is divided into three beats. After I had caught it I thought that salmon fishing was pretty simple. I had to learn the hard way that it wasn't. My father was mechanic and then a gillie on Castle Grant before opening his first shop at the bottom of High Street and after I left school I went into business with him. He retired in 1967 and I moved up to premises at the crossroads and in 1990 opened up here as well in Number 3 High Street. Both shops were usually busy, so there was less time to go fishing, but I'm a bit older now so maybe I will get more time."

When I was writing my book in the 1980s about field sports, I interviewed another great character who was well loved by all who knew him, Jimmy Ross, who gillied on the Delfur Beat of the river when it was owned by Sir Edward Mountain. One of the stories Jimmy told me when I met him concerned the gaffing of a fish for the Duke of Beaufort. Jimmy was sitting on the opposite bank with the other gentlemen on the beat when he saw the Duke hook a small fish. He poled the boat over the river and asked the Duke for his gaff. The gaff was combined with a wading staff with a spring on top to cover the point of the gaff. But Jimmy saw no need to take the spring off because the salmon was still in the middle of the river. The Duke had little or no strain on the fish and Jimmy was convinced that the salmon had no idea that it had been hooked. There they were, both of them, the Duke on the bank and the salmon in the middle of the river. Eventually, the salmon decided to have a swim round and, as luck would have it, came to rest about ten yards from where the Duke was standing.

The Duke roared at Jimmy, "What are you standing there for, Ross! Get in and get it, man! Get in and get it! Good God, man! You haven't even got the gaff ready! What do you think you're playing at?" But the fish was still in deep water, so Jimmy held his peace and stayed on the bank. The Duke was red with anger and shouted at Jimmy, "Will you get that fish when I tell you?" So Jimmy unsprang the gaff, hooked it over the line, grabbed the line, pulled the fish in and killed it. He threw the fly to the Duke, the fish in the boat, and poled back across the river. That night when he got home, Jimmy told his good lady to start packing. "That's it, dear! I've had a terrible row with the Duke today and I am thinking tomorrow we'll be leaving." But not another word was said and Jimmy had no regrets. "No one should speak to another man like that. It was only right that he should be shown how to land a little salmon without all that great fuss."

Grant has had a long commitment as secretary to the Angling Association, which is near to celebrating its hundredth anniversary. The Association offer some of the best and most accessible salmon fishing in Scotland. He has also been a member of the Spey Fishery Board (www.speyfisheryboard.com) for about twenty-five years. Grant said, "When I was a boy, fishing was just one of the things you wanted to do. We used to jump on our bikes after school and away we'd go and our parents would be lucky to see us back at nine o'clock – mind, that's maybe why I didn't do so well at school. There doesn't seem to be the same enthusiasm today for fishing, shooting and that, but we have quite a good little lot here, about thirty-six junior members. We [the association] work with some of the schools, showing the children how to rear fish to get them interested."

During his long career, Grant has fished many of Scotland's most famous salmon streams, including Junction Pool and the Hendersyde Beat on Tweed, the Gorge on the Findhorn – when he remembers a friend struggling up the metal ladders with an 18lb salmon – and the River Naver in Sutherland, where he landed thirteen fish in one day; and a memorable trip to fish for trout in New Zealand's North Island. He started shooting when has was fourteen years old, taught by his father, but because of pressure of work he didn't really come back to the gun until he was in his mid-thirties, mainly with pheasants, but more recently on Aberdeenshire's grouse moors.

I asked Grant what fishing had meant to him and he told me, "It's part of my life and the whole outdoor aspect of it as well. What makes me happy is to see people going away pleased, having enjoyed their visit. That makes me happier more than anything else. You know, up here we do moan and groan a bit, but if we are away for any length of time, we are always very pleased to come back!"

"Have we seen the best of it, Grant," I asked?

"Och well," he replied, smiling, "maybe the best is still to come."

I thanked Grant and as I drove north towards Aberlour by the blue, winding river and I was quite certain that I had left behind me a man with the Spey flowing through his veins. Grant Mortimer is a man entirely devoid of arrogance and was, like Arthur Olgesby, synonymous with everything that is good about our well-loved art.

The Ben Loyal Hotel in Tongue, Sutherland, was mega-busy that night, packed with people all enjoying the music being played by three men: Pete Clark, fiddle; Gregor Lowrey, accordion; and Simon Jauncey, keyboard. They were performing a programme of largely traditional Scottish music, one moment soul-wrenching in its beauty, the next an outrageous, hilarious jig or reel that defied the listener to keep his feet still. This electrifying performance was greeted with wild enthusiasm by the audience, young and old alike.

I spoke to the Pete and Gregor at the interval because they had asked for advice about local trout fishing opportunities. Thus it was that I got to know Pete Clark, who returned on his own later in the year for a couple of days fishing, one of which I spent in his company. Pete is a professional musician who came late to making that career-defining decision. He was born in 1955 in the old Scottish capital city of Dunfermline in the Kingdom of Fife and didn't decide to commit full-time to music until he was forty-five years of age. Since then he has established himself not only as a highly talented performer, but also as a composer and teacher. A recent CD, *Sycamore*, showcases his compositions, including "Loch Moraig", "Dalguise Hall", "The Ghillie and the Otter's Stone" – from www.musicinscotland.com. You may also look in YouTube for other examples of his work, in particular a solo piece written by the legendary Neil Gow and recorded in the great man's living room at Inver by the River Braan near Dunkeld.

There have been four constant factors throughout Pete Clark's life: music, fishing, landscape painting and his love of Scotland's wild places. He began playing the violin at primary school at the age of nine when his teacher was Harry Grant, and continued at Dunfermline High School with David Davies until he left to attend Heriot Watt University in Edinburgh. Pete told me that both teachers were inspirational and that David introduced him to the music of J. S. Bach and his unaccompanied sonatas and partitas. "I have always loved Bach," Pete said.

Pete started fishing with a hand-line when he was about five years old, from a pier at North Queensferry on the Firth of Forth. "I also used to fish the local lochs as well, the Town Loch and Loch Fitty, which was a flooded quarry before it was poisoned and stocked with rainbow trout. I fished it for perch – they were most obliging, and you could fish for them with a float and a worm. But when the father of one of my friends caught a 20lb pike in Fitty, I was amazed and immediately started to fish for the as well," he said.

At Heriot Watt, Pete studied marine biology because he felt that it might help him to find employment in the field of conservation. He ended up teaching biology at Newtown Stewart High School in Galloway for ten years, where he also discovered the joy of fly-fishing; his first sea-trout on the fly came at night from the River Cree, and his first fly-caught salmon from the River Bladnock. "I loved Galloway," he said, "but I wanted a job out of doors." Pete then worked for an outdoor centre in Glen Isla, obtained a three-year contract lecturing for an environmental body based at Stirling University, followed by eighteen months at Hillside School in Aberdour, and, finally, teaching at the prestigious Croftinloan Preparatory School in Pitlochry.

Pete had settled in Birnham, on the banks of the River Tay, close to the birthplace of one of his musical heroes, Neil Gunn, and when Croftinloan School closed he did not want to move from Perthshire. "I had started to play the fiddle at gigs, traditional music, and I figured if I did a bit of private teaching I might be able to make ends meet." It was a bold decision, but it was the right one for Pete, who was now free to concentrate on the things that really mattered to him: his music, fishing and art. Pete was playing regularly at the Tay Bank Hotel in Dunkeld, and one night he floated the idea to his friend, Simon Jauncey, of a Troot Tour; visiting various places in the Highlands, playing in hotels in the evening and fishing the following day. Gregor Lowrey also liked the idea; thus the concept was born, and I met them during their second tour.

Music has also taken Pete to some exotic places when fishing gear and his watercolour paints always go with him. "I have fished for bone fish in Andros Island in the Bahamas when I went there for a St Andrews Night gig, striped bass in Chesapeake Bay, the largest estuary in the USA, and halibut off Vancouver Island in British Columbia. Had I still been doing my nine to five teaching job, I would never have made these trips. People I met in the USA invited me to join them on a trip to India which they called the Himalayan Fiddle Adventure. We were based in Darjeeling, and I was teaching Scottish fiddle and a young Indian man taught Indian style music on the violin. It was wonderful, great country and lovely people. I was only sorry that I didn't get a chance to wet a line because of the hectic schedule. Of course I had masheer in mind, but that didn't happen," he said.

I asked Pete if he could explain why music and fishing were so important to him. He smiled and said, "So many lochs, so many tunes." I am looking forward to the 2012 Troot Tour and to the rare pleasure of fishing again with a man who really is, in every way, the 'complete' angler.

Some come early, some come late, but sooner or later, whenever people discover the joy of fishing, it is 'an ever fixed mark' that stays with them forever. Fiona Armstrong, Lady MacGregor of MacGregor, is married to Malcolm MacGregor, twenty-fourth Chief of Clan Gregor, and is one of Scotland's most noted salmon anglers. However, Fiona owes her introduction to our gentle art to her first husband, Rodney Potts, an experienced and successful angler who regularly fishes the Border Esk.

Fiona's first salmon came from the Cassley in Ross-shire. She told me, "I had been casting very badly and everyone, including the gillies, had washed their hands of me. I was fishing Neil Grasser's water and my line was in a heap at my feet when suddenly it began unravelling and disappearing into the stream. I thought I was stuck on a rock or something, and then realised it was a fish. I shouted for help and eventually the salmon was netted. It weighed about 6 or 7lbs, and because it was my first fish I had to keep it and eat it, which I did."

Fiona is Lancashire lass, born in Preston in 1956. However, her father worked in the Colonial Office, and when Fiona was about two months old the family moved to Nigeria in West Africa where her two brothers, Kit and Patrick, were born. She has very happy memories of these days and time spent in the bush, seeing the wildlife and huge, colourful butterflies, which she was paid a penny for each one she caught for her father's collection; living in houses on stilts and sleeping in a cot on a tray of paraffin to ward off the attention of insects and spiders.

The family returned to England in 1966. Fiona told me, "It was a big shock, going to the local primary school in Preston, marshalled in with all the other children. Suddenly I was in a sensible pair of shoes and a school cap, where, in Nigeria, I used to have lessons from my mother on the veranda, in the sunshine, barefooted and bareheaded. After school I went to University College London. I did a degree in German because when I got there I found that everybody else was practically bilingual.

It did me a favour, however, because I understood I was not going to be academic. I had always wanted to be an actress, but my parents said actresses spent too much time "resting". I was to get a degree and then think about drama collage. Nevertheless,

I got involved in the dramatic society and through this with the student newspaper. I wanted to be with people and talk to people, so I took a year's sabbatical to edit the *London Student* newspaper, at that time the largest circulation student newspaper in Europe, selling 55,000 copies a week. That stood me in good stead when I left university to work with Thomson Newspapers."

It never happened, because a few weeks before she was supposed to start, Fiona visited a friend at a radio station in Reading. There had been a pile-up on the motorway and the station was short-staffed. They gave Fiona a five-minute teach-in on the use of a tape recorder and sent her to the scene. She came back with the story and was asked if she wanted to become a trainee with the station. The rest is history: ITN news reader, presenter for GMTV, *Have I Got News for You*, BBC News 24, TyneTees/Border TV, *Tight Lines*, author of two cookery books and two fishing books, journalism, and a host of other work that keeps her constantly busy.

Ann and I have known Fiona for many years. Her vibrant personality and electrifying smile brightens the darkest of days. Her frankness and honesty is, I think, one of her most enduring traits. Fiona was asked to open the Dee this year, and got a fish, but she also recalled for me one of the times when she was invited to make the first cast on opening day on the Tay. "It was a very bad day, wet and cold, and I was nervous because I hadn't fished since the previous September; leading the procession to the river, piper skirling, then blessing the boat by throwing whisky over it – except that I threw the whisky over myself, which wasn't a great start.

"I got into the boat, and we went out into the middle of the

Eddie McCarthy

Gillie Dougie Reid with 18lb River Thurso salmon

Beat 8.
Thurso River

© BRUCE SANDISON

Fiona Armstrong with Neil Grasser
on the River Cassley

Grant Mortimer

Mike Smith
on River Tay

Bruce Sandison with Pete the Fiddler (right) enjoying lunch in the heather

© CHERRY ALEXANDER

© BRUCE SANDISON

Thornhill. Left to right: Rab Kerr, Ronnie Gibson, Brian Hammon, Bert Wright

Rab with a River Nith salmon

Rab with clients on Thornhill

Sam Bemner,
Wester Elchies

Mike Batey,
Claygate, Langholm

© BRUCE SANDISON

© BRUCE SANDISON

Top dogs: Stan
Payne with
Pippa, Caley,
Ross and Brad

Iain Bell

Skippers Bridge Pool,
Border Esk, Langham

Lady MacGregor of MacGregor with Iain Bell on Border Esk

Iain racing round the track

river – there were hundreds of people watching – I pulled a bit line from the reel to make the cast, but I hadn't pulled enough and the line and fly just flapped around my head. I could sense everybody watching from the bridge gasping in horror. So I pulled out a lot more and managed to get some sort of cast out. Anyway, I thought, 'That's done, that's done.' I went back to the hotel to fortify myself, and there was this old bloke sitting at the bar. He looked at me and said, 'I'll tell you what, lass, you're no bad looking, but that was the worst cast I have ever seen!'"

Finally, I asked Fiona about her favourite salmon fly and she said, "It has got to be the Fiona's Fancy, presented to me after I opened the Tay this year. It hasn't caught anything yet, but I live in hope, and failing that, the good old Ally's Shrimp."

No matter what it is that she is doing – presenting a TV programme, broadcasting, accompanying her husband to Clan Gatherings in America, or fishing – Fiona approaches every task with enthusiasm. She told me that one her mother's guiding principles in life and been to treat every day with vigour, a principal that guides her daughter in fullest measure today.

10
Michael Smith, River Tay and Loch Leven

Mike Smith lives for fishing. He gillies at Stanley on the River Tay and is passionate about the preservation and enhancement of his favourite trout water, Loch Leven. He is one of the most dedicated anglers that I have met and I have known Mike for more than a couple of decades. We served together on the committee of the Salmon & Trout (Scotland) Association in the 1980s when it was chaired by Lord Marnoch and also benefited from the sound advice of the late Lord Hunter, author of the well-regarded 1960s report into the status and future of angling in Scotland.

Mike lives in Kinross-shire and farms at Threapmuir in the shadow of the Cleish Hills. The farm has been in his family since the 1970s and Mike told me, "My son-in-law does all the technical stuff, you know, spraying, combining, whatever, and we grow wheat, barley and potatoes and have summer cattle. It fits in very well with my fishing at Stanley, which finishes on 20 April and starts again in the middle of August. This allows me to fish Loch Leven during the summer months, so I have the best of all worlds."

As a boy, Mike went to Wester Elchies School and then to Aberlour House, a preparatory school for Gordonstoun. Mike remembered, "The highlight of my week was when we would walk from Wester Elchies across the footbridge over the Spey to attend Sunday prayers at Aberlour House. The river looked marvellous, and I never imagined then that one day I would be fishing there. After Gordonstoun I embarked on a career in the textile industry for Dawson International, one of the world's leading cashmere businesses, where my father was chairman. I worked in design and sales, mainly in the Borders, and then in London and New York. Our main customers there were, Brookes Brothers and Saks on 5th Avenue. I would go over and work for two or three months at a time, getting to know our customers. I guess that I got homesick and particularly missed fishing. I started fishing when I was eight years old, for sticklebacks and minnows, and I remember catching my first trophy fish, a perch all of four inches long, on a bent pin and a little mud worm and wondering if I should find a taxidermist."

I asked Mike if his father had fished. "No, not at all. I even tried to introduce him to shooting, but the last time he shot anything was in the Royal Air Force during the war when he flew Spitfires and was the back-up plane to Douglas Bader, guarding the ace-pilot's tail. When Bader was shot down, Father was ill and another pilot was flying as backup. Bader sat out the rest of the war as a POW in Colditz Castle. Father had a very successful career as a Spitfire pilot and after the war married Mother, Magaret Todd, and got into the textile industry. Father's work was his hobby, his life, I was lucky enough to turn my hobby into my work. In 1973 I left the textile industry and started to farm, but my father kindly made funding available for me to buy the Dalguise Beat on the River Tay. I gillied there for twenty-five years and enjoyed every minute of it. In 1999, I sold Dalguise and bought Farleyer from Major Neil Ramsey, a lovely bit of fly-fishing water on the Upper Tay, now sadly damaged by the anti-social behaviour activities of canoeists and whitewater rafters, currently the subject of a legal action to devise an equitable means whereby both anglers and other river users can enjoy the Tay without seriously impinging upon each other's interests."

The heaviest salmon Mike has caught came from Dalguise during an unforgettable Saturday morning's fishing. The river had been taken by a party from Messrs. Tate & Lyle, Monday through to Friday, but due to weather conditions, blue skies and low water, they hardly saw a fish, let alone managed to catch one. When they left, Mike suggested to Callum Gillies, who had been working with him during the Tate & Lyle visitation, that they should have a cast themselves the following morning. Mike said, "Callum was from the Outer Hebrides and a wonderful man and great company and had fished the beat for near thirty years. We had four salmon that morning weighing 102.5lbs, the largest being a cock fish of 43.25lbs taken from the Otterstone Pool. Callum missed it with the gaff at the first attempt, and said, 'Jesus, Michael, it is huge!' He gaffed it well and truly the second time. It was a beautiful fish, sea liced, long and shapely, and from its appearance, I think a River Tummel salmon."

The River Tay is one of the most productive salmon streams in Europe and renowned worldwide for the size and quality of its salmon, including, of course, Miss Georgina Ballantine's record fish of 64lbs caught in 1922 in the Boat Pool of the Glendelvine Beat. The fish was 54 inches long with a girth of 28.5 inches, a head 12 inches long and a tail 11 inches in length.

Her fish was displayed in P. D. Malloch's shop window in Perth and Georgina recounted going to see it. She heard two elderly men discussing that matter. "One said to the other, 'A woman?

Nae woman ever took a fish like that oot of the water, mon. I would need a horse, a block and tackle, tae tak a fish like that oot. A woman – that's a lee anyway.' I had a quiet chuckle," Georgina said, "and ran to catch my bus."

Mike fondly remembered Miss Ballantine. "She had served as a nurse in France during the First World War and never married. As she grew older, she always had a little light in her window at night to assure people in the village that she was all right."

I also remember the late Colin Leslie, head gillie at Cargill, telling me about a huge salmon he saw when he was fishing with a Mrs Morris. Colin said, "The fish jumped clean out of the water about five yards from the boat, and I will never forget it. My stomach took a turn and I asked Mrs Morris if she had seen it." They both saw the fish and estimated it to be about six feet long, three feet deep and to weigh in the order of 100lbs. "I never saw another fish like it, before or since. What a fright I got. I wondered what was coming out of the water. Oh, I wished I had hooked him."

But the Tay can also be a very dangerous river and hardly a year passes without some dreadful tragedy. One of the worst years was 1978 when twenty people drowned, some suicides, some heart attacks, and some fishing accidents. Mike remembered one of the fatalities. "It was a very hot spring and Easter that year with the temperatures in the seventies and the *commis* chef from Dunkeld House Hotel decided to go for a swim, but the water was freezing and he got into difficulties and drowned."

I was reminded of that story when I came as close as I ever want to come to drowning on the Tay. I was in the Boy Scouts at the time and we were camping at Inver Park, just upstream from Dunkeld. A friend, William Calder, and I constructed a raft, as Scouts do, made out of two empty forty-gallon drums with wooden planking across them upon which to sit and a couple of basic paddles with which to propel the vessel. It worked famously, particularly when we had to cross the river to set off on an adventure hike. Two of the boys in our party couldn't swim, so I swam the river, taking one end of a long rope with me. The rest of the group, including the non-swimmers, were thus hauled across the Tay on the raft. Thinking back, I shudder. No life jackets, no adult supervision, but it was in the early 1950s when health and safety regulations were no more than a twinkle in some bureaucrat's eye.

Before leaving Dunkeld and returning to Edinburgh, William and I decided to take the raft into the middle of the river, dive off, and let it go, in a sort of back-to-front Viking funeral. It nearly became our funeral, for the Tay was in spate and coming down in a torrent. With the thoughtlessness of youth, we launched the raft and quickly found ourselves being swept uncontrollably downstream towards Dunkeld Bridge. We were both strong swimmers, and after a quick consultation, we dived in and struck out for the shore. As the water tugged and pulled me downstream, I felt the beginnings of panic. Trying to keep calm, I swam as strongly as I could and after what seemed an eternity, grabbed the roots of a tree overhanging the bank and hauled myself ashore. I struggled upright and saw William hauling himself on to the bank further downstream. The distance we had swum from raft to shore was only a few dozen yards, yet we had been swept hundreds of yards downstream, almost to the bridge. There were steps leading up from the bank of the river up to the road above and we suffered the indignity of walking back to camp through the town in our dripping swimming costumes.

Mike had also had instances when one of his guests decided to go for a swim. He recalled the time when Francis 'Fanny' Lee, a legendary footballer who made twenty-seven appearances for the England National Team and scored 200 goals during his career, was fishing with him at Dalguise. "He was a stocky guy and a great character," Mike said, "and because it was a hot day decided to have a dip in the river. He jumped into the Bridge Pool, which is pretty deep, and the current once it hits a bend takes you out into the middle of the river, whether you have a life jacket on or not. Calum Gillies was with me that day and had stayed behind to keep an eye on things; it was his seventieth birthday and I had gone to pick up Callum's wife because we were taking them out to lunch. Normally, when I leave the river, I lock the boat, but this time, thank goodness, I hadn't done so. Callum managed to get the boat out. Francis had panicked and gone under, but Callum managed to grab him and pull him into the boat. When I got back, I found an uncharacteristically quiet Francis Lee. When he recovered, he headed off for home. We went to lunch. But a few weeks later, Callum received a gold watch from Francis to thank Callum for saving his life.

"Another incident, with a less happy outcome, happened about ten years ago. A guest had taken a boat out on the Catholes Beat on a terrible day and suddenly realised that he couldn't handle it. If he had done nothing, he would probably have ended up at Newburgh in the Tay estuary, but safe and sound. Instead, he did the worst thing and threw out the anchor, which immediately took hold on rocks on the bottom of the river and, through the force of the current sank the boat. It went straight down and it was five weeks before we found the body."

But Mike also remembers happier times. "John and Caroline Hamilton, from Ireland – good friends of mine – used to fish with me. They brought their daughters along, Eva, Nicola and Louise, and I had the great pleasure of seeing them all catch their first salmon. Like their mum and dad, they soon became very competent anglers, like most women are. I have seen Caroline Hamilton go down a pool, after it had been fished by a man and take two or three fish when the man had done so and been fishless. She is always diligent, and where we might be fishing with a big tube fly, she will fish down with a couple of spiders, maybe size twelve's, and produce the goods."

As all the gillies that I have met, Mike subscribes to the theory that one woman angler is invariably far more successful than any ten men. "I had a couple from Glasgow with me one day," Mike told me. "He was an accountant, and that did not immediately endear him to me, given my experience of that breed during my business life, but his wife was a lovely, quiet and gentle woman. I said to them that most of the fish lay within twenty yards of the bank, although the river was nearly 100 yards wide at that point. But he knew better and was casting into the middle of next week, right across to the far side, and catching nothing. On the other hand, his wife had followed my advice and soon had her first fish, a beautiful 10lb salmon. So I told the man again where the fish were, in the channel, not over on the other side. In spite of that, he was still casting across the stream, doing his macho thing. Then his wife took her second salmon and, sadly, I had to say to him, 'Sir, it's not a gillie you need but a lawyer.'" Mike invariably refers to his gentlemen guests as 'sir', not, he told me, in deference but because it avoided the potential embarrassment of forgetting their first names.

Mike has fished in many other Scottish Rivers and particularly enjoyed the times he spent on the Naver in north Sutherland, a famous and exclusive salmon stream, which is also enjoyed by HRH Prince Charles. He remembered seeing Bill von Rutenburg, the American restaurateur, and his wife fishing in the Parson's Nose Pool, with Donald Bruce, a former police sergeant, as their gillie. Mr Rutenburg was not in the best of health and was being supported as he fished on one side by his chauffer and on the other by his physiotherapist, a bit like the Scottish Country Dance, 'The Dashing White Sergeant'. Meanwhile, Mrs Rutenburg had landed two grilse. So Donald persuaded Mr Rutenburgh to go down the stream again, because it was packed with grilse. So in the trio went again, and again failed to connect with a fish. Mrs Rutenburg came down behind them and had another two grilse. So, whereas before it and been 'Well done, darling', it was now, 'Oh, so you think you're cleverer than me!' I think that that was a pivotal moment, because shortly thereafter he sold his beat on the Naver and gave up fishing."

Mike also told me about when he fished with Harry Chapman Pincher, doyen of the espionage/spy catcher market in the days of the Cold War and staff writer on the *Daily Express*. "He and his wife Billie fished with me at Farleyer in May. Billie was a lovely lady and she had just had a hip operation so had to be careful. Anyway, she immediately caught a fish, about 10lbs, and I was delighted for her. Harry was not the best of sportsmen that I have ever met, and was somewhat less than delighted with Billie's success. He went down to the tail of the pool and lost a fish, and then, thank God, he caught one. So we went up to the Aielean

Chraggan Hotel, Alistair Gillespie's hostelry, which now looks after the fishing on the Upper and Lower Farleyer Beats. It was a glorious spring day, sun shining the birds singing. I said to Billie and Harry, 'What a beautiful day! You have both got beautiful fish and we are about to have a lovely lunch, what more could a man ask for?' Harry replied, without a smile, 'More fish.' He was in his eighties then, but I realised that there was nothing I could do with him and never invited him to Farleyer again."

The only time Mike has ever put a guest off the river occurred in the days when the use of prawns as bait was still allowed on the Tay. I remembered Colin Leslie at Cargill, back in the 1980s, commenting to me on the use of prawns. "Any idiot can catch a salmon with prawns, but proper salmon fishing is fly-fishing. It always has been and, as far as I am concerned, always will be." However, other gillies have told me that taking a prawn down a pool can scare off every fish for miles around. Gordon Dagger, the head gillie on the little River Forss in Caithness, recalled an occasion when a friend of his used prawns when salmon fishing in Ireland. In spite of their best efforts, neither Gordon nor his friend had managed to even remotely disturb the fish, and whilst Gordon decided to change his flies yet again, his partner declared that he would "sort them out" with a prawn. He leapt into his car and drove to the nearest village where he purchased a large bag of prawns. Eventually, Gordon left him by the river, furiously hurling a prawn across the stream, completely confident that at any moment a salmon would grab it. An hour later Gordon returned and found his friend sitting by the pool, a dejected heap, still fishless and clutching an empty paper bag with the residue of the prawns scattered round.

"What happened?" enquired Gordon.

"The damned fish wouldn't eat them so I ate them myself," came the disconsolate reply.

Mike continued, "Robert Marshall, a good friend and well-known farmer and civil engineer from the Central Belt, was fishing the beat and he had invited two guests, a father and son, to join him. I hadn't met the son before, but I set him off fishing the Bridge Pool whilst I went down to the Otterstone Pool with his father. The father asked me if I had any prawns, so I went up to the fishing hut and gave him one, then put the rest back in the hut and locked the door. He took a fish with it almost on his first cast, and sometime during the morning, he must have told his son. Because he didn't have any, the son broke into the fishing hut and took the rest of the prawns that were there. So I just told him to get in his car and bugger off, which he did. If there is one thing that I can't abide in an angler it is ill manners. They say that money is the root of all evil, but I think that salmon fishing runs it a close second. It seems to bring out the best and worst in some people."

I asked Mike if he would change anything, if he had the chance to do it all again. "No," he replied. "Although perhaps politically, I would like to have been more involved because I believe that there is too much 'political correctness' around today. People tend to avoid the real issues. For example, we now have buzzards everywhere, and when my oystercatchers sit on their nests, the buzzards get them. Grey partridge have almost been wiped out. But buzzards are a protected species now and nobody does anything to try to control their numbers. We create an imbalance in nature and fail to strive to find a balance. Look at Loch Leven, which I have fished for decades. Apart from the problems with cormorants predating on fish, we now have around 2,000 black back gulls and herring gulls nesting on St Serf's Island where they have displaced the black-headed gulls that used to nest there. They have also decimated the tufted duck population; ninety-four per cent of tufted duck fledglings are eaten by the gulls. The plight of West Highland and Island salmonids, devastated by disease and pollution from factory salmon farms, is an unsupportable act of extreme environmental vandalism, but nothing is done to address the issue. I remember fishing the Moidart River, when Marjorie Leas owned the Upper River and General R. N. Stewart owned the Lower River. I saw sea-trout of up to 16lbs there; now it is virtually fishless. Loch Shiel, which Lord Hunter used to love to fish, is just the same. Sea-trout of over 18lbs used to be caught in Loch Eilt, which is also now devoid of both sea-trout and salmon. If I had the chance to do it all again, these are some of the things that I would fight for."

Finally, I asked Mike if he could explain what fishing meant to him. "Bruce, it's everything. I don't spend hours chatting about fishing, like we used to do, but I savour every minute I spend fishing. My blank days make my good days. Without the black days I wouldn't have any good days. I remember a friend who told me that when he was fishing in Alaska he caught thirty-three salmon from thirty-six casts. He said, 'Michael, it was hell on earth.' That's what I think. Fishing shouldn't be that way. Fishing is somewhere in between your heart and your head."

I left Mike going off to complete urgent business on the farm, and with his very kind invitation to take Ann and me out with him to fish Loch Leven. Mike is generous, courteous and eternally enthusiastic, a wonderful advocate for all the things that I hold dear in my native land.

11

Rab Kerr, Brian Hammond, Ronnie Gibson, Bert Wright, Buccleuch Estate

On an early April afternoon I arrived at Thornhill in Dumfriesshire to meet Rab Kerr, River Manager on the Buccleuch Estate and three of his friends, Brian Hammond, Ronnie Gibson and Bert Wright, who also worked there as keepers. Collectively, they had more than 170 years of experience covering every aspect of life on a major sporting estate – and, of course, wonderful memories of the people they knew and the incidents that they were involved in along the way. We sat together in Rab's comfortable sitting room and I listened whilst they talked.

I firstly asked what they thought of the Langholm Moor study, a ten-year scientific exercise costing an estimated £10 million that investigated the impact hen harriers had on grouse numbers on the moor. The study was prompted by a view that is largely shared by most estate owners and their gamekeepers, that unless hen harrier numbers were controlled, Langholm, as a viable grouse moor, would simply cease to exist. Whereas Scottish National Heritage (SNH) and the Royal Society for the Protection of Birds (RSPB) argued that hen harriers were not the core of the problem of declining grouse numbers and vigorously opposed any proposal that their numbers should be controlled, they believed that a better solution would be found in more effective management of the moor

Ultimately, both sides of the dispute claimed victory for their disparate views. But it seems to me, the facts speak for themselves. During the study no harriers were shot. Today, however, on Langham Moor, there are only two pairs of harriers and virtually no grouse. At one stage there were more than a dozen pairs on the moor and these birds are masterly predators. But because their numbers were not controlled, they simply ate all the grouse. Then harrier numbers started to decline primarily because foxes, also searching for food, were killing harrier fledglings on their nests; time-lapse cameras showed this quite clearly. Other birds and animals moved out because there was nothing left for them eat. If a balance had been preserved between harrier and grouse populations, then the moor, in all probability, would have been viable today.

However, the keepers identified another problem that contributed greatly to destabilising the moor: overshooting on the part of estate guests. Rab said, "It began when the price charged for grouse shooting started to rise. You could easily get a hundred brace in a day on Langham, Sanquhar, Wanlockhead, and with grouse selling at £145 a brace, the temptation to shoot too many was hard to resist. The attitude seems to have been that as long as there were a couple of grouse left at the end of the season then there would still be grouse there the following year. Grouse shooting became an indispensable source of income. In reality, it was the law of diminishing returns and a road that could only lead to disaster."

This was also compounded by the fact that a lot of shooting was, and is, let out by the day, whereas in the past it was generally for several days or a week. Day lets tend to encourage guests to shoot everything that shows, just to make sure they get their money's worth. The signs were already there back in the 1980s. When I spoke to Andrew Hunter, a retired keeper on the estate, in 1986 he told me, "One day last year we had an army of shooters, keepers, beaters and Land Rovers here and they only managed to shoot five grouse between them."

Rab and his friends also agreed that the kind of people shooting today had changed radically since when they began working. Ronnie commented, "Some of them who come to shoot today would never have got on the place in the past. I've worked with prime ministers, princes, queens, dukes and members of Parliament – the whole lot. I remember one telling me that you never needed to worry about the landed gentry because what you saw is what you got, that it was the others, who may have had the money but were not landed gentry and would like to be, who caused all the trouble. Over my working years, that has always proved to be the case."

Bert said, "I think it is because the estates are now run as a commercial business, corporate entertaining and so on – fishing, shooting, whatever – as long as it generates cash."

I believe that this also leads to more frequent shoot accidents. Brian said, "I have been shot about fourteen times, the head, top of my ribs. Shooting me in the head, by the way, was a waste of time because there was nothing up there in the first place!"

Brian asked, "Mind the day when your rear got shot? The guest walked into the hut and you asked him if he had enjoyed himself and he said that he had. You replied, 'Well, I'm glad to hear that, sir, because you have just shot me in the rear.'" Brian also recalled the story of a day with an Italian party of shooters. "We were at Eccles and one of country's top dog handlers and his dog were with us, picking up birds that had been shot. Before the start of the drive the Italians all started taking photographs of each other. They did so, I was told, because it is the Italian custom to put a photograph of the deceased on his tombstone. That should have warned me. At the end of the drive a wounded bird rose and started running up the hillside. I will never forget seeing the dog handler's animal charging after the bird, chased by all the Italians, who were still firing at the bird over the dog's head, pursued by the dog handler yelling at them that he would rip their heads off if they hit his dog."

Brian said, "Well, the last time I was shot it put me in Dumfries Hospital. The guest shot me from about thirty yards. He was the outside gun on the line and he had fired at a pheasant. The first thing I remember was lying at the base of a tree with a man standing looking down at me as though I was dead. He went to the keeper who was working with me and said, 'You had better get up there. Brian has been shot and I think he's dead.' When the keeper found me, my face was covered in blood, but I had recovered. The keeper jumped a wall and raced down to the man who had fired the gun and roared at him, 'Did you fire that shot?' The man said 'No', and the next moment he was flat on his back in the field. The keeper had knocked him down with a single blow. I was taken to hospital and an eye specialist from Carlisle came up to remove the pellets. There were three in the middle of my eyelid and various others through my face and one or two at the top of my ribs. I heard later that the man who fired the shot created merry hell saying that he was going to sue the keeper for hitting him. The keeper turned round to him and said, 'If you didn't fire the shot then I didn't hit you.'"

Ronnie said, "My predecessor, Jim McKnight, was shot badly. He had been out that day with group of ex-army and naval men, colonels and captains and the like, and one of them was an awkward shot. He lifted his gun from below his waist, every time, up and right over his head. He caught Jim in the side and that was another hospital job. Jim had thirty-seven pellets between his leg and his neck.

"On another occasion the guns (guests who were shooting) were walking in line over a turnip field and it couldn't have been a well-formed line because one of them shot his neighbour in the behind."

I asked Rab and his friends about health and safety regulations, and they just laughed and said, "There weren't any regulations in those days, and more often than not, nae common sense either amongst some of the guests.

As much as the guests have changed, so in many ways have the people who manage the affairs of estates. In the 1980s I met Willie Drysdale. Willie was the head keeper on the Hopetoun Estate near Edinburgh, but started his career in Dumfriesshire. Willie was well respected and kindly remembered by Ronnie and his friends. When Willie started at Hopetoun he told me, "Keepers were always provided with a suit of clothes, and for special days, when the great folk came, a kilt. On those occasions the head keeper would line everyone up to make sure that they were properly turned out. Few were not, because jobs were hard to come by in those days. I hated that damned kilt. On a frosty morning, wading through wet turnips, the backs of your legs would be all chapped and raw." The laird's word was law, then, and the factor made sure that it was obeyed.

Donald MacDonald from Invercauld Estate on Deeside recounted this story to me about John Mackay, a keeper from Aboyne. "Lord Dalhousie had arrived one morning and asked John, 'What have you done with the weather, Mackay? Could you not have managed to make it a better day than this?'

"John replied, 'Och, it was fine yesterday. Are you sure you didna bring it with you, my lord?' The next morning he was called to the factor's office and given his notice."

Brian recalled when he first began work on the estate, "I stared with Andrew Hunter and I can remember walking down from where I stayed, about three and a half miles away, to get to his house on time. It was January, pitch black and blowing a blizzard. As I neared the house I heard a voice, 'If you want to continue working here, boy, take your hands out of your pockets.'"

Andrew Hunter's career with Buccleuch Estate began 1938. I met him in the 1980s when he described the then Duke to me as being 'a bit eighteenth century' and a very easy man to get into trouble with. You didn't speak unless spoken to first. Andrew told me, "If you were wrong with the Duke in the morning, then you were wrong with him all day. If the line on the hill was ragged the Duke would roar and shout at all and sundry until it was as he wanted it."

Andrew remembered the Duke of Marlborough at a pheasant shoot getting hell from the Duke for daring to leave his appointed position. Andrew would arrive home some nights after a bad day with the Duke and tell his wife to start packing and get ready to leave. However, more often than not the phone would ring in the evening and the Duke would say, "Hunter, I hope you haven't thought too much about what was said at the butts today?"

"No, my lord. I have forgotten all about it," Andrew would reply, and there was an end to the matter.

Andrew Hunter's welcome to Ronnie that cold January morning when he started work must have been intimidating, but he had mellowed a great deal when I met him. He talked easily about the people he had worked with, including the actress Audrey Hepburn who had starred in such notable films as *The Unforgiven*, *Charade* and as Eliza Doolitle in the hit-musical *My Fair Lady*. She also fished for salmon with Andrew on the River Nith. Andrew told me, "I chose the Otter Pool as being the place with the best chance of a fish. It is not easy to get to, but I thought we could manage. Well, she looked down at the jumble of rocks to the river and announced, firmly, 'I am not going anywhere near that disgusting place!' But I persuaded her, although I had to near carry her to the river. And she got a fish."

Ronnie worked well with Andrew Hunter. "It was a five-year apprenticeship," he said, "and depending on how you got on, at the end of the five years you would be given a wood to look after or a bit of riverbank, and it built up like that until perhaps after eight or nine years you were given a beat of your own. There was none of this walking straight into a beat. You had to prove that you could do it, and if you couldn't you were history."

A keeper's job is still as hard and demanding today as it ever was, but there is now a much more relaxed attitude towards out-dated formalities and a more relaxed relationship between owners, factors, guests and staff who work for them than in days gone by. Most of the keepers, stalkers and gillies that I meet talk nostalgically about the characters they knew in the past, but as I discovered, there are still more than enough characters around today to enliven any day on loch, river, hill or moor.

But it was fascinating to listen to the four friends talking over old times. Bert remembered Kenny Houston, who lived up at Wanlockhead in a row miner's houses. Lead was mined in the surrounding hills and gold as well. The river Wanlock ran by about twenty feet from Kenny's front door, and Kenny said that his father told him that when he and his mother returned from their honeymoon, he noticed a glint of gold in the river. He went over and found a gold nugget as big as horse's nose, so ran to the house to fetch a wheelbarrow and a spade. But there had been a flash flood and by the time he returned the nugget was gone. The only thing that wouldn't float in the spate was the gold, so he searched and searched for it, but in vain.

Brian said, "I had Kenny in the Land Rover with me one night, and before I pulled out on the road, I asked him if there were any cars coming. He said no, so I pulled out, just as a huge petrol tanker came by missing me by inches. 'Kenny!' I roared. 'I thought you said that were no cars coming!'

"'There weren't,' Kenny replied.

"'That was no a car, it was a lorry.' We were almost hit by 15,000 gallons of petrol, but it wasn't a car."

Apparently, Kenny had his own special technique for catching crows on the grouse moor. He would lie buried in the heather with a dead rabbit tied to his chest and when a crow landed on his chest to get the rabbit, he would grab it. Bert caught him out, though, one day. "I had been sea fishing at Kipford and I caught this massive skate, so I took it up to Wanlockhead and put it in the burn. When Kenny passed I called him over, 'See this, Kenny, have you ever seen the likes of that in the burn before?' Kenny was speechless."

Wullie Wilson was also another well-remembered character. Brian said, "Mind the time when we were all sitting in the woods having lunch at a pheasant shoot? We had a fire going and Wullie had picked up this old dead crow that was lying in some branches, skinned it and was toasting it over the fire. As the guests passed by they stopped to look in astonishment. There's Wullie shouting, 'Just about ready, boys. Who's for a leg?' Wullie always cleaned his own chimney, twice a year, but never bothered about a brush. He would go up to the wood and get a fir tree, attach a rope to the tree, then drop the rope down the chimney and shout to those below, 'All right, lads, pull.' They pulled it down, but one day the rope broke and the chimney went on fire."

Other tales of Wally Kirkpatrick followed. Just after an aircraft passed overhead one afternoon, Wally was seen coming off the hill with something circular wrapped in plastic under his arm. "Where are you going with that?" Someone asked. Wally replied, "Hame. God, boys, this'll do the tea for a week." Wally thought that it was a fruitcake. He was convinced that it had rolled out of the Jumbo Jet as it passed overhead because the stewardesses had all been standing at the back door having a fag and looking out.

On another occasion, Wally went to the woods to help with cutting trees. "Where shall I start, boys?" he said. He had an electric saw and they all wondered where he intended to plug it in.

He was at a shoot one morning and had spent the whole morning shouting for his dog. But the dog wasn't with him. It was still in its kennel because Wally had forgotten to bring it.

Finally, they remembered all the keepers sitting at lunch one day on the hill. And of course, their dogs were nosing around, hoping for food. Wally was in his glory because his dog was sitting there looking on, not joining in. "Now you look at that," Wally exclaimed. "There is how a well-trained dog should behave. It is about time you all trained your dogs to do the same." Little did Wally know that a Land Rover had rolled forward in soft mud and was trapping his dog's tail.

Poaching is an ever-present problem and keepers often get little assistance from the police when trying to deal with it. Some officers take the matter seriously; others apparently couldn't care less. Some years ago my wife and I were fishing Loch Garvie in Wester Ross. A small river drains Loch Oscaig and it runs through Loch Garvie before flowing for a short distance north to join the sea over the sands of Garvie Bay. We found a huge monofilament net in the neck of the outlet stream from the loch, clearly set to catch any fish running the river. I collected the net and took it down to Ullapool Police Station. The constable on the desk told me to leave it with him and he would attend to the matter. He didn't even bother to ask me my name, never mind my address or make any note of when and where I said that I had found the net.

The Buccleuch Estate has extensive fishing rights on one of south-west Scotland's most famous salmon and sea-trout streams, the River Nith, and poaching can be a problem because the main road, the A76 from Cumnock to Dumfries, margins the river closely for much of its length. Poachers are always with us, and, I suppose, they always will be. I remember Andrew Hunter telling me that one day he watched nine pairs of spawning salmon on their redds in a little tributary of the Nith, but when he returned the following morning, there was not a fish to be seen. However, footmarks were visible on the riverbank, so he followed them all the way to the estate boundary and then on to the next moor. There, in a gully on the hill, he found two sacks full of salmon. Andrew hurried home for his Land Rover, but by the time he had returned, the sacks and salmon had gone.

The only way the fish could have been removed was by vehicle or by pony, and there were no tyre tracks to be seen. However, grazing peacefully nearby was a shepherd's pony and Andrew could clearly see hoof-prints close to where the salmon had lain. So he went on until he came to the shepherd's house and asked him, "Is that your pony in the field, John?"

"Aye, it is," said John.

"And are you the only one that uses it?"

"Aye," replied John.

"Well," said Andrew, "it's a funny thing, John, but there were two sacks of salmon on the hill this afternoon and now both of them are gone."

The shepherd eventually admitted that he had loaned his pony to two men to carry the salmon away and that they had been bound for Muirkirk. Four hours later, complete with policemen and search warrant, Andrew caught the poachers as they cleaned the salmon, carefully putting to one side the roe for later use as bait, which is a criminal offence. They were fined £250 each, but refused to say to whom they proposed to sell the fish.

Brian Hammond gillied on the river and he told me that he had many a brush with people fishing illegally, which could sometimes result in him being physically attacked. "I remember one of the factors here phoned me at about 1am to tell me that he could see lights in the fishing hut and would I go down and see who was there. 'Just knock on the door,' he said, 'and as they come out get their names and addresses and bring them to me when the office opens at nine in the morning, and I will deal with it.' But I knew that when I knocked on the door I would be very lucky only to be hit on the head, never mind anything else. Was I supposed to write down their names and addresses in the sand as I was lying half-conscious?

"The next morning I was called to the factor's office and he asked me what had happened. I told him that there was nobody there and that they must have realised that they had been spotted and scarpered. 'Jolly good,' he said, 'just keep an eye on the hut and do the same if it happens again, bring me the names and addresses and I'll deal with it'. I thought, 'Aye, right.'"

Sheep rustling is also a problem. Robbie Dickie, a local man, told Brian that he once came upon two men butchering a sheep in the back of a van. Robbie asked them what was going on. One of them said, "Well one thing's for sure, and that is that there is enough room in the van for the sheep and enough room in the boot for you, so shift, now!"

Brian also remembered once sitting with another keeper and a policeman on the side of a hill watching a man in waders working a run in the river using a glass-bottomed box. He was certainly after salmon and sea-trout. They observed him for about half an hour and then arrested him and confiscated the box. He was charged and duly appeared in court, only to have the sheriff throw the case out. The sheriff argued that it couldn't be conclusively proved that the man was intent on poaching fish, because he might have simply been observing them."

Deer poaching can also be a problem. Rab Kerr recounted an

incident when, early one morning, he found a car with four men in it coming off the hill on an estate road. Other than trying to force them off the road, there was not much he could do, but Rab was quite certain that they had been poaching. "I knew where they had probably shot the deer, so I went by them and down to the village policeman's house and hammered on his door until he got out of bed and answered my knock. The car seemed to be making for Dumfries and we tried to follow, but lost it. So the policeman radioed ahead and the Dumfries police managed to find and stop the vehicle. The inside of the car was just a shell, really, with only two seats in the front. In the back was a shotgun, four red deer and four roe deer. Three of the group had left the car before it was stopped and the driver wouldn't give their names. But he got three months for the part he had played in the incident"

Brian also had a poaching tale to tell that allegedly happened thirty to forty years ago on a viaduct near Leadhills on the lower slopes of Broad Law (1,686ft). The viaduct there was opened in 1901 by the Elvanfoot, Wanlockhead Light Railway Company to service the lead mines in the area and was dismantled in December 1992. It was a magnificent structure, with eight spans and length of 400 feet, designed and built by 'Concrete Bob' McAlpine, who also built Britain's first concrete structure, the famous viaduct at the head of Loch Sheil in Lochaber. Kenny Wilson, head keeper at Leadhills, who features in the story and this book, was born close by at the hamlet of Hass. Brian said, "I remember one of the times up there at Leadhills, when Kenny Wilson was head keeper. They caught this man shooting grouse and anything else he could get. They knew that he had to have an accomplice and a car somewhere, but he refused to say where they were." They were standing on the old viaduct and the policeman allegedly picked the man up by the ankles and threatened to topple him over the parapet if he did not disclose the information.

"'I'll ask you again,' the policeman said. 'Where is your pal and the car?' The man said that there were witnesses to what was happening and the policeman said, 'Aye, and they didn't see a thing.' So he told the policeman, who went down to the vehicle. When the accomplice came from where he had been hiding and got in the car, the policeman said, 'Hello, you're nicked.'"

Our talk had turned back to where we had started, the Langholm Moor grouse/hen harrier study, and I mentioned that I had met Brian Mitchell, who had been a head keeper and moorland manager for thirty-six years. Brian has written extensively about the conflict between conservation bodies such as the RSPB and Scottish National Heritage, including a definitive article on the subject in the magazine *Shooting Times*.

Ronnie Gibson remembered a less contentious tale about Brian and his dogs. "He had got this spaniel, and he told his wife, Doris, that he had left the dog in the house whilst he had gone to shoot grouse. Well, when Doris came home from work the dog would not let her in the house. Every time she went to open a door the dog would go wild and try to attack her. Eventually, she had to bring Brian back from the shoot before she could get into the house.

On that note, I asked Rab and his friends if they had the chance, would they follow the same path again. Ronnie said, "I don't think that I would do so now, but at the time, for all the interesting people I met, from the former Prime Minister Harold MacMillan down, and the laughs that I have had, it was great fun.

I remember after a day's grouse shooting with Andrew Hunter, we would hang the birds up in the larder and go in early the following morning to load them into wicker baskets, then up to Kirkconnell Station to put them on the train to London. The next morning we would go back to the station to pick up the empty hampers that had been sent back overnight. Now it's the likes of a game dealer who does all that. For the time I spent at it, aye, it was good, but latterly it's just run by chequebooks and numbers, and all too often by people who don't really know what they are doing. You invariably knew a lot more than they did, but they never asked and they were in charge."

He turned to Rab and his friends and said, "I think that everybody would agree with that?"

I heard no dissenting voices.

12
Sam Bremner, Wester Elchies, River Spey

The first time I saw the River Spey was from the back of a furniture removal van when I was twelve years old. I was in the Boy Scouts and our annual camp that summer was close to the banks of the river near Newtonmore; the vehicle was at the station to take us and our camping bits and pieces, tents, pots and pans, to the site. We spent two weeks there, mostly cold, getting wet from the rain and wet from swimming in a peaty loch nearby, chopping down trees, building bridges and rafts and generally doing what Boy Scouts do and enjoying every moment of it as we did.

Days were much longer then, not like they are now, when they dash past like an express train. Although I was already an embryonic angler, I fished only for brown trout and the sight and sound of mighty salmon splashing upstream in the Spey's fast-flowing waters aroused in me the desire to catch one, a desire that remained unsatisfied until a couple of dozen years later, and then not in the Spey, but further north on the River Thurso in Caithness. During the intervening years I lashed a number of rivers to foam in search of a fish, but remained perennially salmon-less.

Sam Bremner, head gillie on the Wester Elchies beat of the Spey, the man I had come to see one fine April morning, had been more fortunate than me. He was born and bred at Craigellachie, imbued with fishing in his blood from his earliest years. Sam lives in a perfect house, a short cast from the river on the west bank opposite the Speyside town of Aberlour. Sam's house is not easy to find if you don't know the way, and I wandered about for a while before working out that a rough track that appeared to lead nowhere, was in fact the way down the hill, through the trees, to his lair.

Sam came out to meet me, smiling as he shook my hand, and I apologised for being late. On the other side of the river an angler was fishing the Aberlour Angling Association water. His elegant Spey casts sparkled in the sharp sunlight sending crystal droplets flying across the surface. We watched his efforts for a moment.

"What are his chances, Sam?" I asked.

"The river is a bit high today, but you never know," he replied.

Yes indeed, I thought, that is one of the treasures of salmon fishing, you never know.

Sam took me through to the living room where we settled with a cup of coffee and some welcome home-baked scones, comfortably to talk. I asked Sam how he became involved in fishing. "I was born in 1956," he said, "when we didn't have computer games or the like, so we had to make our own fun. My father was wounded during the war and lost a leg, so he couldn't work the farm when he came home. Instead, he worked as a barman in the Craigellachie Hotel. He was there for more than thirty years and mother did early morning breakfasts. My brother and I used to get permits to fish the river from the hotel, and that's where it all began for me when I was seven years old. We boys, about four or five of us, went down to a pool every evening to fish and play in the woods. As I grew older, on Sundays, I started going to the hotel to give guests a hand – you know, with their cases and fishing gear."

"It's a small world, Sam," I said, "because when I came out of the army in 1960 I took my father for a week's salmon fishing on the Spey and we stayed at the Craigellachie Hotel. I fondly remember your dad. He always had an encouraging word for me when I came back fishless. I also used to give some of the guests a bit of hand too. In the army I had been a lowly lieutenant, so I was a bit over-awed to find two retired generals fishing the same week as we were. One of the old gentlemen had some difficulty in getting out of his waders after the day fishing. He sat on the tailgate of his car whilst I heaved them off. In the evening, after dinner, he would sit in the lounge in front of the fire, reading his paper, or so it seemed; in fact, he was sound asleep."

As Sam worked around the hotel, he got to know a lot of the guests and was soon asked to help some of the ladies on the river. After leaving school, he served his apprenticeship as a cooper, a trade much in demand for Speyside's many whisky distilleries. But all Sam's spare time was spent as a gillie at the hotel.

"I was a professional worm digger," he said. "You used to get a couple of pounds for a jar of worms, you know."

"Did you teach yourself to cast?" I asked.

"Yes, I suppose I did. My mother and father bought me a fly rod – I still have the Kingfisher line that came with it – and my oldest brother helped me with the basics, and a friend of father's took me down to the Spey. Prior to that, I had spent most of my time on the River Fiddich and my parents were happy with that. But when I started to go to the Spey, it was an entirely different matter. Funny, because when you think, it was as easy to drown in the Fiddich as it was in the Spey."

Sam gave up coopering to become a full-time gillie about six years after leaving school. At school, the father of one of his friends, was also a keen angler and head gillie on a beat below Craigellachie. When one of the beat's gillies had to go into hospital for an operation, Sam was asked if he would like to 'stand in' during the man's absence. Sam took time off work to do the job and was asked, if a full-time position as a gillie came up in the future, would be interested. "It didn't take me long to think about it," Sam said. "I thought, well, all I have ever wanted to do is to fish and shoot, and here I was in the right place at the right time. So I said yes."

"So when did you begin shooting?" I asked.

"Oh, long before I had any lessons. In those days you could walk about with a gun and nobody would bother. I started shooting duck on the Fiddich, creeping round corners to see if there was a duck sitting on a stone. If I shot one, I would take it home and Mother would pluck it; I will never forget that, last thing at night, Mother sitting close to the hearth as the fire was dying, plucking pheasants, pigeons, or whatever we boys had shot, with the strong draft pulling the down and feathers up the chimney."

Sam and his wife have two children and when they first came to Wester Elchies the children fished, but not so much now. "I never force them," Sam said. "Robert is twenty-nine years old now, and I still hope that he might come back to it. I do the keepering here as well as the fishing, and I have had him out, beating, and he's done some clay pigeon shooting with me but never shot live game."

The Spey has always been regarded, not only as one of Europe's finest salmon streams, but also for the quality and abundance of its sea-trout; in days past over 5,000 sea-trout could be taken each season. In recent years, however, the numbers of sea-trout have declined and the fishery board have put in place measures to try to restore Spey sea-trout stocks. Ann and I enjoyed fishing the Spey for sea-trout many years ago, below the old bridge at Grantown, and I asked Sam what he thought of the situation now. "Well, actually, they came back a wee bit last year, although they arrived earlier than usual, we even got one in April and a couple in May. June was always the best month for sea-trout, but they seemed to run right through our beat without stopping."

Recalling the old days, Sam commented, "Then nobody was really interested in fishing for sea-trout, it was all salmon. The only folk who fished for sea-trout were the locals and the gillies, although a few people did come up to fish for them in June. When I think back, June was a very quiet month for salmon on the Spey, but these last few years we have been catching salmon in June, which rarely happened before. You might pick up a couple fish in the spring then it dies away again and picks up towards August, and dies back in September. Fresh fish enter the river at the back end, but they just stay in the bottom beats where they seem to hang about there until they are ready to spawn. Some might start coming up the system then, but a lot of these fish stay in the lower river and we don't see them here."

In the mid 1980s, when I wrote my first book about Scotland's gillies, stalkers and keepers, *The Sporting Gentleman's Gentleman*, during the course of information-gathering I met a fine man, the late Jimmy Ross of Rothes. I was delighted to learn that Sam had known Jimmy as well and held him in the highest regard. "He was a topper, a gentleman. I knew Jimmy for a long time. One of the last times I saw him was down at Easter Elchies, which was the Rothes Association water in those days. There were a couple of special permits available, so if you got one you could start fishing right from Aberlour downstream for about five or six miles."

When I met Jimmy Ross, he had also talked fondly about the old days. "Oh, bless my soul," he said, "when I think of the numbers of salmon we used to catch down here at Delfur in the old days! Some days, with Sir Edward Mountain we would have forty to fifty salmon. I remember one morning with Sir Edward when we had more than two-dozen before lunch. The best day brought a total of sixty-seven salmon, but the fishing was less commercial in those days. Most of the salmon were sent to local hospitals; indeed, some gentlemen used to dispatch their fish to hospitals all the way down into England."

The largest salmon Jimmy Ross landed was caught by Ronnie Faulkner and it weighed 41lbs 8oz. The fish was hooked in Dewsies Hole and eventually landed away downstream at Green Bank by Croft's Farm. There was a ridge out in river at Green Bank, when Jimmy saw the dorsal fin of the salmon showing above the water. When he gaffed the fish he was almost pulled into the river, and had to kill the fish before he could haul it to the bank. But when Jimmy looked round to congratulate his gentleman, Mr Faulkner was nowhere to be seen; in the excitement of playing the fish, he had suffered a heart attack and was lying on his back on the bank. The Land Rover was some distance away, so Jimmy had to struggle home carrying both angler and the fish. Happily, Ronnie Faulkner recovered, the salmon did not and Jimmy never forgot that incident.

One of the most famous stories of huge Spey salmon was recounted by noted Scottish angler, author and lawyer, Thomas Tod Stoddart (1810–1880). He tells of a fish hooked many years ago by an Aberlour angler, Duncan Grant. "First you must understand that what is now called 'preserving the river' (the introduction of private beats) was formerly unknown, and everyone who chose to take a cast did so without let or hindrance. In pursuance of this custom, in the month of July some thirty years ago, one Duncan Grant, a shoemaker by profession, who was more addicted to fishing than to his craft, (as was Stoddart himself) went up from the village of Aberlour to take a cast in some of the pools above Elchies water. He had no great choice of tackle, as may be conceived – nothing, in fact, but what was useful – and scant supply of that.

"Duncan tried one or two pools without success, till he arrived at a very deep and rapid stream, facetiously termed the Mountebank. Here he paused, as if meditating whether he should throw his line or not. 'The river is very big,' said he to himself, 'but I'll try her; if I grip him he'll be worth the hauding.' He then fished it, a step and a throw, about halfway down, when a heavy splash proclaimed that he had raised him though the fish missed the fly. Going back a few paces he came over him again and hooked him. The first tug verified to Duncan his prognostication, that if he was there 'he would be worth the hauding', and he held fast, nothing daunted. Give and take went on with dubious advantage, the fish occasionally sulking.

"At the Boat of Aberlour, seven hours after he had hooked his fish, with the said fish fast under a stone, he was completely tired. He had some thoughts of breaking his tackle and giving the thing up, but he finally hit upon an expedient to rest himself, and at the same time guard against the surprise and consequence of a sudden movement of the fish. He laid himself down comfortably on the banks, the butt end of his rod in front, and most ingeniously drew out part of his line, which he held in his teeth. 'If he tugs when I'm sleeping,' said he, 'I think I'll find him noo'; and no doubt it is probable that he would. Accordingly, after a comfortable nap of three or four hours, Duncan was awoken by the most unceremonious tug at his jaws. In a moment he was on his feet, his rod well up, and the fish swattering down the stream. He followed as best he could, and was beginning to think of the rock at Craigellachie, when he found to his great relief that he could get a pull on him. He had now comparatively easy work, and exactly twelve hours after hooking him, he clieked him at the head of Lord Fife's water: he weighed 54lbs, Dutch, and had the tide-lice upon him."

The largest catch that Sam experienced was when one of his guests caught a cow on the back cast. "We were standing there blethering, you know," said Sam, "and when he cast he caught the cow. The first we knew about it was when the rod was almost pulled out of his hand and the cow took off across the field like an arrow from a bow, for nearly 100 yards. Fortunately, the fly came out, but the reel was screaming that day."

He also recalled a guest who was spinning when he hooked an otter. "We were just fishing away when he got a pull and the line started coming towards the bank. I had never seen a salmon do that. Then an otter jumped out onto the bank and started rolling around, and luckily enough, the hook came out. The otter did a quick exit back into the stream. We get a lot of the unusual stuff as well – frogs, bats, a swift once. I remember one night down at the hut, fishing for sea-trout, my guest had two pulls and two frogs for his evening."

My own most spectacular and embarrassing catch happened all those years ago when Father and I were fishing at Craigellachie, not in the river, but on the main road that ran parallel to the top beat. We were driving down to the lower beat with our rods poking out of the nearside window of the car, when my reel suddenly began screaming. Father slammed on the breaks, but not until the centre spool of the reel was showing. My fly had caught on the low branch of a tree and nearly all the line had been stripped off in a matter of a few seconds. Still in my waders, I endured the ignominy of walking up the side of the road reeling in, much to the amusement of passing cars, and a busload of American tourists. Father, bless him, never said a word.

But Sam recounted an even more embarrassing situation that happened to him. "I was landing a very good fish for a lady, using one of those Guy nets, and we had half the salmon in the net when my belt broke and my trousers fell down. She dropped the rod and tried to pull my trousers up. I told her, 'Never mind that, just give me a hand with the fish!'"

Sam has also had his fair share of rescuing guests from the river. "Some people seem to be prone to falling in," he explained, "tripping up every time they see water. I remember one guest falling in, but he didn't make a splash or shout for help. His family was having lunch, sitting at the picnic table. Fortunately, I was sitting close by on a bench watching him and managed to get him safely out, but it could have been another story if I had been looking the other way. You generally hear a few swear words, but there was not a thing. I thought that he had actually collapsed."

Sam has known many of his guests for forty years and more. "I have watched a lot of boys grow up, until, of course, they meet girls. After that you don't see them for about four or five years, but eventually they always come back. Nowadays it's their grandchildren that I am teaching to fish."

I asked Sam if he felt that woman anglers were more successful than men. "Yes, I think so. A few of us were talking about this the other day. I think that it has all to do with the distance people want to cast. If you tell a woman how far to cast, then she will generally stick to it. However, with a man, you can tell him anything you like and with a few minutes he will be trying to pull the other bank closer. I say to them, 'Catch the fish on my side of the river first, and then you can catch the fish on the opposite bank.' A lot of men just want to get the fly out as far as they can. But the ladies are fine. They listen, and that's a good thing. Another thing about the ladies is that they never give up. Doesn't matter how cold it is, or if it's raining. If the men see the rain coming, they run for the hut, whereas a woman will say, 'No, it's all right, Sam. I'll just carry on fishing.'"

Finally I asked, "Sam, what does fishing really mean to you? You have been doing it all your life. Why?"

Sam shook his head and said, "You know, that's a very difficult question. It's a hard question, but the first thing that comes into my mind is enjoyment, relaxation, I suppose basically life to me. When I first started, I was paid for doing it, I'm still getting paid for enjoying my fishing, and it's not really a job, is it?"

"Could you do without it?" I said.

"Oh, no. Never. I have been offered keepering jobs down in Essex, but I wouldn't like to live like that. I don't fish as much now as I used to when I was younger. One of my guests said to me the other day, 'Go get your rod, Sam, and have a cast. But I said, 'If you don't mind, I would rather just stand here with you.' He asked me why and I told him that I didn't want to fish and at the same time be worrying about how my guests were getting on. I want to relax when I'm fishing, I don't want to think about anything else. But I have never before thought about what fishing means to me. I have always been by the Spey, and I think that probably I always will be.

"You know, you always remember your first fish, and the ones that get away. I can still remember a very good fish I lost in 1979. I will never forget it because I tried to net it myself, with one of these big iron nets with the wooden handle. I had the fish in the net, dropped the rod, picked up the net, and suddenly the fish was away."

As I watched Sam telling the story, I felt that he was reliving the incident as though it had just happened; the pain that all anglers know when they see a specimen fish returning to its natural habitat.

As I drove away, up the track that had taken me so long to find, I glanced back to wave to Sam. He was standing on the riverbank, the silver Spey shining behind him, and I thought, 'Well there is a fine man who is happy in his natural environment.'

13
Mike Batey, Claygate, Dumfriesshire

I met Mike Batey on a bright April afternoon at his home in the small village of Claygate to the north of Canonbie in Dumfriesshire. He is a robust, tall man, well bearded, brisk and welcoming and was dressed overall in black, topped by a tweed flat cap set at a jaunty angle above smiling eyes. At that time, Mike was employed by the Buccleuch Estates as a head keeper, responsible primarily for rearing thousands of pheasants and partridge for the estate shoots. Today, he performs the same function for John Hammond, formerly of Border Fine Arts, who now owns the business. Mike's house is adjacent to the bird-rearing pens and the kennels, from the latter of which came the sound of thunderous barking.

The name Batey is the Cumbrian version of the Scottish name Beattie, and more likely than not, Mike's ancestors in lawless times were probably Border Rievers, until the Union of the Crowns in 1603 when the borderlands between England and Scotland were virtually a separate country, where the inhabitants did not recognise the authority of kings or queens, whether in London or in Edinburgh. The general rule seemed to have been to align oneself and one's family with whichever local magnate was in the ascendancy at the time. Whilst the Union changed that irrevocably, a feeling of special status still lingers in the borders to this day, as does the more friendly rivalry that exists between once warring families. The story about the infamous fish garth at Netherby Hall, which almost caused all-out war between England and Scotland, and details in connection with the Border Rievers, is more fully outlined in the chapter of this book devoted to the life and times of Iain Bell, the Buccleuch Estate former Fishery Manager.

Mike was born in 1963 near Dalston in Cumbria, about four miles south-west from the city of Carlisle where his family had a farm. Mike went to Caldew School at Dalston, but was far more interested in the countryside than he was in academic study. He said, "I was the one looking out the window all the time and my real schooling was in the woods or in the River Caldew which ran through the village."

As a boy, Mike once shot a fox on a neighbouring estate, unaware that it was being pursued at the time by the local hunt. Angus Chisholm, the keeper on the estate, heard of the incident and thought it a marvellous story and invited Mike to work with him. Mike told me, "I suppose that fox was a turning point in my life. I worked with Angus after school, and when I left school I got a permanent position with Sir Charles Graham at Netherby Hall on the banks of the Border Esk. I worked there for about five years before moving on to Solway Bank where I worked as a keeper for nine years with Lieutenant Colonel Raymond Johnson-Ferguson and his brother, Major Brian."

Mike enjoyed the years he spent at Solway Bank and fondly remembers the Colonel and his brother. "Shooting was the main interest on the estate, pheasant and grouse. Pheasants were not reared, as they are today. These were truly wild birds and wonderful sport. We only shot the cock birds, so you will understand how the stock improved. We were able to shoot three or four hundred pheasants during the season without recourse to artificial rearing. It was the same with grouse, and up to three hundred of them could be taken." Mike learned a lot from the Johnston-Fergusons because both were well-informed amateur naturalists. It also worked the other way. The Colonel recounted to Mike how he was sent out by his father when he was a boy to walk the woods and the moor with the head keeper. "The head keeper taught him how to shoot, and how to shoot safely. There was a lot more contact then between the landowners and their keepers than there is now. Indeed this practice of the head keeper tutoring the young boys was almost compulsory in times past, and in consequence boys grew up understanding the complexities of managing an estate and also an appreciation of the considerable risks involved in field sports."

Mike was twenty-one when he went to Solway Bank, but prior to that he had gained experience in rearing pheasants at Netherby Hall. This wasn't needed at Solway Bank, so Mike spent much of his time on the 9,000-acre estate controlling vermin. This reminded me of a comment made by one retired and rather disgruntled keeper. He said that there were only two kinds of vermin on estates and that they both began with the letter F: foxes and factors. It is difficult for people not engaged in country matters to accept the use of the word 'vermin' to describe creatures other than grouse, pheasant and partridge, because they have no real knowledge of just how much damage some the these species can do to the commercial interests of an estate. During his time at Solway Bank, Mike shot hundreds of foxes and stoats. Now, he told me, because there is no keeper on the estate to control vermin, the game birds, wild pheasant, grouse and waders have all gone.

Thomas Speedy was a gamekeeper, naturalist and author. His most notable work was *Sport in the Highlands and Lowlands of Scotland with Rod and Gun*, published by Blackwood's in Edinburgh in 1886. Included in his list of vermin are all the raptors, from eagles down to merlin, ravens, crows and magpies, badgers, otter, fox, polecats, wildcats, stoat, weasels, hedgehogs and rats. Sir William Jardine, writing in the late 1800s and commenting on eagles said, "Such was the depredation among flocks during the season of lambing that every device was employed and expense incurred by rewards for their destruction. From March 1831 to March 1834 in the country of Sutherland alone, 171 old birds with 53 young and eggs were destroyed." Today, this would never be tolerated, but it is hard to deny the logic of the need for some form of control over the numbers of predators; otherwise, if numbers are allowed to increase naturally, in the end they will destroy themselves by destroying their primary sources of food.

As it is in every aspect of the keeper's work, that which a keeper makes look easy is in fact the product years of experience. Arranging a successful pheasant shoot, for instance, requires careful planning on the part of the keeper; not only to ensure that there are birds to shoot, but also by 'presenting' them to the waiting guns in the best possible fashion; the higher they fly the more exciting and challenging it is for the shooters. Those driving the birds towards the guns – the beaters – must be trained and disciplined, only putting the birds into flight at the right time and in the right place. The pheasants should be pushed as far as possible on their feet, and only flushed from a spot that is higher than where the guns wait. No untrained dogs should ever be allowed on the shoot because they can often cause havoc and ruin an otherwise good day.

Mike said, "I organise the guns, give them a lecture on safety, set them where a peg marks the place from which they will shoot. You can always tell who the best shots will be, generally the old aristocracy. They always turn up wearing worn tweeds with holes in them and you can guarantee that they will be safe; they never walk by you, but come straight up and shake you by the hand. However, if someone arrives in a brand new suit and waterproofs, you wonder how he is going to perform and keep a close eye on him until you are satisfied that he knows what he is doing."

I asked Mike if he had ever been involved in an accident. "No, Bruce," he replied. "I don't think a dangerous shot has ever crossed my bows. I have probably been lucky, because some of the people coming to shoots nowadays can be very dangerous, particularly Italian and French guns. I know moors in Northumberland where they actually put up protective Perspex screens between the butts to avoid the shooters killing each other rather than the grouse." Mike was simply confirming the opinion of the vast majority of keepers that I have spoken to over the years.

Mike said, "The French are very passionate about their shooting. I had a French party here once, shooting woodcock, which for them is a great trophy bird." Messrs. Walker and Mackie, old experts in field sports, say that the best days to shoot woodcock are after clear moonlit nights, or days on which the sun is not too bright. Mike continued, "They had come for a day's rough shooting and I had taken them to a wood up here behind my house. To help with the shoot I had another keeper with me and two men from the village. Somehow, we eventually found ourselves surrounded by the shooters. We had been in the wood driving the woodcock towards their guns, but they were still shooting as they came towards us; not in a line, as they should have been, but acting individually without any apparent thought for the safety of their companions, let alone for us. We all just hit the ground because we knew what was coming. I shouted and managed to stop them and gave them a piece of my mind. Either they shot in the air and walked in a straight line or they could walk home right now. God knows what it is like in France when the hunting season starts. There must be dozens of accidents, because as far as they seem to be concerned, it's every man for himself and the devil take the hindmost."

One of the funniest things that Mike has ever seen happened on a shoot managed by another keeper. "One of the guests arrived with a golden setter dog called Benson and its owner assured the keeper that the dog was well-trained and biddable. On the very first drive the dog shot off into the woods and flushed out all the birds that the beaters had been carefully moving towards the guns. Nobody was very pleased with that, especially the keeper and the other guns. They were even more appalled when the dog did exactly the same on the second drive. Before the start of the third drive, it suddenly became like something out of a *Keystone Cops* movie. The guns were running across the field to try to cut the dog off, piling over fences and hedges, and I couldn't do anything about it for laughing. And after them all ran the owner of the allegedly biddable dog, yelling at the top of his voice, 'Benson! Benson! Benson!'"

I asked Mike what he thought about the Langholm Moor

Raptor Study and, again, he echoed the comments I had heard from other keepers throughout Scotland. "Yes, it was a scientific study, I suppose. But it did show that the hen harriers on the moor had seriously damaged the status of the grouse population. I believe that there are only a couple of harriers nesting there now, but there are a lot of buzzards as well. The grouse have long since gone, having been eaten by the raptors. There are more buzzards today in Scotland than there have been for nearly one hundred years and their numbers are still increasing. To be honest, in the present climate, I don't think that we will ever obtain the right to control raptor numbers, regardless of the damage they do to other species, including smaller moorland and garden birds. There hasn't been any grouse shooting on Langholm Moor for nearly fifteen years. I can't see the study being a success, but hope for the head keeper's sake that it is."

There is huge pressure from environmental groups, primarily from the RSPB and generally supported in its views by the government's Scottish Natural Heritage (SNH) agency, to prevent estates from culling raptors. When raptors are found dead, shot or poisoned, it is front-page news and keepers are invariably blamed for these deaths. Politicians wring their hands and issue streams of high-sounding public statements about 'irresponsible' keepers and calling for estate owners to he held to account for the actions of their employees. However, these same people, politicians, RSPB and SNH, are singularly silent when it comes to the shooting of seals that predate on farmed salmon in their cages in the West Highlands and Islands, in spite of the fact that disease and pollution from these cages is driving one of Scotland's most iconic species, Atlantic salmon, to extinction.

To my mind, this is quite simply duplicitous and degrades public confidence in the substance and veracity of these organisations and the people who manage them.

Mike went through to the kitchen to refill our coffee cups and I looked around the lounge. It was immediately apparent that there was a serious artist in the house and was not entirely surprised to learn that that artist was Mike. He derives his inspiration from the landscape that surrounds him and his works are strikingly bold, full of life and vigour, cathedral-like skies, burnished moorlands and rocky headlands. Mike uses a combination of palette knife and brush to apply oil paint to his canvas and I found the result to be remarkably effective; it was almost as if I could smell the scent of heather moors and sea spray. His paintings are neither figurative nor abstract but movingly combine elements of both styles. It was clear to me from the outset that Mike was fascinated by light and that, to him, light is colour. He told me, "That is how I escape, painting. It's a passion that I can't really understand or explain; it's just something that I have to do. I loved art at school and it was suggested that I went to Art College, but my heart was in the woods, so I stuck to keepering. At that time, the punk craze was in full swing and I didn't want to be part of it. I knew instinctively that I wouldn't fit in, but I have always painted, bits and bobs over the years."

But looking at the extent of work on display, art must have recently become a more important part of Mike's life, so I asked him what had occurred to release such a huge burst of creative energy. "I broke my leg," Mike replied.

"How did that happen?" I said.

"A tree, believe it or not." Apparently, Mike was working in the forest one day and had cut down a tree. As it fell, it formed a sort of bow and catapulted back and smashed his leg against another tree.

"I was lucky it was just one leg," Mike continued, "and lucky that I kept a hold of the chainsaw because I had to cut the tree to get my leg free. I then crawled about 300 or 400 yards to where my vehicle was parked, hauled myself in and drove to the village for help. I was unaware of any pain at the time, probably because the adrenalin was flowing, and I knew that the only way to get help was if I were to do it myself. The pain came soon enough, though, later. An ambulance carted me off to hospital and I was there for three or four months. When I was let out on crutches, I went to a shoot; my boss was great, driving me around in his Range Rover, but in quiet times, when I was sitting around, I got out my paints and just went for it. That's how I found my art. Thinking back, it's funny that a fox and a broken leg should have had such an impact on my life." If you want to have a look at examples of Mike's work, or own one of his paintings, you can either give Mike a ring on tel: 01387 371339, or log on to www.devorgillagallery.co.uk/our-artists/micheal-batey, The Devorgilla Gallery in Dumfries, where Mike's work is displayed.

As we talked, there was still the sound of intermittent barking from the kennels and I asked Mike about his dogs. "I've got a team of cocker spaniels in there. Some of them are as wild as hell, but if I put them in a forestry plantation, they work all the time, putting birds up for the guns. I love rough shooting and think it's the finest thing you can do, rough shooting or woodcock shooting. Working with the dogs, it is real hunting. I have had springer spaniels and Labradors, but I think that cockers are the most reliable and biddable. Jack Windle, an old keeper friend of mine, gone now, always said to me that you have to have a sense of humour to own a cocker because they have minds of their own. One minute they can be your best buddy, the next minute they seem to decide that they know best and they are off. Jack was a famous dog trainer and is remembered in the Cocker Championships by the trophy he left, the Windle Cup."

I went on to ask Mike if any dogs that he had owned were outstanding, and he said, "I've had some really wonderful dogs in my time, particularly a Labrador called Major, he was an absolute star, but I also remember fondly a little springer spaniel named Heather I had at Solway Bank. If I took her out to shoot with the Colonel and Major Brian, she would leave me and go and work in front of the Colonel. It didn't matter where I was, she would just take off. When Heather had a bird in a tussock or wherever she waited until the Colonel had got himself into the right position for a shot, and this could take a few moments as the Colonel was not the young man he used to be. When ready, he would say, 'Go on, Heather. Go on,' and the dog would go in and set the bird up for the Colonel to take a shot. The Colonel and Heather had an understanding, a partnership, and a connection between them that I didn't understand. I should have given him the dog because they were so in love with each other."

Mike has also done a fair bit of stalking for roe deer on the Buccleuch Estate, but only once stalked a stag when he worked with Colonel Raymond Johnson-Ferguson at Solway Bank. The Colonel also owned land on a peninsula in Loch Torridon in Wester Ross, and when he was there on holiday Mike went up to see him. On one occasion, he got a boat from Shieldaig and motored round to where the Colonel had a house by the shore. I will let Mike tell the story. "When we arrived there was smoke coming out of the windows and doors, so we beached the boat and ran like hell to see what was going on. 'Colonel, Colonel,' I called, 'your house is on fire!' He replied, 'No it's not, it's the bedding drying. I turned the electric blanket on and when the smoke stops and steam stops it means that it's dry!' We shook our heads in disbelief, but, I thought, that was the real Highlander, the Ferguson part of the Colonel, showing itself."

Mike used to frequent the bar in the Shieldaig Hotel, which of course was always full of stalkers, keepers, fishermen and shepherds. He was asked by a guest one night what he did for a living and replied that he was a gamekeeper. The guest, Mike couldn't remember his name, other than it was double-barrelled, asked Mike if he would like to work with him for a week. Mike agreed and found himself stalking red deer stags on Ben Damph with the owner of the estate and a Highland pony, Mike's task being to take the shot stags off the hill on the pony's broad back. Dumfriesshire and the Galloway Hills are often referred to as being "the little Highlands of Scotland", but Loch Torridon is the real thing, surrounded by majestic peaks: Liathach (3,456ft), 'the Grey One', to the north, and Beinn Damh (2,957ft), 'the Hill of the Stag', Maol Chean-dearg (3,060ft), the 'Bald Red Head' and the Applecross Mountains to the south, with the misty Isle of Skye across the broken waters of the Minch dominating the western horizon. At the end of Mike's week on the Hill of the Stag, he was asked if he wanted to be paid or if he wanted to shoot a stag. Mike opted for shooting the stag, which he did, a fine nine-pointer. "That's the only stag that I have ever shot and I still have the head today," Mike said.

Mike is not formally involved in fishing in his current position, but he still manages a cast or three whenever he has time to do so. "I have caught loads of brown trout, because I was brought up fishing for brown trout on the River Caldew when I was a boy, and the Esk has always been kind to me with sea-trout, but I have never caught a salmon. I have hooked three, but never managed to land them. But I have landed a lot of fish for other people, tailed them or gaffed them when I was working at Netherby Hall. Netherby is probably the best beat on the river and I remember seeing hundreds and hundreds of salmon in the pools in the '80s, stacked up on three or four levels. It was an amazing sight. I have always been involved in fishing and love it."

Mike's mention of salmon being stacked up reminded me of when I used to travel between Edinburgh and Newcastle each week in the 1960s when I was working for a construction company. I always chose the Coldstream road, the A697, and always stopped on Border Bridge in Coldstream just to make sure that the Tweed still flowed under its graceful arches. The pool below the bridge was often, as Mike described, seeing pools at Netherby 'stacked up with salmon'. I once watched an angler fishing the pool and as his fly passed through the throng, the salmon simply moved to the side to let it past, and then returned to their original position. I watched this happening for about fifteen minutes, and, turning to go, flicked a cigarette end into the stream. Immediately, a salmon rose and took it. Funny things, fish.

Mike Batey has been a gamekeeper for thirty-two years. I asked him if he had any regrets about choosing game-keeping as a career. Mike said, "I think that if I had had doubts I would have packed it in years ago. But I have no doubts, never had any doubts. I've seen it from the beginning, you know, the real old-fashioned keepering, when rearing and putting out 1,000 birds was considered to be for a big shoot. Now I'm rearing 16,000. Every day I go out there is something different. That's the beauty of doing what I do, really. Have I any regrets? No, none at all, and I would do it all over again if I could. I'm positive about that."

As I took my farewell and left the creator of the dramatic paintings I had so enjoyed seeing, I thought of the little boy shooting the fox and of the injured young man in the forest, crawling along the track dragging his broken leg behind him And I also thought of the decent man I glimpsed in my driving mirror, waving goodbye. I put down the window and returned the wave and in doing so caught the happy sound of barking cocker spaniels from the nearby kennels.

14
Iain Bell, Canonbie, Border Esk

Iain Bell was a water bailiff, gillie and the Buccleuch Estates fishery manager on the Border Esk for twenty years. He lives in the town of Canonbie close to the river and retired in summer of 2011. Although I had never met Iain before, for many years he helped me to update the River Esk entry in my book *Rivers and Lochs of Scotland*, and I was delighted when he agreed to talk to me about his life and career for my current project, a new book about Scotland's stalkers, keepers and gillies. My elder daughter Lewis-Ann lives at Glenzierfoot a few miles south of Canonbie, so when Ann and I visited her recently I also arranged to call and see Iain.

When I met Iain in April he was still working with Buccleuch Estates and he greeted me with a firm handshake and a warm smile. Iain is fit and weather-beaten and boasts a neatly trimmed beard. He is a considerable presence, has a ready laugh and a sharp sense of humour, all essential adjuncts in his job. Iain was born in 1959 and his family come from the Border town of Gretna Green – infamously described in 1582 by an English visitor as being the home of 'Scottishe theves' – although, as it is with many Solway families, there is a bit of County Antrim blood somewhere in there as well. Prior to becoming fishery manager on the Esk, Iain worked with the Ministry of Defence (MOD) in Northern Ireland and in England and was a police dog handler on the tactical firearms unit. His father had also worked for the MOD, so Iain was well travelled.

I asked Iain how his interest in fishing began and he said, "I was in Northern Ireland when I was a boy, and you know, as wee lads do, I was always splashing about the burns, pulling up stones, looking at beasties, caddis grubs half out of their shells, and so on. I put one of the caddis grubs on a hook and then, with the cork from a beer bottle as a float, I would flick it into waterfalls in search of trout. That's how I got corrupted into fishing. I really enjoyed observing nature along the rivers and came to realise that catching a fish was just part of a much wider experience." Ian continued, "In later life, I also worked with scientists doing river surveys, electro-fishing. They would tell me that the survey results always showed that the majority of trout and salmon tended to shelter under bankside growth at the side of the burns. However, as a boy, I would creep up to the waterside and lie motionless, watching the water and saw that fish lay everywhere in the run of a pool and that it was only when they were disturbed by, say, predators or perhaps electro-fishing teams, that they would dive for cover."

Iain went to school in Northern Ireland, in County Antrim at a place called Crumlin (The Crooked Glen) on the east shore of Lough Neagh and spent a lot of his childhood exploring the shores of the lough. He told me, "I was a devil for bunking off school. I never liked school. I basically brought myself up, because I had no mother. Perhaps I was a wee bit wild." There were pollan, freshwater herring, in the lough and I used to watch local men going out in boats to net them. One day they asked Iain if he would like to go with them. Of course Iain said yes. "We would steam out and I'd help them cast their nets. Large migratory trout called Dollaghan, pike and the famous Lough Neagh eels were also caught, and I invariably went home with half a dozen pollan in my pocket."

Canonbie, Ian's current home, is an attractive and busy little town that was established more than eight hundred years ago when King David I of Scotland (1124–1153) founded a priory there, hence the name Canonbie, 'The Town of Canons'. The town was immortalised by Sir Walter Scott (1771–1832), 'The Wizard of the North', in his poem 'Young Lochinvar', who famously 'came out of the west' and 'swam the Eske river where ford there was none' to carry off his love from the Graham stronghold at nearby Netherby Hall on the east bank of the river in England. Canonbie lies at the heart of the land of the Border Rievers, the Steel Bonnets, moss-troopers, freebooters, raiders and rogues who plundered the area remorselessly during the Middle Ages; anything that was not firmly nailed down was swiftly removed, and going to bed safely at night did not necessarily guarantee a safe awakening the following morning, or indeed any wakening. Iain showed me a copy of the inscription on a tombstone found at the site of Redkirk Abbey near Gretna Green, now submerged by the Solway. It gives a brief glimpse of what life was like during these turbulent years. Iain reassured me that, as far as he could establish, the subject of the grim epitaph was in no way related to him:

Here lyes ION BELL, who dyed in ye yhere 1510
And of his age 89 yheres
Here, Bluidy Bell, haith skin and bane,
Lyes quietly still aneath this stane.
He was a stark mosstrooper kent,

As ever-drave a bout o're bent.

He buynt ye Lochwood Tow'r and Ha'

And dang ye Ladye ower ye wa.

For whylk ye Johnstone, stoot, and wyte,

Set Blackeath in a low by nyght.

Now cried a voice as if frae Hell,

Haste! open ye gates for Blaidy Bell.

With some thirty miles of the River Esk to manage, Iain was always busy and he was helped in his work by Peter Kinstrey, his assistant and right-hand man. Peter was a farmer, but his business was destroyed during the foot-and-mouth outbreak in 2001, when nearly 300,000 cattle were culled in an attempt to halt the spread of the disease. Iain told me, "I had been looking for an assistant but was having a hard job finding someone suitable. I told the Duke that I thought Peter would be the right man, and he agreed.

"We have had all sorts of people fishing our river, from miners, judges, unemployed lads and factory workers to doctors and vets. Our fishing is available to everyone at a very reasonable cost and I believe our salmon, sea-trout and trout fishing represents some of the best-value-for-money fishing to be found anywhere in Scotland. My policy has always been that if someone who has never fished the river before phones asking me for even just a day ticket, I always offer to show them the river. A lot of anglers coming here for the first time have this vision of being confronted by a stuffy factor with leather patches on his sleeves and a plum in his mouth. I like to, personally, take Joe Soap and show him where I think the best place is for him to start, and if he needs further advice, I tell them to give me a call."

But fishing on the Border Esk has not always been so reasonably organised. The overall management of river, two-thirds of the length of which is in Scotland, is governed by the English Environment Agency. In England, anglers must pay a rod licence to their Environment Agency; whereas in Scotland, anglers pay a fee directly to the river owner for permission to fish. The English Environment Agency has had the right to enforce their regulatory authority on the Esk since 1975, but it is only in recent years that it has begun to try to do so, much to the annoyance of the Scottish estate owners through whose lands the river runs and to Scottish anglers who fish the Esk. This is just one of the legalistic 'quirks' that still exercise the minds of lawyers of both sides of the border. However, the dispute between England and Scotland over fishing in the Esk is not surprising, given that it has been going on for more than six hundred years.

The primary cause of the trouble, which began back in 1450, centred upon where the exact line of the border between the two countries lay – particularly in the south-west, where the ownership of an area of some thirty square miles, bounded in the west by the River Sark and in the east by Liddel Water, was hotly disputed. This area became known as the Debatable Lands, a lawless wilderness, a place of refuge for escaped criminals and ne'er-do-wells, and in 1551 a proclamation, agreed by both sides, was issued warning that: 'All Englishmen and Scottishmen, after this proclamation made, are and shall be free to rob, burn, spoil, slay, murder and destroy all and every such person or persons, their bodies, buildings, goods and cattle as do remain or shall inhabit upon any part of the said Debatable Land, without any redress to be made for the same.'

The problem of ownership was not solved until 1552, when, with the French Ambassador acting as arbiter, a final boundary line was agreed between the two countries. It was ratified by decree at Jedburgh on 9 November. But control of the valuable Esk salmon fishing was coveted by both countries, and this caused one of the longest ever disputes between England and Scotland, as is evidenced by the continuing row over the introduction of the English Environment Agency rod licence.

Sometime before 1474, the English constructed a fish garth in the Esk at Netherby Hall downstream from Canonbie, constructed from pebbles and shingle that acted as a barrier to trap salmon returning to the Esk to spawn. The trap was so efficient that few salmon escaped and Scottish proprietors upstream were left with no fish. The English claimed that the right to build and operate the garth "belonged to the King of England and his subjects by law and custom". James III of Scotland did not agree and the Scots removed the garth.

By 1485, the English had rebuilt the trap, but again it was destroyed by the Scots. Various attempts were made to find a solution in 1487, 1488, 1490 and 1491; however, all were unsuccessful and arguments continued with unabated fury. As soon as the English rebuilt the garth, the Scots raided and destroyed it. By 1513, the dispute had grown to such proportions that before the Battle of Flodden, when James IV challenged the Earl of Surrey to single-handed combat to avoid a full-scale encounter between their two armies, one of the rewards he demanded if he won was the removal of the Esk fish garth. Claim followed counterclaim until 1543 when, under circumstances not recorded, a measure of agreement seems to have been reached regarding the trap. Nevertheless, the dispute continued, and in the mid-eighteenth century there was renewed conflict which almost resulted in civil war between the two nations.

Sir James Graham of Netherby Hall had rebuilt the garth, and the Scots were so angered that they gathered a small army of local people to tear it down. Graham responded by collecting an army of his own, including a detachment of soldiers from the garrison at Carlisle. Bloodshed was only avoided when Sir James agreed to open a gap in the garth to allow salmon passage upstream. Thus, with the imposition of the English Environment Agency rod licence two hundred and fifty years later, the Auld Enemy have finally won their battle for complete control over what is essentially a major Scottish salmon stream. That which they could not achieve by force of arms for five hundred and fifty years, the English have achieved with the stroke of a pen, and without a murmur of dissent from their quisling collaborators in a Scottish government ruled by the freedom-fighters of the Scottish National Party. William Wallace and Robert Bruce must be birling in their graves.

But perhaps they may no longer have any need to do so. Recently at the High Court of Justiciary in Edinburgh, Iain Bell gave evidence in defence of a local angler who stood accused of fishing the river without an English Environment Agency permit. The three judges hearing the case stated that they found it difficult to see where the English Environment Agency jurisdiction began and where it ended. In summing up, they reasoned that if they could not understand where they might need a licence, then how might the average man in the street be expected to understand? The defendant's appeal was allowed.

Iain assured me that although most of his anglers behave responsibly today, there are problems with poaching. Iain recalled, "I remember one time, just upstream from Canonbie, watching a man fishing the river. I guessed that he did not have a permit, and I just walked up quietly and stood behind him; I prefer not to be seen approaching people, just to appear behind them. I asked him if I could have a look at his written permission to fish, his permit, and of course he didn't have one. But he did have a beautiful 16lb salmon on the bank beside him. So I gave him two options, either to take a trip to the Sheriff Court, or hand over the salmon to me so that I could divide it up between the old folk in the village. He chose the latter option. I picked up the fish and escorted him from the river. Unbeknown to me, however, my colleague Peter Kinstrey was fishing nearby with a guest, a Mr Quinnel, who was a regular visitor from the south, and he said to Peter, 'Do you see that, Peter? What a lovely man your Mr Bell is, carrying that angler's salmon around for him.'"

Iain told me about another incident involving poachers. It happened in the deep pool below Skipper's Bridge, a fine old bridge built in 1693 and widened in 1807, that still carries the A7 Langholm/Carhole road over the Esk downstream from Langholm. Iain had a tip-off that someone intended to clean the fish out of the pool, so he and Peter set out one night to watch the pool. It was raining, hard, and Peter had brought a dark green golf umbrella with him, under which they sheltered. Iain wasn't too happy about the umbrella, but said nothing.

All of a sudden, two figures, silhouetted against the moonlight, appeared at the foot of the bridge. They seemed to be very smooth, and Iain concluded that they were wearing wetsuits. They came down from the rocks to the water's edge and looked up and down the river, and then they were gone.

Iain continued, "So I waited for an hour or so and then went up to the brig and looked down to where Peter was still sitting under the umbrella. I could see the bloody thing in the moonlight, with raindrops dancing off it. A plan was hatched. I gathered up some bits of moss and tin of worms then returned to Skipper's Bridge. I pushed the umbrella further out over the rocks and closer to the river and left the moss and the tin of worms under the umbrella. I then got a forked stick and some empty beer cans and scattered them round. My idea was that the poachers would return in daylight and think that there been someone else there that night, with rod and line, also poaching the river.

"The following night, minus the umbrella, we were watching again, and sure enough they appeared with about sixty feet of gill net, one on either side, to drag the net down the pool. They actually made a mess of what they were trying to do, because as a pool is being netted, the fish move down to the end of the pool and as the pressure builds, they turn and bolt upstream into the net. But the poachers stopped halfway down the pool and only got one sea-trout, a fish of about 5lbs 8oz in weight. They were wearing wetsuits, and we got both of them and their net. Interestingly enough, one of them appeared in my office a few years later. 'I know you,' I said. 'The last time we met was in the dark.'

"He replied, 'I don't want any bother, Mr Bell, I just want a permit to fish. Can I have a permit, please?' He paid, I gave him a permit and that was the end of that."

Iain told me that poaching was less of a problem today, although it still goes on. What is of greater concern to the river owners in the area is what is happening when salmon and sea-trout migrate to sea. Salmonid numbers have declined considerably in recent years, particularly the sea-trout populations that made the Solway Rivers amongst the finest sea-trout streams in Europe. Iain recalled that in 1994 he was down at the Willow Pool and Cauldron pools near to where Liddel Water joins the Esk. There had been rain previous night, ending a drought, and the water level in the river had risen by an inch. "I watched the river for just over an hour, from ten in the morning until the back of eleven. During that time I counted over 1,000 sea-trout coming up in pods of between fifteen and twenty fish, with their backs out of the water. I was mesmerised. I went down to Netherby and spoke to auld Dennis Skidmore, who was the gillie there. 'Dennis,' I said, 'have you seen what I have seen?'

"'Aye, lad,' he replied. 'I was on Thistle Bridge and saw thousands of fish moving upstream.'"

It seems that these days are gone, and Iain wonders if illegal netting at sea might be part of the problem, that salmon and sea-trout being caught at sea before they have the chance to return to their natal streams to spawn. I remembered speaking to Dick Graham, the head gillie on the Hoddom Beat of the River Annan, who had said the same. Iain went on, "I remember that it was the same year that I buried my father. I was watching a boat, a drift netter, in the Solway that was laid out on the Solway shore with my night sight. It was strangely close to shore, and I thought to myself, 'These boys are up to no good.' I was on the shore at the time and the boat was about a quarter of a mile off, as near as damn right in the tidal channel of the inner Solway rivers, a zone where drift fishing for salmon was illegal. I was sure that I saw them working a net. I was a water bailiff then with the now defunct National Rivers Authority, but at the same time had a Scottish bailiff's warrant, and so had a responsibility for keeping order on both the Scottish and English sides of the Solway. So the next night I organised a group of colleagues, four of us, and we were waiting in a fast inflatable boat, a rib, to see if the suspicious vessel would appear again.

"Sure enough, in it came, and I was certain that they were netting illegally. We fired the outboard engine of the rib to life and roared out and boarded the boat. They had just over 1,000 feet of net with salmon still in it. We arrested them, and when the case came to the District Court in Annan, the owner of the boat called a friend of his who was a Justice of the Peace to give evidence as to his good character. Anyway, it didn't help much because the skipper and his crew were all found guilty.

"The following week I buried my dad down at Gretna, and I looked at the man driving funeral car. 'I know you,' I said. 'You were in court last week and gave a character reference to the skipper of the boat that was illegally fishing. Why did you do that?'

"'Oh,' he replied. 'I know him well and he would never do anything like that. What really happened was that he had lost his nets when the boat was further out at sea and only reason they entered the restricted zone was to recover them.'

"'Well,' I said to him, 'isn't that funny, because, you know, he lost his nets in exactly the same place the night before.' His face just dropped!"

The decline in sea-trout stocks is also a matter of concern in other areas of Scotland. The reason for the complete collapse in the West Highlands and Islands is easily recognised and understood: disease and pollution from industrial scale factory fish farms in the area, most of which are owned by Norwegian multi-national companies. Parasitic sea lice breed in their billions in these pseudo-salmon-packed cages and they transfer to wild salmonids as they pass by on their migratory journeys to and from their rivers of birth and their feeding grounds in the North Atlantic. This is not only my view, but is widely shared by those who follow these matters, including a former director of the government's Scottish Environment Protection, Professor David Mackay, who once famously said that the link between the decline in wild fish in these areas and fish farm sea lice was "beyond all reasonable doubt", whilst another former government scientist, Dr Richard Shelton, who was chief officer at the freshwater research laboratory in Pitlochry, said during a BBC Scotland radio broadcast that the link was, "as plain as the nose on your face".

Whilst sea-trout numbers have declined in the Moray Firth and in the south-west of Scotland, where there are no fish farms, they have not suffered a complete collapse. River owners, fishery biologists and anglers have established collaborative groups to try to find the cause of the decline and devise means of reversing it. Iain Bell has played, and is playing, a significant role in the South West in this matter. He said, "Over the past year, with lots of help, we have managed to gather DNA samples and 256 sets of sea-trout scale samples, all provided to us by anglers and traditional Solway haaf netsmen, and these samples, along with samples from other Irish Sea catchments – Wales, England, Isle of Man, Northern Ireland and Eire – are being analysed at the

School of Ocean Sciences, Bangor University, in Wales. The more we know about the genetic make-up of the distinct populations of sea-trout in our rivers, the better able we will be to understand what are happening to these fish at sea, why it is happening, and what they feed on and where they go to feed."

Iain also seemed to confirm another problem that Dick Graham from Hoddom mentioned when I spoke to him about the subject: intensive fishing by Spanish boats. There is anecdotal evidence that wild sea-trout from Scotland are frequently on sale in Spain and in the south of France. Another incident seemed to support this view. Iain had spoken to one or two contacts in the MOD who told him that for a couple of years round the millennium they had been receiving radio signals during April and May from what were perceived to be Spanish fishing boats. Iain said, "I might be wrong, of course, but it seems to me that the start of the decline in our sea-trout numbers was around the time when the government opened the Irish Box [UK Fishing Area] to European boats. In truth, we don't yet know where the problem lies, but we do know that if we wish to promote and secure a better future for our sea-trout stocks, then we must keep searching for the answer."

Talking about Spain reminded Iain of another incident that happened some years ago. He told me, "You know these Dumfries tattie sacks, old hessian sacks that were used for storing potatoes? Well, we were out watching the river one night and at about 4am we went down the mouth of the river where I noticed these tattie sacks hanging over a fence. I had a closer look and found a note pinned to the fence. It said, 'Ha, ha, ha, you bastards. Three hundred and eighty quid worth of fish last night. See you when

Bringing home a stag

Peter Fraser,
Invercauld Estate

Invercauld Estate. Left to right: Willie Bain, Roy Davidson, Colin Macintosh, James Davidson, Captain Farquharson, Donald MacDonald, Donald Campbell, Peter Fraser, Ronnie Hepburn

Buchan Burn, Merrick

With guest on
Invercauld Estate

Bill Drury
on the
River Spey

Bill Drury
with a Rio
Grande
sea-trout

Billy Drury casting

Billy Jack and guest
on Junction Pool,
River Tweed

© BILLY JACK

© BRUCE SANDISON

Loch Naver, Sutherland

Junction Pool at Kelso

East Loch Bee,
South Uist

© BRUCE SANDISON

Loch Stilligarry, South Uist

© BRUCE SANDISON

Billy Felton with 3lb 12oz
trout from West Ollay

From Billy's
fly box

© BRUCE SANDISON

Jake and argocat

Ian Smart and son Jake stalking on Ben Loyal Estate

Jake's first stag

© IAN SMART

© JEAN SMART

we get back from Spain.' We watched the river for a few more nights and there was no sign of them."

But the more Iain thought about it, the more convinced he became that the message about Spain was simply a ploy to distract them. He was right, because his colleagues apprehended them a week later poaching the River Eden upstream from the bridge that carries the motorway over the river. They had thirty-six salmon and a sea-trout.

Iain met his future wife, Pamela, when he was with the MOD and they were married in 1981. They have a son, Alasdair, who is a police constable and works with Lothian & Borders Police, and a daughter, Heather, who recently qualified as a midwife in Glasgow, and Iain introduced them both to fishing when they were little. "If you introduce them to fishing and other country sports when they are children, it stays with them for the rest of their lives, it never really leaves them. Heather caught her fist sea-trout when he was about twelve, and I bought Alasdair a new rod last season. His house backs onto the River Whiteadder, so it is quite convenient for a few casts when he has some free time. Alasdair was actually a keeper up at Bentpath, but joined the police when he got married. I suppose I did the same, but only the other way round, I got married and then became a keeper." I followed a similar path with our four children, and also our grandchildren, of which we have been blessed with ten, ranging in age from Jake, who is eight, up to the eldest, Brodie, who is twenty-four.

The world of keepers, stalkers and gillies is small and closely interlinked. They all generally know each other, either as friends and colleagues, or through mutual acquaintances. Iain recalled one of his old colleagues, Billy Bell, who was a stalker, gillie and bailiff with the Buccleuch Estate for many years. "The day he retired we had a presentation for him in the Estate Office and a lovely print of a kingfisher from Border Fine Arts, and I had made him a stick. Anyway, the factor made the presentation and Billy made a wee speech and he told a grand story, he said. 'I mind years ago,' he said, 'when I was working up north and had a client with me who was not just in the peak of fitness. I could see that he was getting out of breath, so I suggested that we stop and have a spy to see where the stags were. So there he was, my gentleman, lying in the heather, and he looked down and saw a great clump of big thistles. He tells me that he was surprised to see that thistles could endure so high above sea level. I turned and said, 'Aye, thistles and factors will thrive anywhere.' That was Billy's parting shot."

Iain also fondly remembered another of his friends, John Lambert, a retired grouse-keeper who used to be called 'The Terror of Fountain Fell'. "He was as real character," Iain said. "Tall, rangy and with great bushy eyebrows. I was butchering sheep with him one day and was amazed at his dexterity with the skinning knife, far better than I could ever be. So I asked him who had taught him that trade and he paused and turned to me and said, 'Hunger, laddie. Hunger.' I have never forgotten that."

Iain has always kept terriers, which he describes as 'mobile mink traps' due their ability to track and kill these unwelcome, foreign predators, descendants of escapees from mink farms in the days when these animals were being farmed for their fur. Iain had a black Patterdale terrier named Pop, of which he was particularly fond; Patterdales are working dogs which originated from the Lake District, Patterdale being a small village to the south of Ullswater and a few miles from one of the Lake District's highest peaks, Helvellyn (3,117ft). I will let Iain take up the story. "I was walking a forest track one day with the dog, through one of the huge commercial forest that we have here in the borders. All of a sudden, his ears cocked up and his eyes hardened into a steely gaze, and after coming on point briefly, he shot off into the dark of the coniferous jungle. Hearing little for ten minutes or so, I picked up a faint sound of a hard-baying dog. I walked on, but in the distance the barking continued. Ah, I thought, Pop has found Charlie Fox, but curiously, the sound appeared to be coming from high above the ground. I battled my way into the thick spruce and for what seemed like a mile blindly fought my way toward the sound of the barking. Just as I guessed that I was getting close, the baying just stopped, but following my nose I came upon a slight clearing with some windblown trees propped against those still upright. The terrier must have chased this fox up the blown spruce trees and had pinned it there by barking. But when the fox got wind of my approach it must have made a break for it. And, of course, Pop went after it. Sure enough, on examining the tree I found pulled tufts of fox hair on branches about eight feet above the ground. With both dog and fox lost in the deep plantation, I fought my way back to where I had parked the car.

"I whistled and shouted, revved up the engine of the vehicle, slammed the doors and tooted the horn, but to no avail. Not a sign of the terrier; these dogs are trained and accustomed to staying tight and pinpointing their prey until you get to them. After a few words of choice Gaelic, I drove home, but returned with my bagpipes, a secret weapon of war. I began to play a number of marches and as I drifted into the third part of Donald Maclean's

'Farewell to Oban', I thought my reed was going a wee bit off and looked down at my chanter. Pop was sitting at my feet and howling like a wolf baying at a full moon. Job done."

I asked Iain about his piping. "Oh, I suppose I have been playing since I was ten. I have played with a lot of different bands, Irish and English bands, as well as Scottish. I got an invitation about three years ago to attend a band reunion in Northern Ireland and was happy to go. The first man I met when I walked into the hotel was my auld pipe major, the man himself, tuning up. When he was finished, I walked up to shake his hand and he said, 'Noo ya wee skitter!' and I thought to myself, 'Well, nothing has changed.' I don't think I was a great piper, but I did manage runner-up once in the British Championship and was pipe major of the Langholm Pipe Band.

"I have played at many functions, from Burns' Suppers to piping for members of the Royal Family. Usually it went well. I remember playing at the Duke of Buccleuch's funeral at Melrose Abbey, and that was a bit embarrassing. I had been standing round the back of the Abbey for probably nearly a couple of hours whilst the service was being held, and it turned cold. Pipes are very temperamental about temperature and because of the service I didn't get a chance to re-tune the pipes. When they came out from the abbey, I had to blow like hell to get a tune out, but I am sure the old Duke would have had a laugh on me."

During my journeys round Scotland speaking to stalkers, keepers and gillies, I have always been surprised by the breadth and scope of their interests. Apparently, being knowledgeable and expert at just about everything to do with country matters, never mind being eminently practical, may have other skills as well. Iain Bell is a prime example. A highly talented piper and composer, artist, stick maker and motorbike racer. Iain, like his father before him, was serious about his motorbike and was Scottish Classic Racing Club Champion in 2008, riding his 1969 Rickman Triumph road racer bike; the trophy he was awarded is named the Jock Weddell Trophy, and Iain's dad, John, raced against Weddell in his racing days.

A number of stunning landscape paintings adorned the walls of his home and now that Iain has retired from the Buccleuch Estates he has time to follow these other interests. Last year, he managed a trip to the Isle of Man TT races, something he always wanted to do but couldn't because of his duties on the river at that time, and he enjoyed every minute of the experience. He has taken up his paintbrushes again and also plans to put together and publish a collection of the music he has written. I have been an immediate benefactor of his decision to do so: Iain has honoured me by composing a marvelous melody, a pipe tune which he has titled 'Bruce MacGregor Sandison'. And, of course, he has a lot more time now to go fishing.

15
Peter Fraser, Invercauld Estate, Deeside

Caenlochan, nine miles or so south from Braemar in the East Grampian Mountains, is a Special Area for Conservation and a Special Protection Area for Birds under European legislation. It touches on some of Scotland's most notable estates, including Invercauld, Airlie Estate, Balmoral and Tulchan. Peter Fraser, the present head stalker on Invercauld Estate, told me, "There were a lot of deer, and sheep as well, when I first knew Caenlochan, but they are largely gone now." Scottish Natural Heritage (SNH), backed by the Deer Commission Scotland (DCS), was concerned about the damage they believed these animals were doing to the natural habitat and to rare alpine plants. They claimed that there was far too many deer and that their numbers would have to be reduced.

Peter remembered one such cull on Caenlochan. "This was a collaborative cull involving stalkers from several neighbouring estates," he said. The cull was carried out under the terms of a Section 7 Control Agreement of the Deer (Scotland) Act 1996. A control agreement may be established where the DCS is satisfied that the deer have caused or are causing damage to woodland, agriculture or the natural heritage, and DSC has consulted with the owners and occupiers and secured agreement that deer management measures are required. As such, there is an enormous amount of pressure put upon keepers, stalkers and landowners by SNH and DCS to reduce the numbers of deer on their ground to the number that these organisations, in their wisdom, believe to be sustainable.

Peter continued, "The wind was from the south that day and the first beasts we stalked were shot on the Tulchan march. After the first stalk, the deer moved into the wind, gathering more animals as they went. The herd was stalked twice after that, with more beasts being shot, before the herd ended up in Dummay Corrie, which was deer-fended on two sides. Their only means of escape was back the way they had come, but this time their escape route was surrounded by marksmen. I estimated that there were about eight hundred deer in this corrie, and they were terrified. They were grouped in an immense circle and they wouldn't move, with the steam from their exhausted bodies rising above them in a cloud.

"So a shepherd walked down to where the deer stood. Many of them were exhausted, lying panting on the ground. He shot three beasts before mass panic ensued and the deer went here, there and everywhere, trying to escape, with everybody shooting at them all the time. Some came past me and I had never in all my life seen deer in such a terrible state, tongues hanging out, eyes rolling. I was sick with what I had witnessed. At the back of the herd I spied a wounded hind with three motherless calves, so I shot them." Peter said that more than ninety beasts were killed that day.

On some occasions a helicopter is used to locate the deer and fly in the stalkers. The stalkers are dropped off at various positions around the herd and the killing commences. When the deer break lose, the helicopter returns and leapfrogs the stalkers ahead of the deer so that they can be shot again when they stop to rest. Meanwhile, the helicopter returns to the first site and lifts the carcasses off the hill. This process can be repeated several times during the day. Peter told me that "These culls with helicopters went on for several years, but I would have nothing to do with them. We carried on reducing our numbers of deer, as we had been ordered to do so by Scottish Natural Heritage, but in the most humane way possible. I feel so sorry for the keepers and stalkers who might be browbeaten by SNH and the DCS into undertaking these mass culls. However, if the estate refuses to do so, or does not do it quickly enough, then the authorities have the power to come onto the estate and conduct the cull themselves."

As I listened in horror to Peter, who is also Vice-Chairman of the Scottish Gamekeepers Association, recounting this story, I was reminded of the slaughter of deer on a similar scale more than four and a half centuries earlier, noted by William Scrope (1772–1852) in his book *The Art of Deer Stalking* and in which he describes Mary, Queen of Scots hunting in 1563:

"The Earl of Atholl prepared for her Majesty's reception by sending out about two thousand Highlanders to gather the deer from Mar, Badenoch, Murray, and Atholl, to the district he had previously appointed. It occupied the Highlanders for several weeks in driving deer, to the amount of two thousand, besides roes, does and other game. The Queen, with her numerous attendants and a great concourse of the nobility, gentry, and people, gathered in the appointed glen, and the spectacle much delighted Her Majesty. The Queen's stag-hounds and those of the nobility were loosed, and a successful chase ensued. Three hundred and sixty deer were killed, five wolves and some roes."

Peter Fraser is a big man, in stature and in personality. He has the quiet air of authority that so many of Scotland's senior keepers, stalkers and gillies exude – exactly the kind of men you would want to be by your side in the event of an emergency. In his capacity as Vice-Chairman of the Scottish Gamekeepers Association, Peter recently presented the results of a study – 'The economic importance of red deer to Scotland's rural economy and the political threat now facing the country's iconic species' – a no-holds-barred exposé of exactly what is being done by Scottish Natural Heritage in the alleged interests of conservation:

"A national scandal is playing out on Scotland's hills. And while our wild red deer are the immediate casualties of the nation's indifference, the price will ultimately be paid the decline and decay of remote rural communities the length and breadth of this country. Our society is allowing exceptional animals to be destroyed, mown down like vermin in the night. It is permitting valuable carcasses to be abandoned to waste where they fall and indiscriminate night shooting that infringes animal welfare codes. Is this the way to manage Scotland's iconic animal, the celebrated Monarch of the Glen? We're laying our greatest wildlife assets to waste without considering the consequences. And it may already be too late in some places to prevent the devastation from being permanent.

Peter Fraser is a working conservationist and has a deep knowledge and a lifelong interest in all of the wildlife on his hills. Experience has taught him that biodiversity is essential to a healthy landscape. He wants to ensure a diversity of bird life, dunlin, ptarmigan, ring ouzel, golden plover and golden eagles.

He wants healthy, nutritious heather that can support grouse and other wildlife. He knows instinctively that unless the landscape is managed, then none of this is possible. A copy of the full transcript of the report is available on the Scottish Gamekeepers Association website at: www.scottishgamekeepers.co.uk.

Peter lives in cottage near Crathie in Royal Deeside and his grandfather was a fishing gillie at Invercauld, on the east part of the estate. "I can't remember how long Grandfather would be there, but he didn't get to retire on the job, because I remember him having to give up work because of ill health."

Peter's father was born in Ellon and went to Australia when he left school to work on a dairy farm. "He came back here for six months and got fed up doing nothing, so took a job on a farm, met my mother and got married." He was caught up in the Second World War and spent three and a half years in a Japanese prisoner of war camp, Peter told me. "When Father came home he was never in the best of health and never really fit enough to do manual work to any great extent, although he lived to be eighty-one years of age."

Peter himself was born in Ballater in 1947 and went to school there. When he left school he worked on a nearby farm for two or three years. A tenant farmer, Charlie Smith, had a sheep farm on Invercauld Estate, a man with a great reputation for the quality of the black-faced sheep he produced and well known in sheep farming circles. Peter said, "I worked with him for a couple of years, but I had always wanted to do keeping and eventually got a start at Glen Tanar with Jimmy Oswald. Now, he was a character. I was with him for two years. But I loved Braemar, and whilst working with Charlie I sometimes met Donald

MacDonald, the head keeper on Invercauld, and got on well with him."

I remembered Jimmy Oswald and Donald MacDonald, both of whom I had met back in 1986 when researching my first book on Scottish gillies, stalkers and keepers. Jimmy took me round the kennels at Glen Tanar and complained that the dogs were better accommodated than the keeper because their kennels had under-floor heating, whereas they had to do make do with open fires in their cottages. I also enormously enjoyed meeting Donald MacDonald, the epitome of Highland gentlemen. Donald had worked all his life as keeper and gillie. He started on Mar Lodge Estate where his father was head keeper, and as a boy, Donald used to go up to Mar in winter to watch the deer being fed. Everything was done in Gaelic, so Donald was constantly being hushed when he asked what was being said. In the days of Donald's father, the estate still employed eighteen keepers and gillies.

I can easily imagine Peter Fraser working well with Donald MacDonald; they were two of a kind. When a young keeper on Innvercauld decided to move to New Zealand, Donald asked Peter if he would like to come to Invercauld. Peter didn't hesitate. He said, "I started at Invercauld in 1969 and have been here ever since." Prior to that, after leaving Glen Tanar, Peter had returned to work with Charlie Smith, and then got a hill lambing job in Glenshee. Peter told me, "I got the chance to stay on there full-time and was going to do so when Donald phoned me about the job at Invercauld. In some ways, I regret leaving Glenshee, because it was a great place, the glen life. Everybody pulled together. Glenshee was a special place then.

"The shepherding was a great way of life. I must admit that I did like the shepherding, especially when I came up to Braemar. Shepherding is just like everything else, just a case of getting to know the ground because the sheep always have their own routes. You have to understand where they are going, what they are going to do, just as you have to do with stalking deer. It's like a game of chess. When you have been on the ground for a wee while and whether its sheep or deer, you will know exactly where they will head to if they have been disturbed."

Peter recalled a day at the clippings in Glenshee. "It was with Finlay Cameron at Old Spittal Farm. Finlay was from the Black Isle and a keeper/stalker on the Rhiedorroch Beat of Invercauld before he went into shepherding. He always wore the kilt when he went up the hill and then changed into dungarees when working at the sheep pens. That day, we went down to the Spittal Hotel for our lunch and, of course, a dram or two was taken, so everyone was quite merry when we went back up the hill to continue our work. Some of the young lads with us said that whoever had the first clipped sheep should keep a hold of it and they would put Finlay's kilt on it. When the first sheep was clipped, we got Finlay's kilt and put it on the animal.

"We had five or six hundred sheep clipped by then, and when you let go of a sheep after it has been clipped it always takes a jump. So did this one, complete with kilt. It went round and round the holding pen, faster and faster and we couldn't stop laughing. Finlay was dipping lambs and hadn't seen the kilted sheep, but he heard us all laughing and came over to see what was going on. He thought that it was quite funny until he realised that it was his kilt. 'You bastards!' he shouted. 'You'll get no pay this day!' When we eventually got hold of the ewe the kilt was in shreds, but Finlay took it all in good fun."

Peter also had a story about his friend and mentor Donald MacDonald. "An exceptionally nice man, he was. Donald used to stay up at Braemar and came down to Invercauld every day and left his Land Rover out the front of the Duncan Wright's joinery shop. Anyway, Donald appeared one morning as usual and was met by Archie Davidson, the keeper at the time who lived where Tom MacPherson used to lived, up at the stables at Invercauld. So off they went to do whatever it was they had to do. As soon as they were gone Duncan came out and jacked Donald's Land Rover up onto blocks, but just enough to clear the wheels off the ground. Duncan and his friends knew roughly what time Archie and Donald would be back from the hill at night, so they came back too. Archie went away home and Donald jumped into his Land Rover. He tried to move it forward, tried to move it backwards and just couldn't understand what was happening. He stopped the engine, got out and soon saw what was wrong and also saw Duncan and his pal peering through the window, laughing at him. He charged across to the door which was already slightly open, and above which Duncan had placed a box of sawdust. Over his head it went. Happily, Donald also saw the funny side of it too and they all had a good laugh."

Tom MacPherson was another name from my past, another glorious gentleman I spoke to in the 1980s. Tom had retired by the time I met him and was losing his eyesight. He lived with his daughter and son-in-law in a small cottage near Ballater, but I will never forget his gentle, soft-spoken voice and kindness, and how his eyes sparkled when he talked about his time on loch, river, moor and hill. Tom, Donald MacDonald, and Peter Fraser remained friends all their working lives. Tom's career had started as a boy when he was staying on his uncle's farm at the head of Loch Laggan. The estate was owned by Sir John Maxwell Stirling and the shooting was let to the Rothschild and the Sasson families. King George V used to shoot there when he was Prince of Wales, and Tom was warned off one evening to mind the gate for the returning gentlemen. He remembers seeing the ponies coming down the hill, the Prince of Wales out in front, at the gallop. He dashed down to open the gate. That evening, a half-sovereign was sent up from the big house as his reward.

The largest salmon Tom ever landed was a fish of 45lbs on the Dee for the legendary angler Arthur Wood. He also recalled fishing on Loch Maree, where his brother worked on a local estate. "In those days," he said, "we would go on the loch and regularly take twenty to thirty sea-trout, grand fish of up to 14lbs in weight. The best fly was always a Red Spider tied on a size 10 hook." Thanks to disease and pollution from Norwegian-owned factory fish farms, Loch Maree is largely devoid of the sea-trout that made it one of the most famous fisheries in the world. Tom also told me about a near miss at the butts at Invercauld when he found the laird crouched on the floor. Tom asked what was wrong. "'First that fellow down there got me and while I was watching him, damn it, the chap on the other side caught me in the shoulder. It's just not safe and I'm staying here until it's over!'"

The following day Tom was loading for the laird, watching carefully. He saw the neighbouring gun, a small man from China swinging round to his left and just had time to call out a warning to the laird. They both flopped like partridge and avoided serious injury by half a second. Tom went over to the man. "Now, sir," he said, "that was very nearly your best shot of the day: the laird with one barrel and his keeper with the second." If the Chinaman had not been told off much during his life, he certainly learned a thing or two that day when the laird got to him, and he was never seen on the hill again. I will always fondly remember Tom MacPherson.

Tom died in October 1993 and as his coffin was being lowered into his grave, a stag roared from Creaig Chlerich, the hill opposite the kirk yard at Braemar. Tom always used to say that the roaring was music to an old stalker's ears.

I asked Peter what his attitude was to the Freedom to Roam legislation and if it had effected his work. His answer was, as always, predictable and practical. "One day I was out stalking. I wasn't actually doing the stalk, one of the lads had the guest out whilst I took the pony. I was just leaving the loch where the ponies were kept, when I saw two walkers going up the hill from the east side of the loch. I went up the other side and eventually we met at the top end of the loch. We stopped to talk and they asked me where I was going and I told that I was going to pick up a stag.

"They hadn't seen anything like that before and asked if they were doing any harm. I said, 'Oh no, just follow me.' I was making for a spot where I knew that I would see Michael, the young stalker with the guest. I stopped and explained that the stalkers would be coming over to the top of a corrie, where they hoped to find deer and they asked if they could stay and watch. I gave them my binoculars and pointed out what was happening. They heard the shot and watched, cameras clicking, as we loaded the stag onto the pony and went on their way delighted with what they had seen. I think that if you just explain to folk in a nice manner, it's amazing how decently they will respond."

The atmosphere on Invercauld estate during Peter's time there very much reflected the character of the laird, Captain Alwyn Compton Farquharson, the sixteenth Farquharson Clan Chief. Peter worked for this laird for twenty-three years. "Aye, and you wouldn't get a nicer man, just a gentleman. It's sad that he didn't have family to carry on the estate. It went into a Trust and just somehow seemed to lose its sparkle, it's all changed. You couldn't have got nicer men than the laird, and the factor too. There was always a great family atmosphere on the estate. The tenants and everybody got on very well. On gathering and clipping day, keepers would give the shepherds a run out to the far end of the ground and help out at the pens, either by catching ewes or rolling up the fleeces. In return, some of the shepherds helped out during the grouse and stalking season and always told the keepers when they spotted signs of a fox, and would tell us when they saw grouse chicks, which gives us an idea of how the grouse were doing.

"It's changed such a lot over the years, the attitude to deer; they are just classified as vermin. And you are restricted now in what you can and can't do. But I thoroughly enjoyed my time keepering. It's a funny thing, when you set out in life you think that thirty or forty years is a long way in front, but when you look back, it's just nothing. If I could go back in time I would choose the same career again, but I wouldn't like to carry on now. I think that I've seen the best of it. I don't know what the future holds for keepering. It's totally different now. It is very sad. I think that we were very lucky to see these estates when they were at their height. I have no objections to who takes over the ground. As long as it is managed in the way it used to be managed, no problem at all.

"I am approaching retirement now and soon won't need to worry about walking out every day over miles and miles of empty hills, endlessly spying for the sight of a stag or a hind. But I won't stop caring about the way we are mismanaging and wasting a precious natural resource, or fearing that the dearth of deer will sound the death knell for many communities in the glens."

I have a wonderful black and white photograph of Captain Farquharson and his keepers on a driven grouse day on the Baddoch Beat of Invercauld Estate, including both Donald MacDonald and a young Peter Fraser. The photograph was taken in 1972 by that great sporting photographer, the late John Tarlton. And, yes indeed, they do look like a very, very happy breed of men.

16
Bill Drury, Aberlour, Spey

Bill Drury's angling life has taken him from the hill lochs of Galloway to the wild rivers of Northern Russia and the wilderness streams of Tierra del Fuego in South America. His working life has been similarly diverse, from the coal face of an Ayrshire mine to acting as consultant and coach in the making of the recently released hit film, now on general release and available on pre-order from Amazon, *Salmon Fishing in the Yemen*. Bill has also designed and launched his own range of superb fly lines and I had the privilege of meeting him last May in the comforting embrace of the whisky bar of the Mash Tun Hotel in Aberlour, conveniently close to the banks of the River Spey where Bill has worked as a head gillie for the past fourteen years.

Bill was born in 1958 in the Ayrshire mining town of Cumnock and went to school there. Lugar Water, a tributary of the River Ayr, flows through the town and Bill began fishing when he was eight years old. He told me, "My mum's in a care home now and her memory is not as good as it once was, but when I showed her the feature in the *Telegraph* newspaper about *Salmon Fishing in the Yemen*, she said, 'I'm really glad that I kept taking you down to the river every morning,' which she did, because it was my mum who introduced me to fishing. I fished with Dad later, but in the early days, it was Mother who encouraged me to fish." Bill left school in 1974 and in his teenage years did some work as a gillie for a local syndicate, to earn some extra money, but like so many of his peers, he went down the pit where he was one of the youngest machine operators at the coalface.

Thinking back on these days, Bill said, "It was a bit scary at times, but that's what I did. However, I would come off night shift on a Saturday and my brother-in-law and mates would be waiting for me in the car park and we would go fishing." I could recognise Bill's reservations in connection with his work at the coalface because I have briefly experienced what it is like to be in such an environment. In the 1970s I went several thousand feet underground in a Yorkshire coalmine, guided by the pit deputy. We came to the end of a long, high-vaulted chamber and the deputy invited us to follow him through a narrow opening in the side of the rock. Our party then crawled on hands and knees along the coalface. The sight and sound of the ripping machine as it passed, tearing the coal from the face, was horrendous. But at regular intervals we were greeted cheerily by the miners on duty. They were as relaxed as I was quite a bit scared. I have never forgotten that experience, or the stolid demeanour of the miners.

As well as fishing more accessible waters, such as Clattering-shaws, Loch Dee and Loch Doon, Bill and his pals explored the lochs in the Galloway hills that cluster round Merrick (2,766ft), the highest peak in the Southern Uplands: Loch Valley, Neldricken, distant Loch Enoch and the little lochs to the east that drain into Cooran Lane. Wild country, as wild as any landscape you will find anywhere in Scotland. Another favourite location Bill frequently fished was the upper reaches of the River Clyde, from Elvanfoot, north to Lamington. He mostly fished with bait in the early months of the season, then flies during the summer, and it was here that Bill developed his enduring love of dry fly-fishing.

Bill mentioned that he had also lived for a while in the little town of Dalmellington, and this reminded me of the days I spent fishing in the area. We often used to call in at a pub in the centre of town for some after-sport refreshment. Dalmellington in those days, like Cumnock, was also a mining community and I am 6'4" in height – not entirely suitable for work down the pit. The ceiling in the pub was so low that I had to sit down to safely get my pint tankard to my lips. I fished vast, bleak Loch Doon and two small lochs to the west, Finlas and Derclach, accessed by a forestry track bordered by the Garnel Burn which drained them into Loch Doon. Our gillies were retired miners, expert anglers and great company.

I also explored Merrick, climbing by the Buchan Burn to the top of adjacent Benyellary (2,380ft) to reach Merrick's summit. The vista from the top is stunning, over the bloodstained moors of the Debatable Lands to the blue and grey mountains of the Lake District in the south, with the stark, dark, rock-plug of Ailsa Craig, 'Paddy's Milestone', and 'the Sleeping Warrior' of the Isle of Arran across the wave-capped waters of the Firth of Clyde to the west. Looking east, the landscape is laid out as though on a map; the lochs and lochans where Bill and his friends found relief and renewal from the harsh reality of their working lives. I descended from Merrick and made my way back to where my car was parked by the Bruce's Stone, a monument erected to commemorate the Battle of Glen Trool in April 1307 when Robert the Bruce defeated an invading English force by rolling mighty stones down upon their unsuspecting heads, thereby causing them great distress and probably quite a few headaches.

Bill was determined to find some kind of employment that involved fishing, so he and his wife Morag and their young daughter Gillian moved to a house just outside Arbroath in Angus, where he found employment on a small estate. Bill said, "It was just general estate work and there wasn't any fishing, but I would check the papers every single week to see if any jobs on a river were being advertised. Eventually, one job did come up, as a river watcher on the River Naver on the Altnaharra Estate in North Sutherland, and I applied for the position. I will never forget coming home from work a few days later and Morag telling me that Lord Marcus Kimball, the owner of the estate, had been on the phone and wanted to know if I could be at Altnaharra the following Saturday for an interview. We set off, all of us and the dogs, early on the Saturday morning and arrived as the sun was setting. I had my interview and Lord Kimball said he would phone me the next day. However, on the way home we got stuck at Bonar Bridge and spent the night there, so I contacted Lord Kimball to say that we were still in Bonar Bridge and could he phone me the following evening. He did, and offered me the job."

Bill's arrival heralded a sea change in the management of the river. He is not a man to be trifled with, and by the time he became a river watcher on the Naver, he was thoroughly experienced in fishing as well as being thoroughly accustomed to hard work and man-management. He watched the river, which was having problems with illegal fishing and poaching. In a small community where everyone knows everyone else, it is not always easy to address these situations and trying to do so can at times create further problems. Consequently, and to avoid conflict, people tend to look the other way and say nothing. Bill played an important part in altering this attitude and in doing so gained the respect of his peers and his employers. Bill was determined to do the job he was paid to do regardless of adverse opinion, as one incident that could have ended in disaster clearly illustrates.

Illegal netting in the sea, in Torrisdale Bay and westwards along the coast to the Kyle of Tongue was predating heavily on stocks of salmon returning to the river to spawn. So Bill arranged to be dropped off at a harbour in the Kyle, where he knew that one of the boats taking salmon at sea was moored. Bill went out to a headland and watched for the vessel going to sea. When he saw it leave, he ran along the headland keeping the boat in sight. At that time, Bill was doing a lot of distance running – up to eight miles a day – so he was the ideal man for the job. He saw the boat stop and put out a net and was able to radio the Naver fishery patrol boat and guide them to exactly where the poacher's boat was lying. The patrol boat was a much lighter vessel than the fishing boat, but got a hold on the net, whereupon a dangerous tug-of-war ensued, with the fishing vessel powering ahead and the patrol boat ploughing ever lower in the water and in serious danger of flooding and sinking. This ended up in court with the poacher being given a paltry fine.

The Altnaharra Estate changed hands in 1991 when Lord Kimball sold it to the Adams family from Aberdeenshire. Bill got on well with Jim Adams, the father, and the family also owned fishing on the River Spey and Bill was invited to look after the beat. It was during this time that Bill became more interested in developing his own casting skills and designing his own lines; also, and almost by accident, the opportunity arrived to go to Russia. Bill told me how that came about. "Iain Neil was a regular visitor to the Spey. He is a writer, photographer, casting tutor and a passionate angler and had worked as a professional guide since 1980. We were talking about Russia, where Ian had been head gillie on the Ponoi River in the Kola Peninsula for five years, and also about the Rio Grande in Tierra del Fuego where I had also been a head gillie. I was looking after a party of six anglers and Iain was impressed with the way I took care of them, you know, got their gear sorted out and all that. Iain said to me, 'You know, Bill, I am sure that Roddy Hall on the Ponoi River would appreciate someone like you out there. Are you interested?' I was. Roddy phoned and asked to meet me the following weekend when he would be on the Spey. The next thing I knew, I was on my way to the Ponoi."

I asked Bill what his wife and Mr Adams had to say about his decision. "I talked it over with Morag, and because I was doing other things as well, such as developing my new fishing lines, we thought that it might open some doors. Mr Adams said that it would not be a problem and that Morag could remain in residence in the estate cottage. So on the first week in May, I was off. A friend, Ian Gordon, another Spey gillie, took me to the airport and about half a mile up the road I asked him to stop the car and said to him, 'I can't do this, Ian, leave Morag and my daughter Gillian for nine months.' Ian said, 'Come on. You will be fine, and so will they.' I was staying overnight in London before flying out in the morning, and I phoned home when I arrived at the hotel. Morag said they were all well and not to worry about them.

"We sent letters every week. I would write a letter and give it to a guest on his way home and he would post it back in the UK."

Bill continued, "A new group of guests arrived every Saturday evening and after getting them settled in I would go to my room to read my letter from Morag which came out with them. For me, it was the best part of the week. Maybe it would have been easier for a younger guy, but for me it was tough being away for that length of time. I had some great highs and some great lows, but it was after all, a once in a lifetime fishing opportunity. I can't pretend that my job was easy because you never knew in advance what the guests would be like, not only as people, but as anglers. The routine was up in the morning, get the guests ready, organise their fishing for the day, make sure that they had everything they needed, help the less experienced with casting lessons and explain to them how to play a fish; in the evening, sort out any problems they had experienced during the day, complete the fishing returns, keep the guests happy and enthusiastic, have dinner with them and then to bed. All to be done again the next day."

As always, there is generally one awkward customer in every party and Bill told about one of his. "He was French, and a huge, elderly guy. He came with his wife, who was tiny. Normally, when fishing from a boat, the bow rod fishing closest to the bank has the best chance of a fish, so after the bow rod has caught a salmon, the rule was that he would swap places with the stern rod to give him the advantage. However, not the Frenchman. He ignored this civilised rule and left his poor wife to get on with it as best she could, which she couldn't, having great difficulty casting and constantly getting her line in a fankle. At lunchtime when we went ashore and into the tent that had been set up for that purpose, his wife was quite miserable. However, on the way back to the river a good salmon rose upstream. 'Did you see that fish!' 1 exclaimed. 'Why don't you go up to the top of the bank and fish that stretch down, the wading is easy?'

"Off the Frenchman went, the light of battle glinting in his eyes. So I said to his wife, 'Jump aboard and we will have a few casts.' She did, and for the next half hour or so had she great sport. The guests all have radios so that they can keep in touch with the staff and I heard this man's radio crackling a bit, but I ignored it. When his wife had caught two or three fish I relented and motored ashore. He was livid, but I couldn't care less because his wife was smiling sweetly. After a few minutes, he calmed down and was as good as gold for the rest of the week." Bill did two seasons on the Ponoi, but turned down the third invitation.

I knew how Bill must have felt, because I had been in a similar position. In 1991, an acquaintance contacted me to ask if I could recommend anyone to look after a fishing lodge for six months on a small island, Isla Monita, in Chilean Patagonia. I couldn't, because very few people can just drop everything and shoot off to the end of the earth to go fishing. However, Ann suggested that I take the job, that it would be a wonderful experience and that they would be fine during my absence; three of our children had left home by then, but we still had the youngest, Jean, with us. As a writer, I could organise my affairs in such a way that would allow me go, and I was eventually persuaded, but when the time came, leaving was one of the bleakest moments of my life. The lodge was idyllically situated at the south end of Lago Yelcho, three hour's drive from the coastal town of Chaitén. Lago Yelcho is twenty-six miles long by three miles wide and dropping to a depth of over 1,000 feet and surrounded by snow-capped mountains rising to over 7,000 feet. My guests were primarily very rich Americans, my staff Chilean, none of whom could speak a word of English, and my Spanish at that stage was basic. I was asked back the following season and I persuaded Ann to come with me; she had recently retired as a dental surgeon and Jean was to stay with her elder sister in Northumberland. As Bill did on the Ponoi, we turned down the third invitation to look after the lodge. But, yes, in retrospect, it was an unforgettable experience.

Bill told me that one of the greatest pleasures that he derives from fishing is working with someone who has hardly fished before and seeing him develop casting skills, finding the rhythm and gaining in confidence, not only in casting but also learning how to play and land a salmon. And Bill has been back to Russia, to the Ponoi and other rivers. In June 2012 on the Lower Varzuga River, he looked after a party of nine anglers, some of whom were complete novices. "At the start of the week," he said, "the beginners were awkward and nervous, not really knowing what to do to hook and play a fish. By the end of the week they were relaxed and cheerful, particularly since the party had more than 330 salmon between them. There were a lot of very happy faces by the last day."

I have also been back to Chile, in 2005, to meet with a group of conservationists who shared my concerns about the huge damage that factory salmon was inflicting on wild stocks and the environment around the world. It was good to see Chaitén again and the friends that I had made there. However, two months after my return, the Chaitén volcano erupted and obliterated the town. Happily today it is being rebuilt.

I asked Bill if his wife and daughter fished. "My daughter

Gillian fished with me when we were in Strathnaver, but only on hill lochs. She was always happiest casting from the stern of the boat whilst I rowed. She has always been wonderfully supportive of everything I have done, full of ideas and innovations, but when it comes to fishing she prefers to wander the bank all day, enjoying just being there and what surrounds her, rather than fishing. Morag fishes and her father was also an angler. She caught a lot of fish on the Naver, spring fish as well, lovely specimens. Morag was the housekeeper at Syre Lodge, about halfway down the Strath, and one of our regular guests, Dr Potts from the Isle of Man, always fished the river in May. He was strictly a nine to five man. He fished by himself and would come round to our door and tell us that if we wanted to fish his beat after 5pm, then we were welcome to do so. Morag had an operation on her shoulder in 2009, so I took her down to the Rio Grande to recuperate."

"How did that happen?" I asked.

Bill said, "Well, since I worked in Russia, I have been taking groups of anglers out there for a week's fishing. I have also done some work with Roxtons – a company which specialise in arranging fishing and shooting holidays around the world – had a spare rod left in a party fishing the Rio Grande and invited me to join it. The next time I went, as a guest, I took Morag. We knew quite a few of the other guests and Morag was the life and soul of the group. She really enjoyed herself, but didn't fish all the time because of her shoulder and the wind. Nevertheless, she caught quite a few sea-trout, her biggest weighing 17lbs. When we came home, Morag went into hospital to have her shoulder attended to, and since then hasn't been able to do much fishing."

I asked Bill to tell me a little about how he came to design lines. "When I was in Russia," Bill said, "I noticed that guests were beginning to arrive with ever more sophisticated tackle, particularly lines. The problem was that very few anglers knew how to use them to their full capacity and watching them trying to perform a Spey cast was sadly worrying. The Spey cast is a method developed on the River Spey to allow the angler to cast without getting caught up behind on bankside undergrowth. In the cast, the line never goes behind the angler, as it does with the traditional and much simpler overhead cast, a technique that allows the angler to get his fly proficiently and comfortably to the right place at the right time." This is, however, neither the place nor the time to go into finite detail about casting techniques. There are hundreds of books and videos available to guide those who wish to improve their skills. But perhaps the best way to do this is to seek personal instruction from people like Bill Drury, who are experts in these matters.

Frontiers, another company who organise fishing expeditions around the world, asked Bill to do a photoshoot on the Yokanga River in Russia. Bill demonstrated to the photographer, Matt Harris, a variety of casting techniques for various angling situations and explained to him why different line designs were required for different situations. Matt mentioned to Bill that he also did work for the Scandinavian fishing tackle company Guideline, and that he was sure they would be interested in Bill's opinions. The result was that Guideline contacted Bill and asked him to design a balanced, longer line for Spey casting. Bill told me, "I wanted to try to bring the benefits of the new lines into a single, long-bellied line that the general angler could handle with ease. The first line I designed was called Impact, two versions, a seventy-four foot line and a sixty-two foot line. It was very well received and revolutionised thinking on the design of Spey casting lines. The shape I made it was so dynamic that it created great line speed and thus was easier to cast. The impact was phenomenal and worldwide and got my name known and established as designer of lines."

The next request for lines came from Sportish, one of the UK's leading suppliers of game fishing tackle for nearly thirty years. Bill said, "They were starting a new brand of line called Speyworks and asked if I would like to develop the brand. And of course I said yes. I kept more or less the same shape as the line I had designed for Guideline, but added in what eventually became known as 'density assisted turnover'. This was a method of adding density nearer the front taper to enhance the turnover of the fly. Everything I have learned about rods and lines has come from watching the river and people fishing day to day. That's where I get all my ideas, watching anglers and seeing what they are doing. My aim has always been to build upon anglers' experiences and to try to design tackle that compliments and enhances their ability to catch fish and to enjoy doing so." Bill also designed a rod for Sportfish, and within six months the rod and the line were their best sellers. Bill worked with Sportfish for a number of years, but recently made the decision to go forward on his own. Everything is in place and Bill will be launching his range on a new website, www.drurylinesandtackle.com.

I can't pretend to be an expert in casting. Nearest and so-called dearest frequently refer to my casting technique as "Father's affliction", conveniently forgetting the fact that, in the first instance, I taught each and every one of them to cast. I have suffered embarrassment on many occasions in this connection and in one such incident, whilst demonstrating my skills to a watching USA journalist and his photographer, connected my tail fly to my right earlobe. It was a terrible South Uist day, windy and pouring, so I managed to break the cast and simply waded out as far as I could in the shallow loch. When I saw them pack up and head for the lodge, I bustled ashore to where Ann was sitting patiently in the car. She removed it, painlessly, using the loop and jerk method. However, my worst came at a Game Fair, courtesy of my younger daughter, Jean. She had spotted a well-known, bearded face at the casting clinic and asked if she could have a lesson. Ignoring the implicit insult that I had been less than satisfactory as her angling mentor, I held my peace and simply agreed, having learned from bitter experience that arguing with Jean is a fruitless undertaking that almost invariably ends in tears – mine.

The instructor soon had Jean under control, which was something I had never managed to achieve, and as I watched, I was amazed at the improvement basic instruction from a professional could effect. But, from time to time I noticed that Jean stopped casting and fell into deep conversation with her tutor. Eventually, she wandered over and smugly announced, "You know what you have been telling me about casting? Well, he says it is a load of rubbish." I spluttered, searching for words with which to defend my reputation. Jean spotted my distress and moved in for the kill. "He wants a word with you, now."

Resigned, I shambled over. "What are you trying to do to me?" I pleaded. "She will never let me forget this, even if I live to be one hundred. You have destroyed my life."

Unperturbed, he handed me a rod and a said, "Come on,

Bruce, and let's try to sort something out. We can't have you going around being a danger to yourself and other anglers, if not to any fish."

Thinking about casting, I asked Bill how he became involved in *Salmon Fishing in the Yemen* and he told me, "It was when I was associated with Sportfish. The filmmakers came to Sportfish for tackle, rods, lines and so on, and the then managing director suggested that they seek my help and advice. He phoned one evening to explain and to tell me that my Speywork rods and lines were being used. The film producers also contacted me and we agreed that I should act as their fishing consultant. They eventually phoned me to say that they had chosen a location on the River Roy in Lochaber, near Fort William, and that the crew all there and would I join them on the following Sunday. Well, I had fished up there before and thought that if the location they had chosen was where the Roy joined the River Spean, a tributary of the River Lochy, then that would probably do. When I got there, I spent the day with Ewan MacGregor, who plays the lead male role, and Amr Waked, who plays the sheik. They had had a couple of casting lessons in London, but nothing much. I explained to them that I wanted to get them to relax, and to look comfortable when they were casting. I told Ewan that he had to look very relaxed because he was the experienced salmon angler, whilst Amr was less so. He was fantastic and really good at following my movements. Amr was OK, but wanted to do all the difficult bits as though he was performing in Billy Smart's circus. It was quite hard to slow him down, but by the end of the day I had managed to do so."

The next morning Bill went down to the administration site

and the transport manager said, "Get you gear together and we will have you up on the next bus." Billy wondered where they were going, as the junction of the Roy and the Spean was just across the road. Billy continued, "Oh no! We were dropped off about a mile downstream from Brae Roy Lodge where the river is entirely unsuitable for the scenes we were about to shoot. I was pulling on my waders when two Mercedes cars arrived. Ewan MacGregor jumped out of one, and Emily Blunt and Amr Waked out of the other. They were all kitted up and ready to go. Ewan came over to me and said, 'You wouldn't fish for salmon here, would you?' I replied no, and we went over to the director. There was a furious argument as I tried to explain what was wrong about the location, that there was not enough water in that part of the river. The crew and the rest of the team, about a hundred people, sat about wondering what the hell was going on.

"Eventually, they gave me a Range Rover and asked me to try to find an alternative location, which I did, about a mile downstream where the river was wider. There was one scene when an attempt is made on the life of the sheik by an assassin, and to foil it, Ewan had to make a cast across the river to hit the assassin with his heavy salmon fly. The director wanted an overhead cast, because he thought it would look better, but the only way it was going work was with a snake-roll cast. Ewan tried to persuade the director to let me make the cast, but he wouldn't have it, so I took Ewan aside and tutored him for half an hour until he managed to get the hang of it." Bill was delighted and relieved when it all went well. Job done.

I haven't seen the film yet, but I am looking forward to doing so, particularly knowing the part played in its making by Bill Drury.

As for casting, he was a member of the Scottish team who took top place in the World Team Championship in Ireland in 2005, along with his friends, Ian Gordon, former World Champion Spey Caster, Scott Mackenzie, another former World Champion Spey Caster, and Eoin Fairgrieve, Scotland's first Angling Development Officer and member of the Professional Game Angling Instructors; a more star-studded bunch of piscators would be hard to find anywhere else in the world.

Given all that Bill Drury has achieved during his lifetime, he is a modest and unassuming man; master angler, master caster, rod and line designer and fisherman extraordinaire. But over and above all, he is simply great company and exactly the man to make any fishing expedition truly memorable.

17
Billy Jack, Junction Pool, Tweed

Billy Jack is head gillie on one of the most famous salmon beats in the world, the Junction Pool, where Tweed and Teviot meet at Kelso. I asked Billy about 'ones that got away'. "Right enough," he replied. "There's been a few, but one in particular sticks in my mind. I was fishing with Robert Beattie – Bob to his friends – a farmer from Northampton. Bob has been fishing this beat longer than I have and one afternoon we sent him down to Hemsford; they used to call it Siberia because there was no gillie there. He had five fish that afternoon, including a huge salmon that weighed 43lbs. Bob brought his uncle up with him one year, Uncle Jim Beattie, who hadn't done much fishing. I took him down to below the old bridge in town. We fished away, but weren't doing much at the bridge because the water was quite high. So I suggested that we went down to the White Dykes, which is a pool just above Hemsford. I knew the pool was suited to high water and that it could fish well.

"I got the boat out and we hadn't been fishing for more than a few minutes when the line came round the back and Jim said, 'Oh, Billy, I've got one!' So he had, and I asked him to raise the rod to get into the fish. At this point the salmon was about twenty or thirty yards downstream of the boat, near the bottom end of White Dykes and the top end of Hemsford. An old, man-made weir, just built with stone, separates the two beats, and it's quite a drop from the one to the other. But when the weir was built, incorporated into it was the top end of an island that runs down

Hemsford, dividing the flow of the river. I thought, 'My God, it's going to go over. We've had it.' But the fish stopped, and then came across the river in front of the weir. By that time we did not have lot of line left on the reel, but we started to get some back. As the salmon came up the far side of the river, it launched itself out of the water, twice, and it was the biggest fish that I had ever seen. I have had few 30lb fish in my time, but this one was really massive.

"I said to Jim, 'If we can get our hands on him it could beat Bob's forty-three pounder.' The salmon headed upstream towards deeper water where we could play him and I thought, 'Brilliant, now we have a chance.' Then all of a sudden he decided to run back downstream. The reel was absolutely screaming and I was back-peddling furiously on the oars to get after it. The fish got to the lip of the weir, and the damned thing went over into Hemsford. Knowing what I know now, I should have just let the boat follow, but then I was worried about the safety of my guest, and myself. Instead, I rowed as fast as I could towards the top of the island, got out of the boat onto the island and asked Jim to give me the rod and follow me down the bank. The reel was a big Hardy's reel and there were only about six turns left on the spindle. I started to run down the bank after the fish, Jim following. As I said, it was biggish water and there were willow bushes on the bank that were virtually covered with water. The line caught on them, I freed it and it got caught again. I had just about managed to get the line free the second time when *ping*, and the fish had broken us. We never saw it again.

"I reeled in and found that the cast had broken just above the fly, but it was one of those fish that every angler dreams about landing. I am sure it was over 40lbs, maybe more. We will never know. But, Bruce, you know the feeling, every angler does. I have had a lot of big fish in my time, mainly down at the bottom end of the Bridge Pool. There is a deep pot there that we call the Maxwheel where we often take fish of 25lbs, 28lbs, 30lbs and more. Many of these fish get away because they are big ones. It's not just anglers telling tall stories. But I have thought, oh, maybe a thousand times since the incident with Uncle Jim Beattie, of how much I would have loved to have landed his big salmon. I suppose it is just one of these things, eh?"

The Tweed is no stranger to tall tales of huge salmon. In 1743, Lord Home was reported to have landed a salmon weighing 69lbs 12oz, and William, Earl of Home, is said to have had one of 61lbs. However, because of uncertainty about matters avoirdupois in these days, the authenticity of the weights cannot be confirmed. But there is no doubt about the heaviest salmon taken in more modern times: a fish of 57lbs 8oz, caught a by a Mr Pryor on a Silver Wilkinson on 27 October 1886 at Upper Floors. Seven other salmon weighing over 50lbs have been taken since then. the heaviest being a fish of 43lbs landed in 1977 by Lady Burnett in the Pot Pool at Tillmouth, and of course, Bob Beattie's 43lb fish mentioned above.

The Tweed is also famous for the number of rod-and-line-caught fish taken during the course of a single day. G. McCulloch took nineteen salmon on 20 November 1903. They weighed a total of 389lbs 8oz, with the heaviest at 39lbs. In more recent times, a Mr Dixon, fishing with gillie Michael Chapman at Tillmouth, had six fish in a morning from Beat 6; their total weight was 121lbs and the heaviest weighed 24lbs 8oz. Sea-trout of great size were also taken most seasons, and in 1985 fish of 18lbs and 17lbs were caught. A sea-trout of more modest size was landed in 1957 below the bridge at Innerleithen by my father. It weighed 4lbs and Father was so excited by his success that he telephoned to tell me the news. At that time I was in the army, stationed 'overseas' on the Isle of Wight and on hearing the news, my heart ached for the feel of a fishing rod in my hand, bent double in action on the Tweed.

I asked Billy if he could account for the huge numbers of salmon returning to the Tweed in recent years; 30,000 fish were taken in 2010. He said, "Tweed is now very much an autumn river, but I don't think that anybody really knows why there has been this sudden upturn in the numbers of returning salmon. It's been increasing for three or four years now and we have being going along here with about 750 salmon each season, although last year we were just three fish short of 1,200. The Tweed has never been a river with two big runs of salmon, spring and autumn. It has always been either one or the other. I remember as a boy going up to the Teviot on 15 February, opening day, when twenty spring salmon were taken. Now this year, with opening day delayed until 10 or 11 April, not a single salmon has been caught and they are still waiting for their first."

I wondered if taking off the majority of the North East Coast drift nets had anything to do with it. "Could be," answered Billy, "as you say, it's just built and built into this massive run of autumn fish over the past three or four years. There are still three netting stations working that take and kill on the order of 10,000 fish a year, although I suppose the river can sustain that, given the high number salmon now returning to the river."

I asked about the effect of industrial fishing for sand eels. Billy felt that that probably also had a lot to do with the resurgence of salmon. He told me, "Last year we had an exceptional run of smolts going to sea and down at Paxton they said the same." I wondered if the introduction of the catch and release policy had made any significant difference. Billy didn't seem to think so. "I'm sure that the proprietors are trying to do the right thing, but in my opinion, it hasn't made any difference. The problems facing salmon today are not in our rivers, but at sea, on the salmon's migratory routes, and that is where the solution lies."

Billy Jack is as much part of his river as the fish that swim in it. The river is his whole life, and as far as I could make out, always has been. I am sure that if you cut Billy you would find the Tweed flowing through his veins.

I met him at his home in Kelso, two doors along from the house where he was born. As a boy, he was always keen on trout fishing. "I could go down the Cobby Riverside Walk and fish for trout at the bottom end of Lower Floors. We used to go out with spinning rods and always caught a few. Now and again the gillies would chase us, but as I grew older I got to know Gordon Lesenger, the head gillie on the Junction Pool at that time, and Joe Allan was second gillie. I often watched them fishing, and one day Gordon asked if I ever fancied doing something like that. 'That would be the job for me,' I told him. I suppose I was about fourteen or fifteen then.

"When I left school at the age of sixteen I got a phone call from Gordon. He told me that old Joe was retiring and asked if I was still interested in being a gillie. I said yes. Gordon told me that his boss, John Cheeseborough, was coming up and would like to see me. I met him for an interview down at the Cross Keys Hotel. As he got up to go, he said, 'As far as I am concerned, the job is yours if you want it.' I said yes, and he told me that they would write to confirm the details, so I went home and told my dad that I had got a job as a gillie on the Junction. He was delighted."

Billy started in August 1978 and since then has never looked back. He worked for eleven years with Gordon Lesenger, who lived in the Friars Cottage, the little white cottage on the other side of Teviot Bridge. Gordon's health was deteriorating, so he gillied on Junction Pool because the rowing there was less arduous. Billy was quite happy to work on the Bridge Pool, which could be more taxing. He remembers both Gordon and Joe very fondly for their patience and courtesy. Billy was also fortunate because he knew the water well; Billy's father was also a keen angler and they often fished for trout together on that part of the river. Billy also had experience rowing a boat on the Teviot and soon got into the rhythm of the Tweed. When Gordon retired, Billy took over as head gillie and advertised for a second gillie. The job was given to Gavin Brown, who had been at school with Billy. Gavin lived close to Billy, and as boys, they also fished together. There was another part-time gillie, because the fishing by then was almost always fully booked.

As it was with Billy Jack, the Tweed also played an important part of my life. My fishing memories were born on the Tweed, and I first committed the sin of angling there nearly sixty years ago in Tweed's little tributary, Lyne Water. Then, for me, bristling with rod, landing net, waders and picnic, it was bus from St Andrews Square, Edinburgh to Romano Bridge, warmed by a wonderful sense of anticipation all the way. I remember catching my first trout. It flew past my ear on a particularly violent back-cast and I spent frantic seconds on hands and knees searching for it in long grass. The fish was about four inches long, sparkling, silver, red-spotted and gasping. I felt that I had never seen anything quite so beautiful nor felt such excitement. I removed the fly and returned the trout to the water, watching breathlessly as it darted off into the depths.

I introduced my father to fishing on Lyne Water. One evening, after his golf match had been cancelled, he decided to drive down and collect me. I was fishing a wide pool near Flemington and saw father park his car by the side of the road. He waved and walked down to where I was casting. "Here, son," he said. "Give me a shot at that." Not long afterwards he abandoned golf and dreamt of little else other than fishing for the rest of his life. Once I had mastered basic techniques, such as filling Wellington boots with water, falling in, retrieving flies from underwater obstructions, the back of my neck and passing cattle, father and I moved downstream to Lyne Station where the Lyne finally mingles with Tweed. Dr Beeching took his axe to the railway station many years ago, but there is still a Victoria Regina letterbox set into the wall of the roadside cottage where we parked.

One evening, full of the scent of meadowsweet and honeysuckle, I was fishing upstream from the railway bridge in fading light. First bats flicked by, and I was engrossed in trying to remove a Grouse and Claret from the back of my jacket. The river had that heady, lingering, evening smell – water bubbling by, caressing moss-capped stones, urgent for the sea. As I twisted and turned, cursing the loss of a few more moments' fishing time, the water by my feet suddenly exploded in a shower of crystal droplets. A huge, silver and gold shape rose majestically from the river and arched back almost in slow motion, the broad tail, sail-like, powering the salmon upstream. The noise of its landing echoed through the night sending moorhens clucking angrily amongst reeds, annoyed at being disturbed.

I slumped to the ground, watching the salmon's arrow-like wake until it faded from sight and silence settled once more over the river. In that moment, I was confirmed into the angling fraternity and have remained forever within its embrace. Everything I wanted lay around me and I knew then that no matter what outrageous or malicious slings came my way in the future, I could always escape to the river.

But the Tweed has changed over the years, not necessarily in its character – it is still as lovely as it ever was – but rather in the status of the river's salmon, sea-trout and brown trout populations. Billy seemed to agree when I asked him what he thought. "When I first started the spring fishing was quite good." I told Billy that I used to fish for salmon in the early 1950s and again when I came out of the army in the 1960s. This was up at Innerleithen, on the New Water, and above Peebles where Manor Water flows in. There were always salmon about in the early months of the season. Billy said, "I caught the tail end of this, before the Tweed became essentially an autumn river. I had a few years when the spring fishing was excellent in February and March, then tailed off in May. You could get a day let on Junction Pool from the middle of May until the beginning of September for a very modest sum. We gillies spent that period cutting weeds, repairing banks, cutting grass, maintain the fishing huts and paths. Nowadays, we have lets from 1 February every week right through to the end of November. It's just chock-a-block."

As I found when I was speaking to gillies in other parts of Scotland, the sort of people fishing for salmon today has also changed. "I remember," Billy said, "we used to have, predominantly, ex-army types, old colonels and generals, judges, lawyers and farmers, whereas now we have more businessmen – in effect, those who can afford to pay the price. I mean no disrespect, indeed the opposite. When I began, a gillie was treated very much as a servant, having lunch separate from his guests, waiting on them hand and foot. It was hard at times. You were expected to get out there, no matter what the weather, and row away as hard as you could for as long as they wanted to fish. Nowadays, you are accepted as much as a friend as a gillie, and very much a key member of the party. I remember fishing with a fruit merchant from Glasgow – Ian was his name, a great lad – and we had some good laughs together. If the fishing was quiet, or the weather wild, he would say, 'Billy, this is not much fun, let's have an early lunch.'

"One day his party had an extremely good lunch and in the afternoon I took him down to the White Dykes. He was sitting on the casting stool and I said, 'Right, get your line in over there,' which he did, but five to ten minutes later he was still just sitting there, his back to me, and I'm rowing away like mad, waiting and waiting to see the fly come round the back of the boat. So eventually I called to him, 'Ian, have you started hand-lining that line in yet?' He gave such a start that he almost fell out of the boat. He had gone to sleep holding the rod, although how he had managed to do so from one of these boat stools is beyond me."

Billy said, "We are a very sociable fishery, here on the Junction, and all get on pretty well with each other. Even if the river is fishing well, most guests will still enjoy an extra half hour at lunch, talking and swapping stories. And if the fishing is difficult, then they will perhaps give it a go in the morning then get the barbecue lit at lunchtime and have a party. I have seen us still there at seven or eight in the evening, laughing and playing silly games. It wasn't like that when I started. We have had some great times, and, hopefully will have many, many more in the future."

For me, one of the greatest pleasures in researching and writing this book was hearing about old friends, the gillies, stalkers and keepers that I had met twenty-five years earlier when I first addressed the subject. Meeting Billy Jack was no exception. He well remembered two remarkable characters that I had spoken to who were gillies on the Tweed, Frank Binnie at Tweed Mill and Jimmy Wallace at Tillmouth, both now fishing that great river in the sky. Billy said, "I remember them both, they were highly respected." Billy also knew Michael Chapman, who I mentioned earlier, and who has recently retired as head gillie at Tillmouth. Michael told me a wonderful story about Frank Binnie and the then head gillie at Tillmouth, David. I can't remember David's second name, but he and Frank Binnie were great rivals, their beats being on opposite banks of the river. They had many a slagging match across the stream. One morning David saw Frank standing on his bank, and called across, 'Have you no one with you today, Binnie?'

"'Aye,' replied Frank, 'he will be here in about an hour.'

"'Get yourself in then, man' roared David, 'and make your Woodbine money before he arrives!'"

Michael recalled another morning when walking to the river with David. David suddenly stopped and said to Michael, "Look, there's Binnie. What's he up to? What's he doing?" Michael handed David his binoculars and told him to see for himself.

Frank seemed to be hiding behind a bush looking over the river towards where they were standing. "What's he doing? What's he doing? I still can't see!" David said. Michael took the binoculars and focused on Frank. The old man was crouched behind the bush, his own binoculars pressed to his eyes, staring across at them. Turning to his agitated companion, Michael said, "Doing, doing? He is as daft as you are. He is spying on you just as you are spying on him and it's damned few fish either of you will catch until you stop this nonsense."

Frank Binnie was a wonderful old man and lived in a cottage within casting distance of the river. I will never forget him. He had retired when I called to see him and he was full of tales and stories about his days at Tweed Mill. We sat and talked in the kitchen, his black Labrador by his side. One of the great angling characters who used to fish with Frank was the author and naturalist, G. P. R. Balfour Kinnear. Frank and Mr Kinnear had a tempestuous relationship, each regarding the other with a high degree of competitive respect. Frank would say to him, "You know as much about fishing as my foot. All you've learned and put in your books has been gleaned from the likes of me, and very little thanks do we get for it."

One morning Frank was pottering in the garden, keeping one eye on his vegetables and the other on Balfour Kinnear, who was fiddling about on the riverbank doing something to his line which was laid out in the grass round his feet. Unable to restrain his curiosity, Frank wandered over to see what was going on. "What are you up to this morning, Mr Kinnear?" he enquired.

"You wouldn't understand, Frank, but I'm greasing my line. That's what I'm doing."

"Greasing your line are you? And why would you want to do a thing like that?" Frank asked. He then received a long lecture on the merits of greased-line fishing for salmon, as recently demonstrated by the acclaimed angler Arthur Wood on the Aberdeenshire Dee, and Frank was told the great numbers of fish to be caught using this new method.

"Oh, is that so, sir?" said Frank.

"You'll catch nothing today, Frank, unless you are fishing with a greased line, so be a good fellow and stop bothering me. I've fish to catch before lunch."

Frank turned, walked back to the cottage in contemplative mood, and shortly afterwards returned, carrying his old Greenheart salmon rod. When Balfour Kinnear looked up and saw the rod, he stopped and asked Frank what he was going to do. "Well, just to prove how little I know about fishing and how much you do, I'll tell you what we'll do. I'll fish down the pool before you. You'll know perfectly well that I won't catch anything because my line's not greased. Then you come down behind me and catch three or four.'" But Balfour Kinnear would have none of it and insisted that Frank fish behind him.

"But that wouldn't be proving anything at all," explained Frank. "Let me go down first and when I don't catch anything and you do then you'll see me greasing my line." Balfour Kinnear still wouldn't agree, and Frank sat and watched him as he fished down the pool, taking a grand salmon of 17lbs after about the fourth cast. But Frank knew that if he had gone down the pool first that fish would have been his, and he claimed Balfour Kinnear was as well aware of that fact as he was.

Billy Jack has also had the odd difficult guest. I think it goes with the territory. I know that when I used to host fishing holidays there was always one awkward customer, invariably the kind of angler who knows it all and won't listen to or accept advice, no matter how tactfully it is given. Billy recalled a party booking Junction one September and whilst the leader of the group was fine, his son was somewhat arrogant. "The young man had done very little fishing, so I took him down to Hemsford. I got him casting well enough, and explained that when a fish took he should let it pull line of the reel and then raise the point of the rod to set the hook. All I got in return was a muttered, 'Yes, yes, OK.' Anyway, after three or four casts, sure enough, he hooked a fish, a good fish of about 18lbs. But instead of letting it run, he held it tight and the salmon was leaping about on the top of the water. No matter what I said, he just would not listen. When the salmon tired and came near the bank, I warned him that when it saw the net, it'd go off again like a rocket. 'Yes, yes, OK,' was the only acknowledgment. Of course, that is exactly what the salmon did, and he, once again, held it tight and did not allow it to run.

"The cast broke and the salmon turned on its side, wallowing in the shallows. 'Get it!' roared the young man. 'Get it with the net!' I told him that the fish had broken the cast; it was gone. 'No it's not. Get it with the net!' I walked back up the riverbank with the net, and eventually he came and stood beside me. 'Have you got another fly?' he asked. I told him no because he was the fisher, not me. 'Oh,' he replied. 'I'll have to go and find Father to see if he as any more.' I watched him turn on his heel, walk across the field and get into his car and drive off in search of his father, who was further up the beat. I was left standing there, I suppose, to await his pleasure. Well, as I said, the Junction is a very sociable beat and in the years that I have worked here there has very rarely been any trouble. The owners are supportive of the gillies, and if they find that a guest has been less than well behaved, we don't see them again. And that is the last we ever saw of that arrogant young man, or any of the other members of his party."

The general consensus amongst the gillies I have spoken to is that women are often far more successful than men in the pursuit of salmon, and Billy Jack was no exception. "Our old boss's wife, Mrs Florence Miller, sadly, she died a few years ago, but she could out-fish the men hands down, no problem. I don't know exactly how many fish she caught, but a good number were over 30lbs in weight. The ladies are far more patient than men and they do what their gillie tells them. If you ask the lady to cast a certain length of line, she does it, and keeps doing it. Whereas men invariably after a few casts begin stripping off a bit more line, then a bit more until they are in danger of catching the far bank and the fly is whizzing round your ears like a lethal weapon," he said.

That reminded me of a story that Jimmy Wallace from Tillmouth, told me about one of his ladies. "The lady was so strong," he said, "she used a big Tweed rod and punched the line, straight out into the teeth of the wildest storm. She never seemed to notice the weather. Wind, rain, hail, snow, sleet or flood, she concentrated on the job in hand with single-minded determination. And the moment a salmon touched her fly she would leap up from the stool and give the rod an almighty yank."

"Dear God, lady," Jimmy would exclaim, "if you hit the poor creatures as hard as that you'll have one come flying from the river and knock you overboard." The best Jimmy could do was to keep his wits about him and his head down. But by the end of the day she had hooked six fish and landed every one. Her husband had slaved away without as much as a touch. In the bar of Ednam House Hotel that evening, before dinner, her husband asked Jimmy how his wife had got on and if she had lost any fish. "Lost them," Jimmy exploded. "She hooked them so hard that she damned near pulled their heads clean off. You'll have to tell her be more gentle with them." But he was not keen on that idea and suggested that such advice would be better coming from Jimmy. "Look," he said, "I have a phone call to make. Here she comes, you tell he whilst I'm gone." But Jimmy held his peace. "I was not brave enough or stupid enough to do so, which is probably why I'm still here today and able to tell you this tale."

Billy Jack has fished extensively throughout Scotland, on the Spey at the Brae Water, Castle Grant and Tulchan, and also on the Tay at Stanley, being invited to do so by his Junction Pool guests. As I discovered, it is a small world, and most of the gillies I met were well acquainted with their colleagues on other rivers, past and present.

I asked Billy when he would be retiring. "Well, to be honest," he said, "I think I will go on for as long as I am fit enough to do so, why not? Unless, of course, people decide that they have had enough of me. I just don't know what else I would do. I would be lost if I had to retire."

"Would you do it all over again if you had a chance?"

Billy didn't hesitate. "Of course I would. I wouldn't change it one little bit."

As I left I thought, 'There is a very happy man with about as much chance of him being asked to retire as there is of me growing wings.'

18

Billy Felton, South Uist, Western Isles

Billy Felton is one of the most knowledgeable and likeable anglers that I have ever known. He and his wife Marion arrived in the Outer Hebrides in 1981, when Billy, a sergeant major in the Royal Artillery, was posted to the rocket range on Benbecula. The posting was supposed to be for three years, but Billy and Marion ended up spending more than thirty years of their lives there, living on a croft at Iochdar at the north end of the Island of South Uist where, eventually, on Billy's retirement from the army, they established their famous guest house, The Angler's Retreat.

It is easy to fall in love with the Hebrides. These magical islands, Lewis, Harris, North Uist, Benbecula, South Uist and Barra ensnare most visitors with their gentle charm, wild moorlands, blue-grey mountains, endless green, white-tipped Atlantic waves washing against deserted golden beaches backed by fertile machair lands. The grasslands of the machair have been built up over the centuries by the prevailing winds and they are rich in lime and a paradise for wildflowers, bright with buttercups, marsh marigolds, yellow rattle, kidney vetch, Irish lady's tresses, orchids, yellow rattle, red clover and Scottish bluebells.

I first visited the Uists and Benbecula in 1976 on a family holiday when we stayed in a caravan near a loch close to Balavanich, known locally and appropriately as The Caravan

Loch, noted for the size and quality of its brown trout and for their reluctance to be caught. All our children fish. I think the Chinese call it 'brainwashing', but it never did our lot any harm and limited arguments about where we should go on holiday. We went fishing in the North of Scotland. My son Blair's first job after graduation as a computer scientist was with the Ministry of Defence at the rocket range on Benbecula, where he soon found himself appointed as secretary of the South Uist Angling Club.

He was friendly with Billy Felton and I got to know Billy during further fishing expeditions to the Hebrides when Ann and I stayed with Blair and his wife Barbara. The most immediately striking thing about Billy Felton is his boundless enthusiasm for fishing, almost with a complete disregard for prevailing weather conditions. Billy always knows exactly where to go to have the best possible opportunity of sport, and invariably, he is right. Having Billy as a gillie is not only a delight, but a significant honour.

Billy was born in the east end of London in 1940, but during Mr Hitler's bombing blitz his parents moved to the relative calm of rural Essex. His father introduced him to fishing. "All the holidays we ever had were on the Norfolk Broads, on boats, fishing," Billy said. "I also used to go hop-picking with my grandmother and my mother. Men who worked during the week used to come down at weekends – for the drinking and the fighting. As a small boy I can remember being fascinated watching people fish.

"When I was older, I used to run home from school on a Friday afternoon, get my tent and bike, pedal to the railway station, get into the guard's van with my bike and go fishing, camping and looking after myself by the Medway or the River Thurne in Norfolk or the little Ouse outside Cambridge. Until the day I die I will always remember being by the river on a quiet Sunday morning and hearing the birds singing and the church bells pealing from far and wide. I fished for bream, roach, dace and chub and would go home in the evening to be ready for school on the Monday morning. I loved fishing."

When he was eleven, Billy went off to boarding school at Kennylands Park School for Boys near Reading, and when he left school, he went to work as a trainee draughtsman under his father who was the Chief Chemical Engineer of the Hemingway Chemical Company. Their factory was at Marshgate Lane in Stratford, where the Olympic Stadium now stands.

That's when Billy discovered the other great love of his early years, boxing. Billy said, "I began boxing, first with the West Ham Boys Amateur Boxing Club, then when I wasn't so keen and had discovered other things like girls, with a lesser club, the East Ham Boys Amateur Boxing Club. But I must have been quite useful, because I won the London Federation Boys Boxing Championship in 1959." Billy also was the Army Cadet Boxing Champion in 1957, and in 1966 whilst serving in Germany, was BAOR Champion, an event that Billy told me was held in the same stadium as the 1936 Olympics.

But Billy was not happy as a trainee draughtsman and felt that he was missing something. So he joined the railways, working for three years as a fireman on the Elizabethan Line from London King's Cross to Edinburgh Waverly. One of his colleague firemen was Joe Brow,n who later found fame as a singer whose hits included 'The Darktown Strutters Ball', 'I'm Henry the Eighth I Am' and 'Crazy Mixed Up Kid'. But when diesel engines replaced stream, Billy was bored and left the railways to join the army, initially as a trainee commando but eventually with the 2nd Field Regiment, Royal Artillery.

Ironically, he met his future wife, Marion, on a fishing trip to Maldon in Essex. "A group of us lads used to go down there at weekends, camping and fishing the Blackwater River for eels. I saw her at the swimming pool and she smiled at me and sort of waved. We were courting for five years and married in 1965. Our three boys, Danny, Gavin and Fraser, all followed me into the army. Gavin was Garrison Sergeant Major in Brunei in Borneo, Danny is a regimental sergeant major and Fraser is now a captain," he told me.

Billy had done some fly-fishing on the River Tees near Barnard Castle when he was posted to Yorkshire, and when he was posted to Benbecula in 1981 he instantly fell in love with the islands. He was much influenced by his friendship with John Kennedy, a fellow soldier, a well-known South Uist angler and author of the definitive book of fishing the South Uist lochs. "John and one of his colleagues, Brian Concannon, ran a fly-fishing and fly-tying course and I joined. I remember John saying to me after two or three lessons, 'You don't need this anymore. Just go off and fish.'"

Billy said, "I will always be thankful to John for his kindness and courtesy. He really introduced me to the magic of fly-fishing and to my favourite South Uist water, East Loch Bee. He taught me how to fish it, and I can't put down the hours of pleasure I have had on that loch; finishing on the Range, coming home and then out on the loch by nine p.m., there sometimes until 3am, just me and my Jack Russell dog, Beau."

I asked Billy how he had become a gillie and he said, "John had gone off to do his bit in the Falklands and I took over the courses he had been running with my son, Fraser, helping me, teaching people to fish, and this and that and when I retired from the army Marion and I decided to set up a guesthouse specifically for anglers. When your son Blair left the Range, I took over from him as secretary of the Angling Club."

Because of his military career, Billy was invariably asked to look after visiting VIPs, who were anglers and shooters, to the rocket range. One pair of VIPs he took fishing were Viscount Cranborne, a Conservative politician who during the 1990s was leader of the House of Lords, along with a serving colonel whose secondary job was as Army Conservation Officer.

Billy recounted, "I knew they only had a short time to fish, so I took them to West Olavat. They arrived at the loch in a grand convoy consisting of the Brigadier's car, carrying Lord Cranborne and the Colonel, the commanding officer's car and the regimental sergeant major's Land Rover full of regimental policemen. When I asked the purpose of all these people, I was told it was to ensure the safety of the VIPs. I explained that such security was unnecessary in the Outer Hebrides; in any case, they would be perfectly safe in the boat with me.

"Back then West Olavat had a small boat with a bung in the bottom to stop water getting in. After we had been on the loch for an hour, I noticed a large puddle collecting beneath me. The Colonel had accidentally knocked the bung out with his feet, water was coming in fast, and we were in danger of sinking. So much for my reassurances about the VIPs' safety. I quickly rowed ashore, feeling somewhat self-conscious.

"The next day I received a letter from Lord Cranborne on the House of Lords' notepaper, saying he had just sat through a very boring debate and that his heart had still been in the Hebrides. I didn't get a letter from the Colonel. Maybe he was too embarrassed about not taking adequate precautions to conserve the life of his Lordship!"

Another VIP who came to the range was Field Marshall Sir John Stannier, CCB, MBE, Chief of the General Staff, the most senior officer in the British Army. Billy told me, "In honour of his visit, it was decided to organise a day of shooting and fishing. John Kennedy arranged the fishing and got a salmon ready for him in case Sir John failed to catch one. I arranged the shooting, and on the day before did a recce to establish where he would have the best chance of getting a shot. I also shot a goose, just in case Sir John didn't shoot one himself.

At the pre-shoot briefing at 4.30am, in the Commandant's house, I briefed the shooting party, consisting of Sir John and his two lieutenant colonel aides. I explained that I had prepared three hides – one for each of them, with Sir John in the middle – and that I had laid out a spread of around twenty decoys to lure the geese in towards the hides.

The plan was that just after dawn a small flight of about twenty geese would lift off and fly into the field area in front of the hides. I made it clear that if this happened, Sir John should take a shot at them, but if they flew out of his range they should be left undisturbed as the main body of geese would lift off later and fly into the same area, whereupon all three of them would get a shot.

Six geese duly headed in our direction, and I could see from my position behind the hides that if they kept on the same flight path, they would come well within range of Sir John. They did, but no shot was fired. Thinking that he had either fallen asleep in the hide or that his gun had malfunctioned, I crawled Indian-style to his hide, found him wide awake and alert and asked why he hadn't shot. He said he was waiting for the main flight to come in. I said something along the lines of 'For f**k's sake, that's not what you were supposed to do!' True to form, around a hundred geese lifted off later, flew towards the hides but then scattered in all directions when disturbed by two local shooters. Neither Sir John nor his aides got to fire a shot.

Around midnight that night, after Sir John and his aides had dined in the sergeant's mess, he got up to make a speech. He thanked the mess for their hospitality and said what a great day it had been. He had got a salmon that he hadn't caught a goose that he hadn't shot and, for the first time since he was a young sub-lieutenant, he had been given a verbal bollocking by a sergeant major."

Billy, with a smile on his face also told the story of The Brigadier's Scallops. "When John Kennedy was posted outside the island in the 1980s, I started running the fishing course for the local angling club. Participants included serving soldiers and their families. We would take them to a loch, get them started fishing then take it in turns to walk round to see how they were getting on. One of the participants was Brigadier Bugs Hughes, who due to a rugby accident walked with a noticeable waddle.

One day when I was teaching a group on Diesel Loch, a friend of mine drew up on the road beside the loch and gave me a gift of a dozen scallops that he had just caught. A few minutes later I saw the Brigadier walking round the loch towards me. He was some distance away, but his waddle was instantly recognisable. Knowing that he had a good sense of humour, I decided to take advantage of the situation.

I put ten of the scallops in the back of my car and carefully placed the other two in the loch. When the Brigadier arrived beside me, he asked how the fishing had been. I said the trout fishing had not been too good and that I had had more success catching scallops. I showed him the ten in my car. The Brigadier then proceeded to look for some in the loch and quickly found one of the two that I had planted. At that point I said I was going home. The Brigadier said he would stay to look for more scallops.

The next day I got a telephone call from the Brigadier's personal assistant, warning me that I had better keep out of the Brigadier's way; he had been going round all morning muttering something about Billy Felton and scallops. Someone had obviously told him that scallops don't live in freshwater lochs!"

I also served in the army, at home and in Southern Arabia, so I empathised with Billy's attitude. As a newly commissioned sub-lieutenant on my first battalion parade I received a public bollicking from our regimental sergeant major. I discussed it with him later and thereafter we formed a close friendship. My platoon sergeant in Arabia, 'Spud' Murphy, was also a close friend. Both these men, to me, epitomised all that is best in army life; they were as devoted to duty as they were to those with whom they served, and above all, they had a sense of humour that lightened the most difficult of situations. In all the time that I have spent with Billy Felton, I have recognized in him these same attributes. Outstanding men upon whom one could always rely.

It is not surprising that The Angler's Retreat soon became a Mecca for anglers. One such devotee was James Paterson, an accountant from Berwickshire who I have known as a friend for more than twenty-five years. James and Billy have had some famous adventures and some famous disputes. Spending a day afloat with them, listening to their banter and constant bickering is unforgettable. They went at it hammer and tongs, about which fly to use, how to fish it, where the boat should be, even about how to fire up the Kelly Kettle at lunch.

James told the story of one such day and it is a pretty accurate account. "It would probably be the late '80s, early '90s when Mr Felton started to gillie for us, just after he left the army. This particular week, my son Jeremy and I had managed to get Loch East Bee for three out of our six days. At that time, Bee was regarded as an enigmatic loch, sometimes good but mostly difficult. Billy knows more about Bee and its moods than anyone else. It is my favourite South Uist loch. You never know what you might catch, a stickleback or a salmon.

"Regulars to South Uist will know that the sun is an absolute killer with or without the wind. Unless you screen up, your face tends to become very tender. After a couple of days Billy's lips were very tender and sore. Jeremy and I were using Zinc Oxide lifted straight from the repertoire of American-Australian surfers which came in such colours as Shocking Pink, Brilliant Blue and Blinding White. It acts as a total sun block and also makes you look cool!

"On applying this, Billy remarked that we looked like a couple of girls, to which I replied, 'That maybe so, but at least (a) we didn't have sore lips and (b) we could eat hot curry with impunity.' Billy couldn't eat anything hot because of the state of his lips and Billy loves his food, especially Marion's Indian curries.

"On the Wednesday, Billy asked us about the state of our lips, and I replied that they were fine. Billy's lips were in a pretty bad state and he had resorted to rubbing them with suntan lotion, which not only comes off easily but tastes hellish (so he tells me!). Lunchtime came around and he asked to see the Zinc Oxide, which comes in a little plastic container.

"'So this stuff really works then?' was the cry.

"'Of course it does, as long as you don't mind looking like a girl,' was the response.

"'I was a sergeant major in the army and I couldn't risk my reputation being seen with this stuff on my choppers,' Billy said.

"'Fair enough, William, you'll just have to sit there and suffer for your reputation.' I believe he used several profanities at this point, which I could not possibly repeat here.

"That night he suffered badly for his reputation and I believe his usual sunny disposition was affected by being unable to sleep because of his lips. Next day as we headed up the first drift, he asked if he could use some of the Zinc, as his lips were very painful. I deliberately gave him the Shocking Pink. As he looked very like the joker in *The Dark Knight*, Jeremy and I fell about the boat with laughter.

"'So, cameras aren't allowed today then?' we said, which was met with another stream of profanities. You need to remember that, at that time, there were no digital cameras, otherwise I would have a photograph to this day.

"'Listen, you two bastards, especially you, Paterson. Not a word of this to anyone, understand? I spent over thirty years building up a reputation as a hard man in the army. If any of my squaddies saw me now, my reputation would be totally shot.'

"The Zinc worked its magic and every morning before the first drift, he would apply another violent shade to his choppers and on the Saturday he could even eat Marion's curry without any pain. At close of play on the Saturday, I offered Billy three tubs of the ointment, but these were declined, his reason being that if anyone else saw him applying coloured substances to his lips it might be interpreted in the wrong way."

It is Billy's unquenchable enthusiasm that has made the Angler's Retreat synonymous with everything that is wonderful about fishing in the Uists and Benbecula, as well as the outstanding standard of hospitality and cooking that Marion provides her guests. Over the years the Angler's Retreat has built up a loyal following of regulars, and a group of these guests organised the publication of a book in tribute to Billy and Marion, *Tales from The Angler's Retreat: Fishing Stories from South Uist*. The book was published by Muddler Books in 2009 and is still available on Amazon. It is a must-read for anyone intent on fishing in these islands.

During his life Billy Felton has caught every species of UK freshwater fish, except for catfish, sturgeon and powen, and he has also caught trout, mahseer and murrel in India.

Now, when Billy and Marion are moving to Elgin to be nearer to their family, he faces a new challenge: salmon fishing. The River Findhorn awaits his pleasure and, knowing Billy, I don't think that it is going to be too long before he is as competent and confident in that pastime, as he has proved himself to be in almost every other branch of our well-loved art. However, Billy will always have a second home where he can practice his first love, fishing for the wonderful wild brown trout of South Uist.

Epilogue

Jake Gilroy Smart is my youngest grandchild, the son of my daughter Jean and her husband, Ian Smart, the head keeper on the Ben Loyal Estate in North Sutherland. Jake goes to school at Altnaharra, where he is one of the six children on the school register. His classmates' parents all work on neighbouring estates as stalkers, keepers or gillies, and from his earliest years Jake has shown every sign that he will follow in his father's not inconsiderable footsteps; his paternal grandfather was a keeper and stalker and his great grandfather a drover. Jake was born in 2004. In 2010 he caught his first brown trout and in July 2012 he shot his first stag.

I sometimes look at Jake and think, 'Yes, eight years old going on thirty'. He is responsible, articulate and determined in all he does, and yet he is as mischievous as only an eight-year-old boy can be and has a vivid appreciation of the ridiculous matched by his wicked sense of humour. I thought that an appropriate way to bring this book to a close would be to interview Jake about his experiences so far as a stalker. Getting him to sit still long enough to do so was another matter, but eventually, with the help of his mum and dad and his big sister, Jessica, we managed to extract two stories, one of stalking with Ian and a guest, Rene Brunn, the previous year, the other about shooting his first stag.

Jake is accustomed to stalking with his father and well versed in what is required, quite happy to crawl hundreds of yards up damp ditches to get into position for a shot and well aware of the necessity to have the wind in the right direction so as not to alert the animals of the stalker's approach. One afternoon, whilst taking him home from school, a substantial herd of deer crossed the road in front of my car and I asked Jake to tell me something about them. For the next half a dozen miles I was regaled with details about where to aim the rifle, at the stag's heart, and where the heart was.

"How do you know that, Jake?" I asked. He told me that Ian had shown him where the heart was when they were in the deer larder butchering carcasses.

"Dad and Rene took me with them," Jake said, "and we drove through the forestry at Inchkinloch down to the end of the track and had a spy. Then we got into the Argo, Dad and Rene in the front and me in the back. Dad drove to the back of the forest and we got out and started walking up a green hill. There was a beautiful green ditch with water in it, and then we reached some flat ground. We had a pit stop so that I could go to the bathroom. We carried on uphill and started turning right at the top of the hill. Then we started to crawl and there were stags in front of us, about fifty yards away. Rene and Dad stopped. Dad gave me the binoculars so that I could have a spy, and they told me to scare the deer away. So I crawled forward and shouted and they ran away."

I presumed that Ian had decided not to shoot any of the stags they had found. They walked on to a lochan and had lunch. Jake continued, "After lunch, we started crawling up the side of a burn. The water got deeper, but we kept crawling until Rene fell into the water and I had to tell him to keep going. Then my foot got stuck in a hole, so I just pulled it out. We found a stag, and a hummock where Dad set up the rifle. Rene aimed and fired and shot the stag. Then Dad walked back to get the Argo. My hands were frozen, so I put my gloves on and covered them in deer blood to keep them warm. Sometime later, Dad arrived with the Argo. I helped Rene pull the stag into the Argo. I sat in the back with the stag and we drove to the truck and went home to the larder. Dad and Rene had a can of beer, whilst I cleaned up all the blood on the larder floor."

Jake then told us the story of his first stag. "Dad said he was off out for a spy and I went to join him. We went along the road towards Altnaharra, stopping every now and again to scan the hills for a stag. We went down to the end of the track at the second forestry block and Dad took out his glass and scanned the hill. He spotted a single hind in the distance. We left the truck and headed to the trees, creeping along the edge of the forest so as not to be seen. We reached a clearing behind the hind and getting low to the ground we crawled as far as we could to see her better. Having a better view of the hind, we could see that she had two stags with her. Moving back into the woods, Dad thought it would be best to move down wind to the right of the group so we could get a better shot.

"Once we were in position for the shot we nestled low. Dad handed me the rifle, but the stag sensed something and turned its head to face us. As Dad told me, I aimed for the middle of the chest and, taking a deep breath, I fired. I hit the stag but didn't kill it instantly. Dad, not wanting the stag to run away, took the gun and fired a second shot only to miss the stag completely. The stag had reached the edge of the forest and was about ready to run into the trees. Dad handed the rifle back to me and told me to try again and not to mind if I hit it or missed it. I took aim and shot the stag in the head. Dad looked at me, a bit shocked at first, before clapping me on the shoulder with a big smile on his face and said, 'Well done!' We walked over to the stag and Dad blooded my face with three lines on each cheek. I didn't want a line on my forehead because it might have got blood on my stalking cap. Dad took photographs and then we loaded the stag into the back of the truck and headed home to show my prize to Mum and my sister."

I suppose there are moments in all our lives that shape the direction in which we will travel. For me, they were seeing my first otter and losing my first salmon. Also, one sharp winter morning, standing in the snow by a tree, arm outstretched, palm upwards with bread for the birds, and the feeling of excitement when a robin perched on the edge of my palm, 'with tiny-eyed caution, jerkily to eat'. For Jake, it is probably going to be the snapshot that brought down his first stag, perhaps confirming the birth of another glorious gentleman?